COMPETITION CAR
DOWNFORCE

As part of our ongoing market research, we are always pleased to receive comments about our books, suggestions for new titles, or requests for catalogues. Please write to: The Editorial Director, G. T. Foulis & Company, Sparkford, Nr Yeovil, Somerset BA22 7JJ.

COMPETITION CAR
DOWNFORCE
A PRACTICAL GUIDE

Simon McBeath
Foreword by Gordon Murray

First published January 1998

A catalogue record for this book is available from the British Library

Published by G.T. Foulis & Company, an imprint of Haynes Publishing, Sparkford, Nr Yeovil, Somerset BA22 7JJ.

Tel: 01963 440635 Fax: 01963 440001
Int. tel: +44 1963 440635 Fax: +44 1963 440001

E-mail: sales@haynes-manuals.co.uk
Web site: http://www.haynes.com

ISBN 0 85429 977 7

Library of Congress catalog card number 97-76816

Haynes North America, Inc.
861 Lawrence Drive, Newbury Park, California 91320 USA

Designed & typeset by G&M, Raunds, Northamptonshire
Printed and bound in Great Britain by Biddles Ltd, Guildford and King's Lynn

Contents

Author's preface

WHILST RESEARCHING AND writing this book, I have been privileged to listen to a great many interesting folk from varied motorsport backgrounds, and if there's one thing I've learned, it's that you can never learn enough. Indeed, one professional aerodynamicist, whose candour deserves anonymity, told me that if aerodynamicists actually knew enough about the subject, most of them, including him, would be out of a job! This is what makes the whole topic so interesting: it is engineering, science, technology, and art all at once. Which is why there is scope for professionals and amateurs alike to study, dabble, experiment, and sometimes to make a breakthrough – perhaps not one that is of industry-shaking proportions, but sufficient to gain a fraction of a second improvement in performance. In the competitive arena of the late-1990s, fractions of a second tend to be pretty important.

Acknowledgements

SO MANY PEOPLE have helped me, directly and indirectly, with the production of this book that I just hope I haven't left anyone out of the following list. I have to say a particular thank you to a few individuals for whose help I am especially grateful; to Tracey, who, despite undoubtedly coming to think of a drag coefficient as a measure of what I have put her through these past many months, stood by me all the way, and took some of the photos too; to my brother, Andy, with whom I have shared the driving and development of a variety of hillclimb cars since 1979 – he allowed me to fiddle about with the aerodynamics of those vehicles more or less to my heart's content, and this undoubtedly taught me as much as any of the text books I ever read; David Jeffrey, of the Department of Aeronautics and Astronautics at Southampton University, who, with the help of sponsorship from Penske Cars, will have attained his doctorate by the time this book is published – he somehow found the time not only to check the technical accuracy of my efforts, but also enabled me to put to rest some popular misconceptions on how wings and flaps *really* work; Gordon Murray, for taking the time and trouble to write the Foreword; and Allan Staniforth, who set me on the right road at the beginning – you were right, Allan, it *was* a large undertaking

Thanks, too, to Darryl Reach, Alison Roelich, and Flora Myer at Haynes; John Wood, Graham Kendall, Paul Atkin, Anthony Baxendale, Keith Read, and Geoff Carr (who sadly passed away just a few weeks before I finished the manuscript) of MIRA; Nick Goozee and David Johnson-Newell, Penske Cars; Brian O'Rourke, Williams GPE; John Russell, Williams TCE; Stuart Featherstone, Fluent Europe; Andy Scriven, Penske Racing South; Mike Pilbeam; Tom Hammonds; Dave Longhurst, Dave Longhurst Racing Developments; Rob Dominy; Chris Bernard; Jack Brown and Bernie (Smitty) Smith, Reclamation Racing; Andrew Chisholm and Mick Kouros, Martello Racing; Tony Broster; Tony Pashley; Bob Le Sueur, Haggispeed; Ed Nicholls, Professional Sports Car Racing Inc; Martin Taylor-Wilde, Multi-Sports Composites; Eric Taylor, Carr Reinforcements; Vic Claydon; Steve Bagnall and Steve Black, SBG Sport; Matthew Lait, Benetton Formula; Giselle Davies, Jordan GP; Peter Coleby, GPC Motorsport; Quentin Spurring, Steve Bennett, John Colley, and Peter Wright; the FIA, RAC Motorsports Association, Silverstone Circuits Ltd, Brands Hatch Circuits Ltd, Castle Combe Circuit, Watkins Glen International, Gurston Down Hillclimb, Goodwood Motorsport, and Santa Pod Raceway; those numerous other hillclimbers who have run my wings on their cars; and lastly my parents, who paid for me to go through University so I could get a proper job, only to see me, 20 years on, still playing with racecars.

And not forgetting all the other fellow motorsport enthusiasts I've exchanged ideas with over the years.

Foreword

by Gordon Murray,
Technical Director, McLaren Cars Motorsport

DURING MOTOR RACING'S short history, there have been very few technical books written on the design, development, and aerodynamics of competition cars which have been accessible in their style of writing. I can remember studying Phipps and Costin's *Racing and Sports Car Chassis Design* from cover to cover when I was designing my first racecar at 18, and as this was 1965 there was no section on aerodynamics or downforce! The book was invaluable to me at the time, as it represented the only practical work on the subject of racecar chassis design.

Competition Car Downforce is surely one of those golden rarities in the text book library, and probably represents the first really practical guide to racecar aerodynamic downforce.

I feel this book will appeal to a wide range of readers, from the non-technical enthusiast right through to designers and constructors in the hundreds of different motorsport categories which employ aerodynamics as a tool.

After consultation with some of the world's foremost manufacturers and race teams, Simon McBeath has done an excellent job of presenting his information in an easy-to-read style, covering such diverse subjects as essential theory (with a minimum of mathematics), and the creation of downforce by aerodynamic devices, with an explanation of how they work. At the same time he puts some popular misconceptions to rest. He also covers how the amateur competitor can attempt to visualise, measure, and quantify the aerodynamic performance of a car, and investigates how professional teams and constructors approach the subject.

The author has used his own experience – gathered during 18 years' driving and experimenting with downforce on racecars – to good effect, and he rounds off the book with case studies in competition categories across the spectrum of motorsport on both sides of the Atlantic.

I would thoroughly recommend this book to enthusiast and constructor alike, as it is unique in its subject and style and is a very useful tool when tackling the 'black art' of aerodynamic downforce.

Chapter 1

From then until now

THERE IS, PERHAPS, no other aspect of competition car technology that has had as big an influence on performance as the exploitation of downforce. In all the world's current major single seater championships, including Formula 1, Indycars, Formula 3000 and Formula 3, aerodynamic downforce is the most important single element in the performance of the cars. In Sports and GT cars, and saloon cars too, downforce has a large part to play. In rallying, drag racing, sprinting and hillclimbing, short oval racing, and a myriad of motorsport categories around the world, downforce is now a crucial element in performance.

Downforce has become so significant that in most leading formulae, the governing bodies have seen fit to regularly review the regulations concerning downforce-inducing devices in an effort to try to keep things in check. In some cases this has involved drastic, sometimes almost panicky, changes to rules as lap speeds have escalated and lap times tumbled to the extent that things seemed to be getting unsafe – cars were hurtling around corners at unimaginable speeds, producing driver-battering sideways forces; braking distances were being cut to tens of metres where 20 years ago hundreds of metres were required. But in other categories more regular reviews, in consultation with the racecar constructors and designers, has produced a more measured, on-going response to the problem. Other things being equal, this helped to stabilise lap times, more or less.

Downforce plays such a large part in performance that devices to create it are expressly forbidden in some of the junior training formulae, like Formula Ford and Formula Vauxhall Junior. And the more senior training formulae permit only limited, and strictly controlled, downforce creation so that drivers may learn in a gradual way how to handle it, how to exploit it, and how to 'tune' it to best advantage, before progressing to the top level where it is so crucial.

Downforce has come a long way in just 40 years. The first known attempt to run an aerofoil on a racecar is generally thought to have been made by a Swiss engineer, Michael May, on a Porsche Spyder as long ago as 1956. The car had an aerofoil mounted above the cockpit, acting through the centre of gravity of the car, which tilted from –3° to +17°. The scrutineers at both the Nurburgring and Monza, where he was hoping to compete, wouldn't permit its use, and it never actually raced.

During the early 1960s designers and engineers made further attempts at gaining an advantage from aerodynamics other than by simply reducing the drag of the car by making it 'streamlined', or by building a lower car to reduce its frontal area. Drag reduction enabled faster top speeds to be achieved from a car with unchanged horsepower, but although this would improve the speed on the straights, it was only going to produce faster lap speeds if cornering speeds could be maintained or improved as well. And in the special case of prototype sports cars for example, making a lower, more streamlined car may well have produced the very opposite of downforce – aerodynamic *lift*.

It would be difficult to tell if this was the case, because other areas of improved performance, such as suspension and tyre development, would contribute to higher cornering speeds, thus masking, or at least reducing the effect of any disadvantage caused by lift. But these cars had the biggest plan areas of all competition cars, and at places like Le Mans top speeds were faster than in other competition categories, and, as we shall see in the next chapter, these two parameters, plan area and speed, are both related to the production of aerodynamic lift (and downforce . . .). As such, the problem was probably of greater significance to sports cars than any other category at the time. Thus it was most likely in sports car racing that the first real attempts to lessen the problem of aerodynamic lift were made, with the fitting of 'spoilers' that disturbed the smooth, lift inducing flow over the large upper surface of the car.

Racers have continually and habitually experimented with ideas that seem to produce benefits to performance, and it wasn't long before spoilers started appearing on sports cars and saloon cars the world over. It was found that even though straight-line speeds were coming *down*, through increases in drag, so too were lap times reducing. The inescapable conclusion was that cornering speeds were actually increasing, and this could only be happening because grip had increased between the tyres and the road. And this meant that real *downforce* was being generated.

Then a particularly innovative racer/engineer remembered again (everybody, presumably, had forgotten about – or had never heard of – May's earlier experiments) that wings kept aeroplanes in the air by creating a lifting force at least as great as the weight of the plane. If that was the case, why couldn't racers bolt wings onto their cars *upside down*, and create a force that pushed the cars more firmly onto the road to increase the available grip still further? The innovative racer was American Jim Hall, who appeared with wings on his Chaparral 2E racer at Bridgehampton, New York State, in 1966, and it is Hall who is universally credited with being the first to actually race a car with aerofoils fitted.

Sports cars like this Ferrari 330 P3/4 were amongst the first to use 'spoilers'.

It was the start of a revolution in race-car performance. Almost straight away Formula 1 took up the idea, and simple aluminium fabrications mounted on struts little bigger than flamingo legs appeared like a rash. But regrettably, it would appear that insufficient thought was put into the design of some installations, because a spate of accidents caused by structural failures of wings and wing supports led the then current ruling body of Formula 1, the CSI, to attempt to ban wings altogether. But after some re-thinking and rapid talking by the constructors, new rules were drawn up by the CSI, and wings were allowed back, in modified and restricted form. Very soon they were in universal use on all Grand Prix cars, and it wasn't long before they began to pervade in other formulae too. The 1970s saw gradual development and refinement of wings in single seater and sports car categories, and saloon racers were doing their bit too. In Europe, the famous Group 2 saloons were sprouting more than mere spoilers, with 'airdams' and 'splitters' at the front end of the cars, and genuine aerofoil section wings at the rear.

The next mental leap, that produced possibly the biggest *performance* leap of all, came in the late-1970s, when another clever engineer, Peter Wright, working for Colin Chapman at Lotus Grand Prix, with Chapman's encouragement successfully introduced the concept of 'ground effect' into Formula 1, with the Lotus type 78. The general concept, however, wasn't new. A patent taken out in the 1930s described how a symmetrical wing created downforce when in proximity to the ground, and the designer of Sir Malcolm Campbell's speed record vehicles had found some downforce from the underbody too. Then Jim Hall showed what could be done with a car that created low pressure over its entire underside, with his Chaparral 2J in 1970. The effect was to suck the car down onto the road really firmly, and Hall did it by using large fans powered by auxiliary motors to remove air from the underside, whilst 'skirts' (a

The Chaparral 2F, similar to the first 'winged racer', the 2E.

term which became infamous in the late-1970s and early-1980s) did their best to seal the underside from the outside, and allow the creation of the low pressure area below the car.

But in Formula 1, 'aerodynamic devices' were forbidden from moving relative to the car (a result of earlier frowned-upon attempts at making wings change their angles of incidence, from steep on the slow bits of circuits to shallow on the fast bits), which rendered the fan concept illegal. There was one attempt at circumventing this rule in 1978 by the Brabham 'fan car', when the fan's primary purpose was said by designer Gordon Murray to be engine cooling, which enabled them to win one race before it was banned. So Wright and

The Chaparral 2J 'sucker car'.

Chapman's great step forward was realising that it was possible to create substantial suction beneath the car using only the car's forward speed through the air, and clever shaping of its underside. In crude terms, the whole centre structure of the car became an inverted wing which generated low pressure over a very large area. This enabled the production of hitherto unknown levels of downforce, and correspondingly greater cornering forces. The resultant increase in cornering speeds, and reduction in braking distances (and, in some cases, the removal of the *need* for braking), saw rival designers begin to take the 'wing car' concept very seriously. And it has to be said that the first ground effect design, on the Lotus 78 car, was relatively inefficient. The following year's Lotus 79, though, was a beautiful and highly effective refinement that enabled Mario Andretti to dominate the 1978 World Championship, and Lotus to take the Constructors' title.

But the other teams played catch-up very rapidly indeed, and it wasn't long before Lotus were being beaten at their own game, so to speak, with Williams producing perhaps the most elegant ground effect car of all in the FW07 series. The ground effect principle proceeded to pervade formulae all over the world wherever downforce was permitted, and a number of other classic designs were born during this era, such as the ubiquitous Ralt RT2/3/4 series, which was so successful in Formulae 2, 3, and Atlantic/Pacific the world over. Sports cars exploited the principle too, and benefited from their huge plan areas to produce literally tons of downforce.

But then the ruling body produced one of its famous 'rapid reactions', and all of a sudden ground effect was banned in Formula 1 with the introduction of a mandatory 'flat bottom' between the front and rear axle lines. The axe fell on other categories somewhat later, but fall it did, although Indycar racing – governed by its own rule-makers – retains ground effect (through profiled sidepods) to this day, albeit in a strictly controlled form.

In Europe, Formula 1, Formula 3000 (which replaced Formula 2 in the early 1980s) and Formula 3 had to pursue other means of regaining the downforce taken away by the changes in technical regulations. Formula 1 cars began a less than elegant looking development route involving extra 'winglets' attached to the outer, forward-most parts of the rear wings. It was around this period that some of Grand Prix racing's most powerful engines were being used, during the

The beautiful and highly effective Lotus 79.

so called 'turbo era', and every bit of downforce that could be won at the rear of the car was needed to assist putting prodigious quantities of power onto the road. Drag became almost an irrelevance with four figure brake horse power levels being generated by the turbocharged 1.5 litre engines. The less powerful single seater categories had to rely on striking a balance between downforce and drag, and wing designs were not quite as outrageous as in Formula 1. Sports cars con-

Sports prototypes like this 1990 Le Mans winning Jaguar XJR-12 Group C car produced tons of downforce.

tinued along the ground effect route, exploiting the relative freedom that their rules permitted as well as the huge plan form area available to them for downforce generation.

1989 saw the return, in Formula 1, to normally aspirated engines of 3.5-litre capacity, with a reduction to more modest power levels. The question of downforce versus drag had to be reconsidered anew, and designers started looking at the underside of the car again as a potential downforce-inducer. It was realised that with a sufficiently small ground clearance, and the right amount of nose-down attitude, a crude form of venturi section could be created beneath the cars in spite of the flat bottom, and we were back to ground effect. It proved vital to cause the air from the underside to escape as efficiently as possible at the rear of the cars, and 'diffusers' came into being to do just that. A whole new aspect to downforce production had been discovered, and refinements continually appeared over the following few years.

Formula 3000 and Formula 3 followed this route too, producing a generation of cars with incredibly low ground clearance, and high spring stiffnesses to maintain as constant a car-to-ground gap as possible. Formula 1 went one better in this area of control, and produced so called 'active suspension' systems, which offered the ability to control the cars' attitude as well as their ground clearance far better than a conventional mechanically sprung vehicle. The prime reason for doing this was quite clearly for aerodynamic reasons, rather than for any possible handling benefits, so in truth, active suspension was illegal – the cars were now themselves moveable aerodynamic devices, with controls built in specifically to move things around for aerodynamic reasons. Presumably the powers that be couldn't separate this aspect from the fact that a car has to move, and as it does so it then becomes an 'aerodynamic device (moveable)'!

Other categories around the world wouldn't allow the use of active suspension systems, and ultimately it was banned in Formula 1 as well. But development of the underside and diffusers continued. Wings, too, came in for more attention, and more complex shapes began to appear as designers started thinking in three dimensions, and 'airflow management' became a trendy phrase. Other attachments were bolted on which were all about gaining critical percentages of extra downforce, hopefully without any extra drag penalty.

Then, after that disastrous weekend at Imola in 1994, when Roland Ratzenburger and Ayrton Senna lost their lives in separate accidents, the FIA, the governing body of motorsport, produced some rapidly imposed rule changes which had the effect of cutting back downforce quite significantly. Some rule changes were immediate, and removed perhaps a few per cent of downforce. But a rule brought in for 1995, which was also applied in Formula 3000 and Formula 3, saw a large increase in the minimum permitted ground clearance over a large proportion of the underbody; the so-called 'stepped floor' was in. This produced a substantial reduction to downforce levels (maybe by as much as 40 per cent), and also lessened the cars' sensitivity to their attitude relative to the ground, which made them more predictable, and hence safer to drive.

Throughout this period of turmoil in the European administered formulae, the rule-makers of Indycar had been regularly reviewing their technical regulations in the light of performance gains from the cars, and imposing almost annual rule changes. This approach seemed to ensure that really drastic changes were never actually necessary – the rule-makers just chipped away at what was allowed in order to keep performance in check. Naturally, the designers and aerodynamicists always did their utmost to win back at least as much as was lost. Recent aerodynamic rule changes in the face of tyre and engine development progress have been somewhat controversial, and it remains to be seen whether the changes work as intended.

Sports cars, meanwhile, had undergone a total change, and the glorious sports prototype cars had been replaced, essentially, with road going GT cars. Downforce-inducing devices were permitted, including splitters, wings, and profiled undersides, but in emasculated form compared to the previous formula.

Saloon car racing had undergone changes during this period too, and now consisted of Class 1 and Class 2 categories. Class 1 permitted quite extensive modifications from the 'silhouette' of the base vehicle, and some serious downforce was available. Class 2 started out looking pretty much like showroom shape, but from 1995 limited splitters and wings were permitted. At the time of writing, though, the rules were being studied very carefully.

Throughout the whole of the period described briefly here, some formulae have come and gone, some have remained unchanged, and others have adapted to rule changes and trends. But wherever its exploitation has been

Right *Since 1995, Formula 1 cars have been obliged to run 'stepped underbodies', as on this 1996 Ferrari F310.*

Below *'GT cars' have replaced the sports prototypes; this is the 1996 McLaren F1 GTR.*

Class 2 'Super Touring' cars allow limited downforce generation with small wings and splitters; this is the Volvo S40.

allowed, downforce has had a dominant influence on racecar performance. There are, of course, other important contributors to continually improving racecar performance, and these obviously include the tyres – the four little contact patches between the tyres and the ground ultimately define and limit how much grip a car can generate. But in the case of racing categories where significant downforce is permitted, tyres have developed in response to the gains that the aerodynamicists have found.

It is interesting that the perpetual struggle of racecar designers to make cars go faster is sometimes seen to be at odds with what might be said to be the main purposes of motorsport – to provide racing and entertainment for participants and spectators. Indeed, downforce itself is seen by some to be the main cause of the perceived lack of overtaking in many racing categories. Drivers are often heard to complain that as soon as they attempt

to get close behind another car in a corner, so as to slipstream past on the ensuing straight, their own car loses so much downforce at the front that significant grip is lost, and they cannot sustain the passing attempt. Further, the finger is pointed at downforce for reducing braking distances to mere tens of yards, which, it is said, also makes overtaking with the so-called 'out-braking manoeuvre' very difficult to carry out.

Undeniably these effects exist, but whether they are the primary causes of this apparent difficulty to overtake is a moot point. Other factors such as track design, car dimensions, and 'Maginot Line' driver mentality ('they *shall* not pass . . .') must all be to blame in some part as well. However, during 1996 the FIA commissioned studies into the aerodynamics of cars following each other closely, in an apparent attempt to find a general configuration that would enable close running and overtaking to occur.

Where would *the sponsors' names go if wings were banned?*

Interestingly, the emphasis of these studies switched for a while from aerodynamics to tyres. It seems the studies indicated that if total downforce was reduced, far from making it easier for cars to follow each other, things actually got worse, and the adverse effect on the following car was, relatively speaking, greater in this guise. But ultimately the FIA decided to introduce 'treaded' tyres into Formula 1 in 1998, in the hope that reducing the amount of rubber in contact with the road will reduce grip, and hence cornering speeds, with a commensurate increase in braking distances. At the same time, the cars are to be made 20cm (almost 8in) narrower too, which will reduce the plan area that can be used for downforce creation by the cars' underbodies; the simultaneous reduction of their frontal areas should increase straight-line speeds. It remains to be seen what the results will be. But it is to be hoped that not too much technical freedom is taken away by the imposition of further rules banning wings and other downforce-inducing devices as some observers seem to want. The science (and art) of producing aerodynamic downforce is far too fascinating to allow that to happen. And where would all those sponsors' names go? But notwithstanding that slightly facetious argument, there is also a legitimate case that can be put on safety grounds for the retention of downforce as an aid to keeping cars firmly planted on the ground. There are, mercifully, very few cases of competition cars in any category doing 'back flips' these days except in the most extreme and freakish of circumstances, so a unilateral ban on 'wings' would be most unsafe.

There are a great many motorsport categories that permit the exploitation of downforce, and the remainder of this book will look at the theory and practice involved in creating downforce in a wide range of these, across the whole motorsport spectrum.

Chapter 2

Out
of thin air

May the Force be with you

As you watch it hurtle down a runway, it always seems amazing that a machine as vast and heavy as an airliner can actually lift off the ground. Yet the forces that lift it and hold it up are created solely by its slender-looking wings cutting through the air as the plane moves along. It seems equally incredible that a current Formula 1 or Indycar single seater racecar can generate sufficient negative lift, or downforce, that it could drive across the ceiling of a large room, and, by virtue of its own downforce, hold itself there, upside down, defying gravity. Of course, it would need to be a pretty big room to allow for sufficient speed, and we'll gloss over just how it gets there in the first place. But the principle is valid, even if the practicalities have to remain a little vague. So how is it that such large forces can be created out of thin air?

Intuitively we have a natural feeling for some aerodynamic forces. If we are travelling along in a car, and we stick an arm out of an open window (which is easier than sticking it through a closed one . . .), we can feel the quite substantial force exerted by the air impacting on the arm. If the palm of the hand is opened and tilted one way and then the other, we can feel upward and downward forces as well as the force that tries to drag the arm horizontally backwards.

But these are only the obvious elements of the forces involved. There are more subtle, yet highly significant effects, which create forces which are at an angle to the airflow, rather than in the same direction. My A-level physics teacher taught me the following experiment, which graphically illustrates how lift is created by air flowing over a surface. Take hold of an ordinary A4-sized (297 by 210mm, 11.7 by 8.3in) piece of writing paper by the corners along one of the shorter edges, between the fingers and thumbs of each hand. Now hold the piece of paper up to just below your mouth, touching your lower lip, so that the edge near to your mouth is horizontal, and the flexibility of the paper allows it to hang downwards from your fingers. Now blow horizontally, across the top surface of the piece of paper; do you see what happens? The piece of paper bends upwards towards the stream of air blowing out of your mouth. Clearly a force is being exerted on the piece of paper, causing it to flex upwards against the pull of gravity. It is the airflow which is causing this lifting force, yet the force is acting at right angles to the airflow. *This* is the force which keeps aeroplanes in the air. It is also the force that pushes racecars firmly into the ground, when so directed.

From Aristotle to Bernoulli

So how are these obvious and not so obvious forces generated? Aristotle, that well-known Ancient Greek who lived from 384 to 322 BC – a modest chap whose specialised subject was 'the whole field of knowledge' – had a stab at it. He reckoned that as a body moved through air, a vacuum was formed ahead of it, which caused the body to continue moving. Well, you can see what he was getting at . . . Then, in 1726, Sir Isaac Newton came up with some more plausible ideas when he realised that air and water moved in response to similar physical laws, and that the forces involved depended on the density and velocity of the fluid flowing past an object, and also on the shape and size of the 'displacing' object.

This was getting much closer to what we know today, but sadly his first go at quantifying things was wide of the mark, and greatly under-estimated the reality. He assumed that the forces on an object were caused by air particles rebounding from the object in a, well, Newtonian sort of way, as shown in Figure 2–1. In this case, the lift and drag forces were thought to be the result of momentum transfer between the air particles and the plate with which they collided. This is clearly part of the cause of the forces involved – go back to the arm-out-of-the-window example, and you can *feel* that this is so. Drag can be partly explained by the Newtonian 'collision' effect. But the calculations for the lift and drag cre-

ated did not agree with experiment.

About 150 years later, another chap called Rayleigh likened the airflow around our inclined plate to the flow set up by the plate planing on the surface of a body of water. But there was still a large difference between this theory and the results from actual experiments, in which the lift force was measured at various angles of inclination, or angles of 'attack'.

It was not until 1907, when a Russian called Joukowski turned his mind to the problem, that the flow patterns were correctly visualised, and the formulae derived for the lift force were found to very closely match experimental results. Joukowski realised that the influence of the inclined plate extended, by the effects of viscosity, into the air, some considerable distance from the plate itself, and this allowed him to come up with theories to match observed results. It is interesting to note that the Wright brothers had got their powered plane to remain in the air for a distance of 852ft (259.8m) in 1903, some four years before Joukowski found 'The Formula' – which goes to prove that you don't have to be fully versed in the theory in order to make something work in practice! Just as well, because this seems to be the basis on

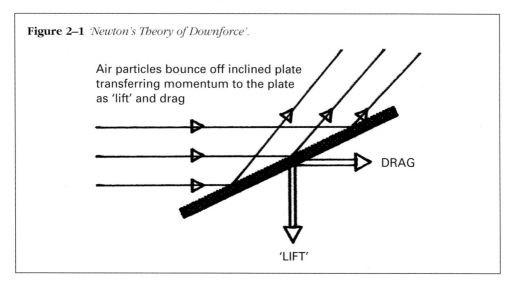

Figure 2–1 *'Newton's Theory of Downforce'.*

Air particles bounce off inclined plate
transferring momentum to the plate
as 'lift' and drag

DRAG

'LIFT'

which much aerodynamic research is done in motorsport even nowadays . . .

But we have to go back in history again, to the 18th century, to find the first explanations of the relationship between flow and pressure in a general fluid dynamics context. An Italian physicist by the name of Daniel Bernoulli is said to have hinted at a direct relationship between pressure and velocity in 1738, in a hydrodynamics text book. But the equation now named after Bernoulli, which mathematically describes this relationship, was actually derived in a series of papers in 1755 by Leonhard Euler. However, for reasons we won't attempt to analyse here, Euler seemed to get no credit, whilst, however unfair it may have been, Bernoulli got his very own equation, and here it is:

$$p + 1/2\rho v^2 = \text{a constant}$$

(ρ, the Greek letter rho, is air density, v is flow velocity)

where p is the 'static pressure', and $1/2\rho v^2$ is the 'dynamic pressure'. So what does this tell us? Well, my physics teacher came to the rescue again, and para-phrased this mathematical formula as 'where the flow is fastest, the pressure is least.' In other words, if the flow velocity is forced to increase, the local pressure must decrease. Note that the equation is valid along a given 'streamline', or mean flow path.

The Bernoulli Principle is what makes a carburettor work. Figure 2–2 schemati-cally shows a carburettor choke tube. Air is being drawn through the tube by the induction stroke of the engine. The flow velocity at line 2 has been accelerated because of the reduced cross-sectional area of the choke tube, so there is a drop in pressure in the restricted part of the choke tube, and it is this pressure reduc-tion which sucks petrol through the car-burettor jet(s) and into the inlet charge to the engine.

Go back now to the experiment in which you blew over the piece of paper, and you can see what caused the lifting force. The air above the paper moved faster than the air below it as you blew over it, and as such the local pressure decreased. This pressure reduction over the surface of the piece of paper created a large enough force to lift the paper upwards, against the force of gravity.

And the principle also applies to a wing section, in the inverted, downforce-induc-

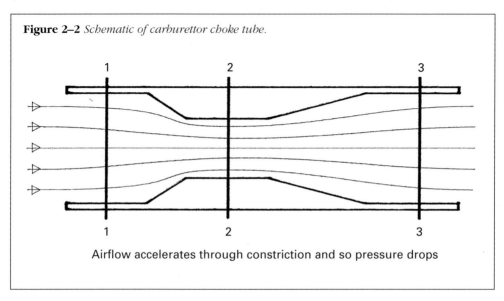

Figure 2–2 *Schematic of carburettor choke tube.*

Airflow accelerates through constriction and so pressure drops

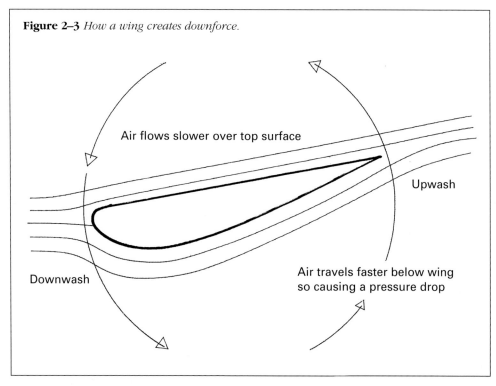

Figure 2–3 *How a wing creates downforce.*

Air flows slower over top surface

Upwash

Downwash

Air travels faster below wing
so causing a pressure drop

ing configuration, as shown in Figure 2–3. The air which flows beneath the wing, where the wing's maximum curvature exists, has to travel a greater distance to get from the leading edge to the trailing edge than the air travelling above the wing. So the air taking the longer route beneath the wing accelerates to a greater velocity. And, as in the carburettor choke tube example, this causes a reduction in local pressure, which this time acts on the lower wing surface, and creates down-force by sucking the wing downwards.

Professional aerodynamicists explain the creation of lift by an aerofoil in terms of the apparent circulation of air around it. They look at the velocity vectors above and below the wing, together with the 'downwash' ahead of the wing and the 'upwash' behind it (in the downforce-producing context), and then refer to this as the circulation that the wing has imposed on the airflow. The streamlines indeed do behave as if there was a rotating and moving cylinder of air, a cylindrical

vortex if you will, aligned with the axis of the wing. The lift forces can actually be calculated in terms of the strength of the vortex. This is all very well if you're a mathematician, but the concept seems rather abstract if you're not – it is, after all, a mathematical model rather than something which is physical and real. And in any case, having once considered the circulatory pattern, they then pass on to the principles of Bernoulli anyway, so for the purposes of this book, this mathematical principle of circulation will be passed over. Serious students will need to consult one of the more theoretical texts listed in Appendix 2 for further reading on this topic. For the rest of us, Bernoulli will do the job.

The forces involved

The two components of aerodynamic force are *drag* and *lift* (see Figure 2–4). These combine together as vectors to give the resultant *total aerodynamic force*, and this is the net effect of all the

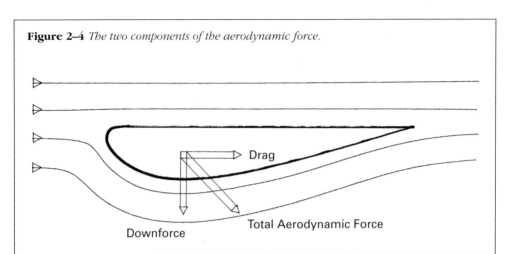

Figure 2–4 *The two components of the aerodynamic force.*

Drag

Downforce

Total Aerodynamic Force

pressures acting upon a body, such as a wing. The pressure differences felt can be expressed mathematically as the pressure coefficient multiplied by the dynamic pressure, viz:

$$p = C_p \times 1/2\rho v^2$$

To resolve a pressure into a force, it is necessary to multiply by the area that the pressure is acting upon, since

pressure = force/area.

So from the equation for pressure above, we can establish equations for lift and drag as follows:

$$\text{Lift} = C_L \times 1/2\rho v^2 \times A$$
$$\text{Drag} = C_D \times 1/2\rho v^2 \times A$$

where C_L is the coefficient of lift, C_D is the coefficient of drag, and A is the refer-

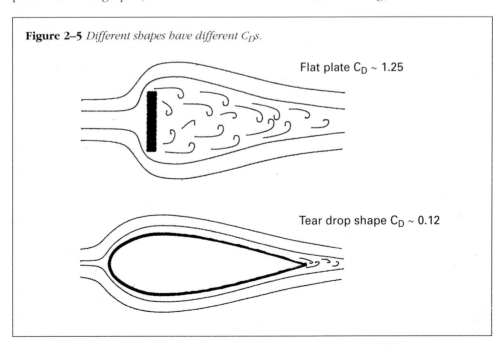

Figure 2–5 *Different shapes have different C_Ds.*

Flat plate $C_D \sim 1.25$

Tear drop shape $C_D \sim 0.12$

ence area. (NB For an aerofoil this is always taken to be the plan area, because this is how the coefficients are expressed, but in the case of whole vehicles, the convention is to use frontal area for both drag and lift.)

The lift and drag coefficients are relative measures of how much lift and drag a particular shape generates. If we look at drag first, again our intuition is surprisingly helpful, to the extent that we *know* that a flat plate turned perpendicular to an airflow will create more drag than a similar width tear-drop shaped object (see Figure 2–5). However, we cannot tell, just by looking, that the flat plate has a drag coefficient (C_D) of perhaps 1.25, and the tear-drop shape, if its length is four or five times longer than its width, has a C_D of about 0.12. But we can usually tell by looking at a car whether it has a high or a low C_D – a (road-car based) McLaren F1 GTR sports racecar looks to be an inherently less draggy shape than a McLaren Formula 1 single seater racecar, and the facts bear out this crude assessment.

When it comes to lift coefficients, subjective judgement is not so easy (unless you happen to be measuring such things on a regular basis), although some examples lend themselves to guesstimates. Taking the McLarens cited above again, the Formula 1 car just *has* to have a higher (negative) lift coefficient, with its multi-element aerofoils. The Formula 1 sports car, in road trim, has no aerofoils, and despite a profiled underbody – of which more in a later chapter – it simply doesn't look to have a downforce-induc-

The McLaren F1 GTR sports racer looks less 'draggy' than . . . the McLaren Formula 1 car.

ing shape. Even in racing trim, as the F1 GTR with front 'splitter' and rear wing, the sports car looks to be a long way short of the single seater in terms of lift coefficient, and hence, downforce production.

But what these assessments of coefficients do not take into account is, as Newton observed an awfully long time before racecars appeared, that *size* is just as important as shape when it comes to the magnitude of the aerodynamic forces created. Look back at the formulae for lift and drag again, and note that 'A', for area, is present in both equations. Clearly, then, if the frontal area of one car is bigger than another, it will produce more drag for the same C_D (at the same speed).

Life is never quite that simple, though, so let's look at an example based on real (1996 vintage) racecars, drawing on several sources for the data. A typical Formula 1 car might have a frontal area of roughly 16sq ft (1.5m²), as estimated in the manner shown in Figure 2–6, and a C_D of around 0.75, according to various references. Taking the density of air (and using this as our convention from here on, to avoid confusing units like 'slugs/ft³') to be 0.00238lb/ft³ (1.22kg/m³), then at 200mph, or 293.33ft/sec (89.4m/sec) drag works out at 1,228lb (560kg approx). At the same speed, a McLaren F1 GTR GT Endurance 'sports racer', with an estimated frontal area of about 19.5sq ft (1.81m²), calculated as width multiplied by height in this case, was said to have generated around 1,000lb (455kg) of drag at 200mph. Thus, the car with the larger frontal area produces significantly less drag, which implies that its C_D is lower. Do the sums in reverse, and this drag coefficient works out at around 0.5. So our subjective appraisal of Gordon Murray's sports car masterpiece was right, it *is* a less draggy shape than a Formula 1 car! And it is to be expected that the road-going version of the sports car has a much lower C_D again, because it doesn't have all the downforce-creating and drag-inducing appendages of the racing model.

It is interesting to do the same comparison with the downforce generated by the two types of car, and calculate overall C_L values. It is reckoned that one 1996 Formula 1 car was producing a figure 'approaching 4,000lb' (1,820kg) of down-

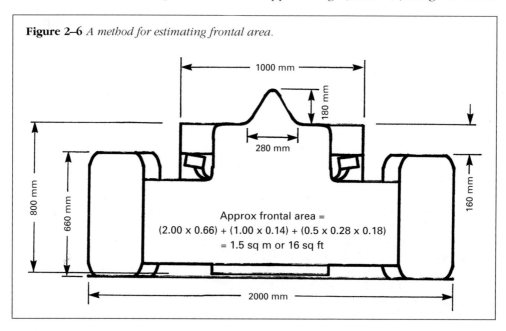

Figure 2–6 *A method for estimating frontal area.*

1000 mm

180 mm

280 mm

800 mm

660 mm

160 mm

Approx frontal area =
(2.00 x 0.66) + (1.00 x 0.14) + (0.5 x 0.28 x 0.18)
= 1.5 sq m or 16 sq ft

2000 mm

force at 200mph (320kmh) in the high speed circuit ('low' drag) configuration used at the Monza and Hockenheim circuits, where speeds this high were not only possible, but regularly exceeded. If we take 'approaching 4,000lb' to actually mean a more conservative 3,800lb (1,725kg) for the purposes of these calculations we will, no doubt, be somewhere nearer the truth. The McLaren F1 GTR generated in the region of 600 to 1,500lb (273 to 682kg) of downforce, depending on configuration. For comparison we will use the lower value for the GTR, since it is presumably analogous to the high speed set-up of the Formula 1 car we are using here. So, the sports racer was producing about 15 per cent of the downforce of the Formula 1 car at the same speed. Running the calculations in reverse again, we see that the respective overall C_L values are 2.32 for the Formula 1 car and 0.30 for the sports racer. This is a significant difference, and reflects, amongst other factors, the efforts of the technical regulators to cap downforce in the sports car category, as well as the success of the Formula 1 aerodynamicists at defeating their regulators! Note that these C_Ls should really have negative signs in front of them to demonstrate that downforce is being generated as opposed to positive lift. But since this book is all about downforce, we'll adopt the convention of treating downforce as normal, and differentiate it from positive lift by using the '+' sign where relevant.

The ratio of lift (that is, downforce) to drag (L/D) is often quoted as a measure of aerodynamic efficiency. In the examples worked through here, the Formula 1 car has an L/D ratio of 3.1:1, whereas the GT car's L/D ratio is 0.6:1. The implication is that the single seater is five times as aerodynamically efficient as the GT racer. This is a slightly simplistic way of looking at things, though, since it doesn't take into account the purpose of the two vehicles, the aims of the competitions in which they take part, or the rules pertaining to each category. So L/D ratios are interesting for comparing cars within a given category, and maybe for studying how a given manufacturer develops his cars over time, but perhaps they should not be used to compare cars in different categories.

Staying with Formula 1 for the moment, in the years 1994 to 1996 there were concerted efforts by the regulators to cut back on levels of downforce, with rule changes to wing dimensions, wing positions, and also to permitted underbody shapes. There seems to be a general acceptance that there has been a substantial reduction in achievable downforce as a result of these measures. One designer has been quoted as saying that his team tends to run as much downforce as possible at most circuits. Taken against the background of regulatory reductions to downforce, this has necessitated the use of less efficient L/D ratios, so the cars now create relatively more drag than they did just two or three years ago. Somehow, though, lap records still get broken almost every year, as a result of technical progress in all areas of performance. Not the least of the critical performance factors is engine power, and fierce competition between the engine manufacturers has actually seen top speeds in Formula 1 reach record levels, in spite of the apparently draggy aerodynamic packages being utilised. At Hockenheim in 1996, the McLaren-Mercedes cars were apparently measured at over 211mph (339kmh) on the circuit's long straights, and one of them, with the benefit of a slipstream 'tow' from another car, was clocked at over 214mph (344kmh).

Drag and power

There is a direct mathematical relationship between top speed and available brake horsepower, which is based on the equation for calculating drag force. In simplified, imperial units form it is:

$$\text{bhp absorbed by drag} = \frac{C_D \times A \times v^3}{146,600}$$

A is in square feet and v is now in mph.

For semi-metricated readers, who still use brake horsepower, the equation becomes:

$$\text{bhp absorbed} = \frac{C_D \times A \times v^3}{1,225}$$

where A is now in m² and v in m/sec. To convert bhp to kilowatts, multiply by 0.746.

Notice that in this equation the velocity now has to be cubed (that is, multiplied by itself three times), so it is evident that 'drag bhp' is a very velocity-sensitive parameter. Notice too the phrase 'available horsepower', which refers to the fact that the figure to use in this equation is the power available at the wheels. This is power which is available to accelerate the car, and to overcome air resistance. Allan Staniforth, in *The Race and Rally Car Source Book* (revised edition, Haynes, 1989) gives a handy table from which it is possible to estimate available horsepower if the bhp at the flywheel is known. The 'correction factors' quoted are said to take into account a range of variables such as alternator loads, fans, tyre rolling resistance and so forth. The corrections, in modified form, are quoted here for a selection of competition categories:

Type of car	Multiply flywheel bhp by
Rear engine single seater with cold or narrow tyres (eg Formula Ford, small hillclimb)	0.91
Circuit single seater with hot and wide tyres (eg Formula 1, Formula 3000, Formula 3)	0.875
Full race saloon/sports with engine at same end of car as driven wheels (eg Le Mans, Imp, Mini)	0.85
Front engine, rear wheel drive competition car (eg Clubmans)	0.82

If we now make some top speed estimates for our two example cars, the 'generic' Formula 1 and the McLaren GT Endurance racer, we get the following results; (see also Figure 2–7):

Car	C_D	A	bhp	Av.bhp	Max spd
Formula 1	0.75	16	700	612.5	195.6mph / 314.5kmh
McLaren GTR	0.50	19.5	600	510	197.2mph / 317.0kmh

A is in square feet, and the bhp values used are ones readily bandied about in the motorsport press in 1996, so they will serve to illustrate, even if they are not true! Available bhp figures have been corrected according to the previous table.

Clearly, a much lower C_D than 0.75 must have been used on the McLaren Formula 1 car when over 211mph (339.2kmh) was recorded, a value of 0.60 or under being necessary to achieve that speed with the power and frontal area figures used here.

The vast majority of racers do not have the luxury of access to a wind-tunnel, which means that, generally speaking, C_D values will have to be guesstimated somehow or other. If, however, a test track with sufficient room to reach absolute maximum speed is available, and all the necessary gear ratios to attain that speed are also to hand, then it will be possible to estimate the C_D, once the frontal area has been measured. But whilst it is an academically interesting exercise, it has to be asked 'does it really matter?'. Top speed is rarely of any significance in most forms of motorsport (with the obvious exception of high speed oval racing). And yet, as we shall see in a later chapter, it *is* of benefit to be able to estimate the C_D when it comes to calculating how much additional drag, induced by extra downforce creation, may be tolerated at certain venues, or how much needs to be removed at others.

Downforce and grip

But why is downforce useful? Why does it make cars go quicker around a given bend or circuit when clearly it creates a penalty in the form of extra drag? It's all to do with friction, and grip. Imagine an object being pulled along by a piece of string across a surface at a constant

Figure 2–7 *Power absorbed by aerodynamic drag.*

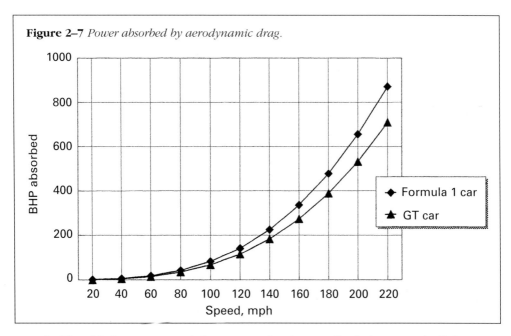

speed. The friction generated between the object and the surface is given by yet another equation:

The frictional force $F = \mu R$

where μ, the Greek letter 'mu', represents the coefficient of friction, and R is the 'normal force' (normal being a synonym for 'perpendicular', or vertical) between the object and the surface, which, ordinarily, is the object's weight (the earth's gravity pulling its mass onto the surface). The coefficient of friction is governed by the nature of the object and the surface it rests upon. So, for example, an ice hockey puck on wet ice exhibits a very low coefficient of friction, and the ice

It's all to do with friction and grip (Pilbeam MP72).

exerts practically no grip on the puck at all. In contrast, the driving tyres of a Top Fuel dragster on sticky asphalt generate an extraordinarily high coefficient of friction, and a correspondingly high level of grip exists between the tyre and the road surface. Notice that the area of contact between the body and the surface does not come into the equation. So why do wide racing tyres generate more grip than narrow ones? That's a topic outside our scope here, so you'll have to ask your tyre technician the next time you see him or her.

The 'normal force' is, as stated above, usually the object's own weight. So, an object weighing 5lb (2.27kg) exerts twice the normal force of an object weighing 2.5lb (1.13kg), and as such it generates twice as much friction when it is being pulled along by the string. Thus it requires twice the force to pull it along at a constant speed as does the lighter object. Now turn this concept around so that the object is a car, moving on an asphalt road. For the car to accelerate, or brake, or corner, the tyres must be able to utilise the friction between their contact patches and the road surface. The maximum limit of this friction is a function of the normal force, and the coefficient of friction between the tyres and the road, as defined by $F = \mu R$. In this case, R is the vehicle's own weight, and so the maximum horizontal forces that can be generated are limited by the weight of the car, and how grippy the tyres are.

That would be true on the moon, or any other place where there is no air to speak of. But here on Planet Earth, where the air is dense and viscous, aerodynamics come into play, and interact with this simplistic view of vehicle dynamics. As we have already seen, it is possible for a car to create substantial vertical forces by virtue of its passage through the air, and these add to or subtract from the vehicle's own weight to modify the normal force, R, and as such, alter the maximum frictional force that the car's tyres can generate. If a car creates positive lift, then the

maximum frictional forces that can be generated are reduced, whereas if the car creates downforce, the maximum frictional forces are correspondingly increased. Thus, all other things being equal, a car with downforce can accelerate, brake, and corner with greater force than a car with no downforce, or one with positive lift. Providing these increased limiting forces can be exploited, the car with downforce should be able to cover a given set of corners and straights in less time than one without downforce, because it will be able to accelerate and brake harder, and corner faster. And this is what it's all about. Naturally, nothing ever comes free, and, as we have already seen, downforce is no exception. The inherent drag penalties involved mean that the whole science (and art) is about trading off the gains against the losses to achieve a net benefit.

Let's work through a simplistic example for a mythical racecar travelling around a single, constant radius corner to see the benefit of downforce. Assume the car travels around the corner in a steady state, that is with no acceleration or deceleration forces, just a perfectly balanced cornering force (not very realistic perhaps, but the maths is simpler!). The line taken by the car makes it a right angled (90°), 164ft (50m) radius corner. We have seen that the limiting force which can be generated is given by $F = \mu R$, and we'll assume μ is an average racing tyre value of 1.4. The car's mass is 1,100lb (500kg). The equation for the force which keeps a body moving in a circular path, known as the centripetal, or 'centre seeking' force, is given by

$$F = (mv^2)/r$$

where m is the body's mass, and r is the radius of the circle. So now, we can say that

$$\mu R = (mv^2)/r$$

because the limiting friction is exactly

balancing the force required to maintain the circular path, and no tractive forces (acceleration or braking) are being fed in. This means our driver is very skilful indeed, and can balance the car precisely on the limit of adhesion available to him! Oh, if only that were possible . . .

Now let's indulge in a spot of algebraic jiggery-pokery, and rearrange this equation to make v, the velocity, the subject, viz:

$$v = \sqrt{[\mu Rr/m]}$$

From this, we can feed in values for the coefficient of friction, the weight, or effective weight of the car, the corner radius, and the car's mass, and calculate the maximum cornering speed possible in those conditions.

If we start with zero downforce generation, then R is equal to the car's weight, and the calculation becomes

$$v_{max} = \sqrt{[1.4 \times 1{,}100 \times 32.2 \times 164/1{,}100]}$$

which comes out to

$$v_{max} = 86.0\text{ft/sec (26.2m/sec), or}$$
58.6mph (94.3kmh)

Notice that the car's weight is expressed in this equation as its mass, which is what the 1,100lb really is, multiplied by the force due to gravity, of 32.2lb force per lb mass.

Using the equation for aerodynamic lift, and substituting the previously determined values for the C_L of 2.32, and for the reference area, A, of 16sq ft (1.5m²), we can calculate how much downforce such a car would produce at this speed:

$$\text{Downforce} = 0.5 \times 0.00238 \times 2.32 \times 16 \times (86.0)^2$$
= 326.7lb (148.5kg, or 1,457 Newtons)

This figure is added to the vehicle's weight to produce an effective weight value – the car is now being pressed onto the ground with more force than just its own weight, and the value for R is the car's weight plus the downforce value. Thus, the maximum cornering speed now becomes

$$v_{max} = \sqrt{[1.4 \times (1{,}100 + 326.7) \times 32.2 \times 164/1{,}100]}$$
= 97.9ft/sec (29.9m/sec), or 66.8mph (107.6kmh)

This is clearly a significant increase in cornering speed compared to the unassisted value, and to bring this gain into even sharper focus, we can calculate the time saving achieved by this gain in speed. Having said that the corner was a 90°, 164ft (50m) constant radius, the distance through it is one quarter of the circumference of a 164ft radius circle, which distance would be given by $2\pi r/4$, or 257.6ft (78.5m).

Time taken = distance/speed

So in the unassisted case, the corner takes 257.6/86.0 = 2.995 sec, and in the assisted case, the corner takes 257.6/97.9 = 2.631 sec, a saving in this one short section of track of 0.364 sec. Add to this the fact that the car now enters the next section of track 8.2mph (13.2kmh) faster than the unassisted car, and yet more gains are to be had from carrying that extra speed. Then one has to take account of the *extra* downforce created because the car is now able to corner faster than before! The process is an iterative one.

Actually, the situation is not quite this simple, because tyres do not behave in a totally linear way. As the normal force on them increases, their coefficient of friction actually tails off, which means two things – firstly, the maths gets more complicated, and secondly, the gains are not as big as in our simple example. But nevertheless, there are still significant benefits to be had, and clearly downforce has a major role to play in racecar performance.

Production cars and aerodynamic lift
The case of the production car is, generally speaking, rather different, with

modern shapes tending to generate *posi-tive* lift. For the racers of production-based machines, the reduction or reversal, wherever possible and wherever permitted by the regulations, of this propensity to create positive aerodynamic lift is a matter of considerable interest. Over the years, this tendency for positive lift production has tended to worsen, especially during that period when volume car manufacturers were vying for the lowest C_D they could achieve. The reason that so many production cars pro-duce positive lift is, of course, tied up in their shape. Design trends have seen a general smoothing out of shapes, with raked back windscreens, and rounding of transitions to give much sleeker shapes, with the benefit, naturally, of low drag coefficients. But, the downside of this effort has been to ensure that the air flowing over the upper surfaces of vehi-cles is smoothly accelerated, and is kept as smooth, fast, and undisturbed as pos-sible. In fact in side view, some modern saloon profiles bear a striking resem-blance to an aerofoil in the positive lift orientation (see Figure 2–8). This, of course, means that low pressure is cre-ated above the vehicle, which is the cause of the upward lifting force.

To put this effect into perspective, it's worth stopping to look at some more fig-ures. Hard downforce values on current racing machines are always difficult to come by, but an unimpeachable source suggested to the author during 1996 that the best of the British Touring Car Championship (BTCC) or 'Super Touring' cars were probably generating in the region of 120 to 130lb (55 to 59kg) of downforce at 100mph (160kmh). This doesn't sound a vast amount, but then the regulations are such that downforce is bound to be restricted. However, when this figure is compared with the produc-tion vehicles, which do not carry the deep front airdams, or the splitters, or the rear wings of their racing counterparts, and which are said to produce positive lift of the order of +160 to +180lb (+72 to +82kg) at 100mph (160kmh) then 120lb (55kg) of downforce seems quite reason-able. This means, in fact, that the effec-tive weight of the cars is up to 300lb (136kg) greater in racing trim than in road trim at 100mph (160kmh) as the result of the downforce. This represents about 13 per cent extra 'normal' force acting on the tyres at this speed, which simplistically translates to 13 per cent greater cornering forces being possible. In a racing category where hundredths of a second count, this is highly significant.

Viscous complications
There are some other definitions that we cannot ignore, and which would seem to further complicate an already complex subject. But consideration of these addi-tional factors is pretty crucial if we are to understand their potential influences. First let's consider the two types of flow which can exist, and define them. Flow may be either 'laminar' or 'turbulent' (Figure 2–9). If all the particles within a parcel of air

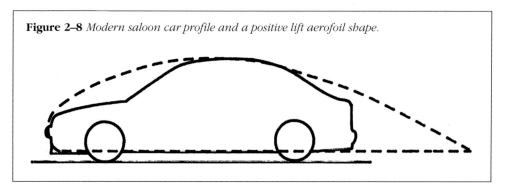

Figure 2–8 *Modern saloon car profile and a positive lift aerofoil shape.*

are moving in the same direction as the average air velocity, and the mean paths, or 'streamlines', traced by the air particles are parallel, then the flow may be said to be laminar. If, on the other hand, the air particles trace out erratic, non-parallel paths, even though the average velocity may be of the same magnitude and direction as in the laminar case, then the flow is said to be turbulent. These two types of flow may be visualised shortly after lighting a fire, as smoke rises from the, as yet, inefficiently combusting fuel. Initially the smoke may be seen to rise in more or less straight streamlines, and this is laminar flow. However, as the smoke rises, it starts to mix and swirl, and the streamlines cease to be parallel. The flow has become turbulent.

Getting back to specifics, as air flows around a body like a car, it may precisely follow the shape of the vehicle, in which case it is referred to as 'attached' flow; if it departs from following the vehicle's shape, it is referred to instead as 'separated' flow (Figure 2–10). The maintenance of an attached flow has a great influence on drag and downforce, as we

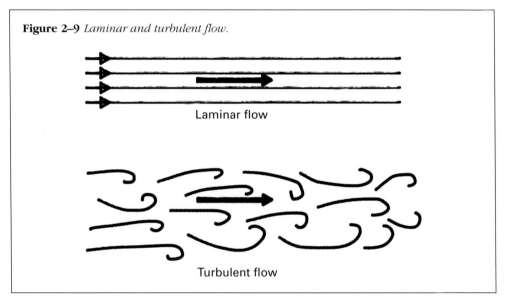

Figure 2–9 *Laminar and turbulent flow.*

Laminar flow

Turbulent flow

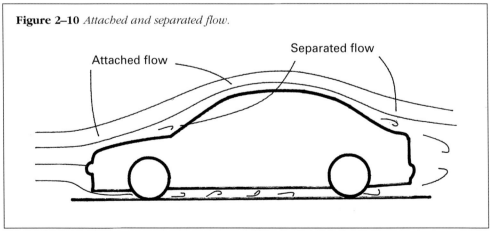

Figure 2–10 *Attached and separated flow.*

Separated flow

Attached flow

shall see in later chapters.

Up to now we have made some implicit and simple assumptions about the way air flows around bodies. If air were an 'ideal gas', with no viscosity, then our simple assumptions might be valid, but in reality, air is a viscous fluid, and, as such, when a body is moving through it, the air in proximity to the body's surface displays internal friction. Air particles which are in contact with the surface are actually held back by friction with the surface, and the air layer immediately adjacent to the body's surface has zero velocity relative to the body – it actually 'sticks' to the surface. The layers of air further away from the surface are slowed down by this viscous friction too, but as the distance from the surface increases, this effect becomes smaller and smaller, until, at a certain distance, the air speed around the body is unaffected, and becomes known as the 'mainstream' air velocity. Thus there is a layer of air around the body through which there is a velocity gradient, from zero at the surface, to the local mainstream velocity at its outer edge. This layer is called the 'boundary layer'.

If the velocity differences between the sub-layers in the boundary layer are small, they will slide over each other with little interaction, so giving a 'laminar' boundary layer. If, on the other hand, something disturbs the laminar boundary layer, such as a change of curvature or surface 'roughness', then the boundary layer can become turbulent (see Figure 2–11). The boundary layer will also increase in thickness further along the surface of a body, so that it may be thin and laminar over the front, upper parts of, say, a saloon car, but will increase in thickness and become turbulent further back along the vehicle (see Figure 2–12) as the result of disturbances caused by the vehicle's passage through the air.

A laminar boundary layer creates less surface friction than does a turbulent one, and so drag is less so long as the boundary layer remains laminar. But a turbulent boundary layer may also delay the onset of flow separation in certain circumstances, or even cause the re-attachment of a separated flow. This can have important positive benefits for drag reduction and downforce creation, and so it would be wrong to say that the laminar condition is what we are always aiming for. Whilst a laminar boundary layer is benefi-

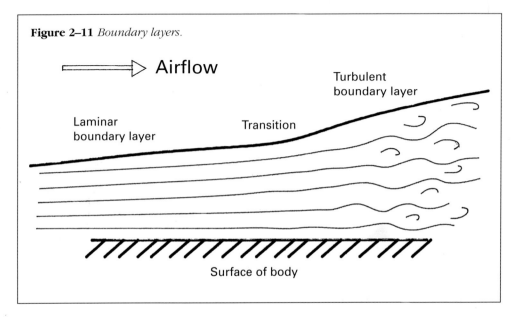

Figure 2–11 *Boundary layers.*

Airflow

Turbulent boundary layer

Laminar boundary layer

Transition

Surface of body

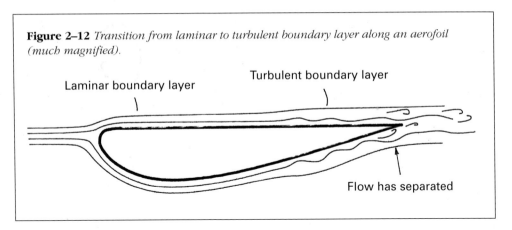

Figure 2–12 *Transition from laminar to turbulent boundary layer along an aerofoil (much magnified).*

Laminar boundary layer

Turbulent boundary layer

Flow has separated

cial in some circumstances, 'vortex generators' on a wing surface, for example, may be used to re-energise a turbulent boundary layer to prevent separation.

Reynolds Numbers

One of the more bizarre ideas to try to understand within aerodynamics is the concept of the Reynolds Number. Defined by yet another mathematical formula as

$$Re = \frac{\rho vL}{\mu}$$

where ρ is air density, μ now represents viscosity, v is velocity and L is 'some characteristic length' such as the length of a car or the chord dimension of a wing, the Reynolds Number is perhaps most simply thought of as a means of comparing data obtained at different speeds and different scales. If we wish to use metric units, this equation comes down to

$Re = 67,778 \times vL$, with v in m/sec and L in metres

For users of imperial units

$Re = 6,300 \times vL$, with v in ft/sec and L in feet

It is interesting to note that the Reynolds Number is another dimensionless quantity; that is, when the units of density, speed, length and viscosity are all resolved in the full equation, they cancel out and produce simply a number.

Take as an example a typical medium sized passenger car of 4.5m (14.76ft) length travelling at 25m/sec (56mph), then the Reynolds Number calculates to 7.6 million, or 7.6×10^6 in 'scientific notation'. So what? Well, consider the case of the testing of a 25 per cent, or 1/4 scale, model of the same car. At the same air speed, the Reynolds Number will be a quarter of the full scale value, or 1.9 million (1.9×10^6). Now, if the wind-tunnel being used for these tests was only capable of producing speeds of, say, 10m/sec, then the Reynolds Number would fall to 760,000, or 7.6×10^5, which is a whole order of magnitude lower. It is now possible that results obtained at this scale and at this speed might not be at all applicable to the full size, full speed case, because the effects of viscosity and density mean that the flow patterns could be very different. Remember that the boundary layer starts off being fairly thin and laminar at the front of a moving body, but further along the body it thickens, and quite probably becomes turbulent. It's not hard to envisage, then, that on a small scale model, the transition of that boundary layer from thin and laminar to thick and turbulent is likely to occur further along, relatively speaking, than on the full size body.

So the Reynolds Number is a convenient way of indicating the scale and speed at which data were obtained, in order that they might be interpreted in context, and compared with data obtained at similar scale and speed. But the Reynolds Number can also be used as an indicator to whether flow is likely to be laminar or turbulent, since, in general, flow becomes more turbulent with increasing speed, and also increasing distance ('L') along a body. Thus a high Reynolds Number might be used to indicate that the flow is turbulent.

Flow is three-dimensional

Because it is common practice to display flow around a shape in simple two-dimensional ways, largely, no doubt, because it is easier to draw things in two dimensions, it is all too easy to *think* only in two dimensions as well. But a car is a three-dimensional body, and air will seek to use all three dimensions as it takes its entirely natural path along the line of least resistance. Professional race team designers now have sophisticated computer-based software packages capable not only of 'drawing' representations of three-dimensional objects (components like aerofoils, or whole cars), but also of displaying an airflow around these objects in a three-dimensional way. The rest of us are probably not blessed with such facilities, and we therefore have to use our mental faculties to attempt to envision flows in three dimensions. In a later chapter we shall look at ways of visualising flow that do not necessarily require either a computer or a wind-tunnel. In the meantime, try to think not just in terms of side elevation or plan view, but in three dimensions and from all angles.

Pressure gradients

Fluids always flow most easily from areas of high pressure to areas of low pressure. This is a result of compliance with the laws of nature, and in the context of air-flow around a car, is not something which usually causes any problems. But air which has accelerated into a low pressure region – over the roof of a passenger based racer, for example, or underneath a ground effect single seater – usually then has to slow down again as the local pressure rises and returns back to ambient. A region of rising pressure is known as an 'adverse pressure gradient'. This in itself is not necessarily problematic, unless the airflow is expected to make too rapid a change of direction in such a region in order to return to ambient pressure. In such a case, the airflow is quite likely to separate from the surface in question, such as at the sharp angle change at the rear of the roof line of a passenger based competition car. This would cause an increase in drag, and often a decrease in downforce too if the flow separates from a downforce-inducing surface. Flow separation on the critical surfaces of aerofoils can also occur if the profile creates too rapid a change of direction. Thus, careful management of airflow in adverse pressure gradient regions is important in achieving efficient downforce.

But enough of abstract theory, for now at least. The following chapters will examine a variety of downforce-inducing devices, looking at the *practical* application of the theory that explains their function.

Chapter 3

Spoiling things

Years of instability

As we discovered in Chapter 1, Michael May's ill-fated attempt at introducing real downforce to motorsport back in 1956 was either ignored, or – more likely, perhaps – just not understood. Whichever it was, his efforts must have been completely forgotten about, because it was quite some time before racers once more 'discovered' downforce, and even then it seems as if it was almost by accident. It was during the 1960s that production-based and sports GT racers (that is, racers of closed wheel cars) got really concerned about aerodynamic lift at speed. By this time top speeds had risen to the extent that the aerodynamic forces were pretty large, and drag-reducing streamlining was beginning to create shapes that could actually cause positive lift. The effect of such lift was, literally, very unsettling, especially for the drivers, because cars could become unstable at speed. This problem would have undoubtedly attracted most attention in the faster sporting arenas such as Le Mans, and the Superspeedways of the United States. However, because their shape is intrinsically less lift-inducing, open wheel single seater racecars didn't experience this high speed instability to the same extent as their closed wheel brethren.

So, it was in the closed wheel categories that lift reducing attachments first materialised. 'Chin spoilers' and 'airdams' at the front and 'ridge' spoilers at the rear were amongst the first anti-lift devices. Front 'splitters' later augmented airdams at the front, and over the years since the 1960s, as these items have been refined and developed, other variations have been added with the same lift reducing purpose. This chapter will attempt to explain how these devices work, and what can be expected from them in terms of lift reduction and downforce production.

Whether it was rear ridge spoilers or front airdams that appeared first in motor racing is a matter for the historians to argue over. In a practical sense, the end of the car that those 1960s racers would have been most likely to study first, aerodynamically speaking, would have been influenced predominantly by which end started to lose grip first at speed! But as far as we are concerned here, we have to start at one end or the other, and, by the flip of a coin, the rear wins!

Rear spoilers

Rear spoilers come in all shapes and sizes, from a simple inclined flat plate as defined by NASCAR and fitted to Winston Cup stock-cars, to a three-dimensional, carefully integrated shape that smoothly follows the lines of the rear of a car. Whatever its shape, for our purposes here we shall consider the definition of a rear spoiler to be a device which is continuous with the upper surface of the car, with no gaps between itself and the car's bodywork. Spoilers with a gap between

Rear spoiler on a NASCAR Winston Cup car.

themselves and the bodywork will be regarded as wings, however crude they may be, and wings will be looked at in a separate chapter.

The purpose of the spoiler is, as its name suggests, to spoil the fast, smooth, low drag airflow that is, unfortunately, the cause of positive lift, and in so doing, to reduce or even cancel out that positive lift. By protruding up into the airflow over the rear of a car, as shown in Figure 3–1, the spoiler causes the flow to separate in front of itself, and creates a separation bubble rather similar to that shown at the bottom of the windshield. If the flow has already separated over the rear of the car, then a rear spoiler will induce the flow to separate sooner. The effect of this is to drastically reduce the local airflow velocity over the rear surface, which

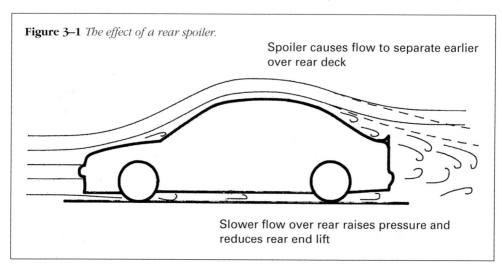

Figure 3–1 *The effect of a rear spoiler.*

Spoiler causes flow to separate earlier over rear deck

Slower flow over rear raises pressure and reduces rear end lift in turn causes a rise in pressure over this area. This therefore reduces the natural lift created by the unadorned car profile.

Curiously, fitting a rear spoiler doesn't necessarily increase a car's drag. There are circumstances where the fitting of a rear spoiler actually decreases drag, but, as a generalisation, it would be wise to simply look for a lift reduction and not be too greedy! Those 1960s pioneers found that the height of the spoiler could be increased without initially hurting top speed, and, indeed, in some circumstances, top speed did actually increase, demonstrating that drag reductions were a possibility. Then at a particular spoiler height top speed started to come down, but so too did lap times. This, of course, shows that although drag had increased, the overall net benefit was positive and good, and derived from increased stability and grip.

It seems that there may be an optimal height for a rear spoiler, though it is important to bear in mind that what works well on one car may not transfer to another with comparable gains. In one study it was determined that the greatest gain, represented by the change to the rear lift coefficient (ΔC_{Lr}) was achieved at a spoiler height which was about 8 per cent of the car's wheelbase (this equates to about 8 to 9in (20 to 23cm) height for a medium size production car of 106in [2,700mm] wheelbase), and gave a ΔC_{Lr} value of –0.45 – that is, it created a sub-stantial reduction in rear end lift which turned the coefficient of lift at the rear axle from about +0.10 (that is, *positive* lift) without a spoiler to –0.35 (genuine *downforce*, in the case studied) with one of that height. If 8 or 9in seems like a rather large spoiler, look at the back end of a NASCAR Winston Cup car.

In another study, ΔC_{Lr} values of –0.30 and –0.40 for rear spoiler heights of just 2in and 4in (50 and 100mm) were indicated, for negligible drag increments. Indeed, at a spoiler height of just 1in (25mm), ΔC_{Lr} was around –0.20, and drag had also been reduced by about –0.03. The marked difference between the two sets of data in these two studies arises, in all probability, because they *were* two different studies, on two different car profiles, and this serves to illustrate how a spoiler's effectiveness is dependant on the individual car it is fitted to, and on what has happened to the airflow on its way to the rear of the car. It is clearly difficult to generalise, and to further emphasise this we could visualise an extreme case of a 1990s hatchback shape with a spoiler mounted at the bottom of the tailgate, where it is situated entirely in the turbulent wake in a position that can do nothing for downforce production or lift reduction (Figure 3–2)

The angle of a flat plate spoiler has also been shown, on a production-based car shape, to influence the aerodynamic benefit, and, not surprisingly, the more

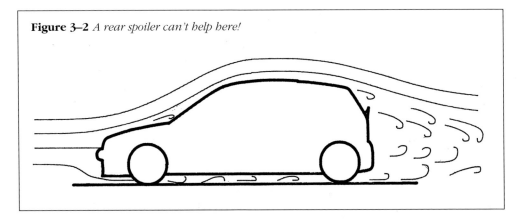

Figure 3–2 *A rear spoiler can't help here!*

steeply inclined the spoiler was, the greater the benefit, with a ΔC_{Lr} of around −0.12 at 30°, rising to about −0.19 at 60°. The benefit did seem to be tailing off after 40 to 50°. Drag increased more or less linearly with increasing inclination angle, to a maximum of about ΔC_D +0.08 at 60°. Whether this drag increment would be regarded as significant or not would depend on the type of competition the car was engaged in, which would determine the speed regime it operated in, as well as how large the increment was compared to the drag coefficient of the whole car without the spoiler. Such a change in drag would be much less of a worry if the car was competing in, for example, a British hillclimb, where top speeds for a production-based car might be limited to about 100 to 120mph, than if it was a NASCAR stocker lapping at 190mph. Equally, if the car started with a drag coefficient of, say, 0.30, then an increase of 0.08 would be far more noticeable than the same increase on a car with a C_D of 0.50.

We'll discuss in more detail the choices and compromises to be made in selecting how much downforce is needed versus how much drag can be tolerated in a later chapter. But the key points of rear spoiler design are that a bigger rear spoiler, up to a point which can only really be determined by some form of testing of the car concerned, gives more benefit in reducing lift; drag increases need not be huge, and in some situations, drag can actually be reduced. And a larger spoiler inclination also creates greater lift reduction benefit, though an increase in drag will follow.

It's interesting to look at what these changes in lift coefficient actually mean in terms of forces felt by a car, by looking at an example. If we consider a standard production family car with a reference frontal area of 25sq ft (2.32sq m) travelling at 100mph (160kmh), we can feed in some incremental changes to C_{Lr} values into the equation for aerodynamic lift and calculate the actual forces involved.

ΔC_{Lr}	Lift force
0.10	64lb (29kg)
0.15	96lb (43.6kg)
0.20	128lb (58.2kg)
0.25	160lb (72.7kg)
0.30	192lb (87.3kg)
0.35	224lb (101.8kg)
0.40	256lb (116.3kg)

Remember, when calculating the forces at any other speed, that the force is proportional to the square of the speed, so at 50mph (80kmh), divide these figures by four, and at 200mph (320kmh) multiply them by four. At any intermediate speed of interest, say 75mph, multiply by the ratio of the speeds squared, that is, $(75/100)^2$. For a clearer picture, look at the graph in Figure 3–3, which shows the forces created by a range of C_L values across a wide speed range for a car of reference area 25sq ft (2.32sq m).

Clearly, even with modest changes to the C_L values the forces can be substantial, and it would be far better to have a negative sign on them, so that they represented downforce working for us, than a positive sign, indicating aerodynamic lift which was trying to float the car off the road! The significance of the forces can be assessed by relating them to the static weight of the car involved, as described in Chapter 2. For example, if our reference car weighed 2,200lb (1,000kg), with, say, a 50/50 weight distribution, and we achieved a ΔC_{Lr} of −0.25, then at 100mph (160kmh) the effective weight at the rear will be aerodynamically increased by 160lb (72.7kg), which is 14.5 per cent of the static weight on the rear of the car. In simple terms, this translates to 14.5 per cent extra grip at that speed, and who *wouldn't* want that much extra grip? And even at half the speed, where the gains are a quarter as great, this represents an increase in grip of over 3.6 per cent. This may not sound much, but taken together with the possibility of very little drag penalty, even this small a gain could translate into vital hundredths or even tenths of a second off a lap or a run time.

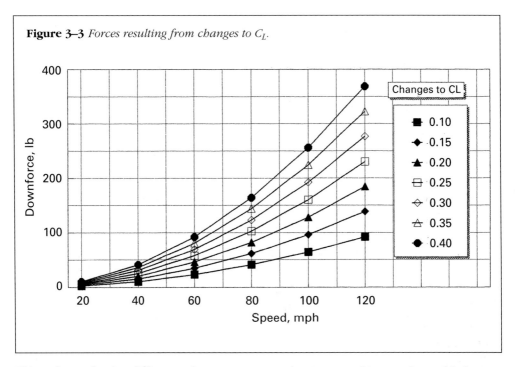

Figure 3–3 *Forces resulting from changes to C_L.*

If it only made the difference between a 1min 30.01sec lap and a 1min 29.99sec lap, the boost to driver and team morale alone would make it all worthwhile! But increasing grip at the rear alone may not help our cause as much as we hoped – unless it produced a lot of aerodynamic lift at the rear in the first place, of course. It's more likely, particularly with a passenger car, that somewhat more lift will be created towards the front of the car, and so we have to look at ways of combating, and possibly reversing, that lift in order to increase grip at the front end too.

Front spoilers

Front spoilers also vary in design complexity, from simple 'chin' spoilers, which are little more than a vertical or near-vertical piece of rigid, flat sheet bolted to the lower front panel of a car, to the beautifully shaped 'airdam' spoilers now integrated into road car designs, and extended in dimensions and effectiveness on competition cars. For the purposes of definition here, let's assume that a front spoiler is something to be *added* to an existing car shape, whether or not some form of spoiler or airdam already exists.

Finding a truly adequate explanation for how a front spoiler works is a bit like looking for the Holy Grail. What's more, there are some variations on the theme which quite clearly have different functions, and provide benefits using different principles. However, because all these devices get lumped together under the same heading, descriptions of their workings get rather confusing. So let's see if we can unravel some of the mystery without adding to the confusion.

In its simplest form, an 'airdam' front spoiler extends downwards from the lower front panel of the car to reduce the car-to-ground gap, and this reduces the amount of air which passes beneath the car when it is in motion. Some of the air which would have passed under the car is now diverted down the sides. So how does this help? There are two potential benefits, depending on the type and form of car. If the car is a production-based vehicle which has not been, or – because

Front spoilers can be complex, as on the Ford Mondeo Super Tourer . . . or very simple, as on this Austin Healey Sprite.

of regulations – cannot be much altered from standard, then in all probability it will have an underside which is far from smooth. There will be crankcases, gearboxes, exhausts, driveshafts, wheels, wheel cavities, fuel tanks, and all manner of lumps, bumps, and holes. Clearly, air passing under a car with such an underside will not have a smooth passage, and it is easy to understand that this situation causes significant drag. So, if the mass of air flowing through this region is

reduced, it follows that drag should reduce, and this proves to be the case. Thus, even though the frontal area of a car may actually be increased by the addition of this type of spoiler, the drag coefficient can be reduced sufficiently to more than compensate for this, and a net reduction in drag ensues. However, for a car that has already been fitted with a smooth underside, perhaps in a search for reduced drag, a further drag reduction should not be expected from an airdam;

in reality, an increase in drag may well occur in this case by virtue of the increase to frontal area. Nevertheless, the positive effects of lift reduction/down-force may still be achieved, to the overall benefit of the car's on-track performance.

The second benefit, and the one in which we are most interested here, is that the pressure beneath the car is reduced by the fitting of this type of front spoiler. But how does this happen? Let's take an extreme example and consider what happens if you block off the flow to the underside at the front completely, with an airdam which reaches to the ground. This wouldn't be practical, and nor would most competition regulations allow it, but let's stick with the notion for a while. If a car with this very deep airdam *could* move along, the air under the car would be in much the same state as the air in its wake, which is to say, turbulent, and being hauled along behind the car.

The wake is a low pressure region (we know this intuitively because not only can we see leaves, dust and debris being sucked along behind a car, but we can *feel* our own car get sucked into the wake of another car we are following closely), and in the configuration described here, the underside of the car becomes, like the wake, a low pressure region (see Figure 3–4). The low pressure has the entire planform area of the car to act upon, and the theoretical result is a car with a decidedly negative lift coefficient – that is, one which would create significant downforce (remember, force = pressure × area). Of course, the impracticality of such a ground-scraping spoiler means that the theoretical benefits cannot be achieved, but the effect, though much reduced, is still obtainable even with the type of ground clearance that doesn't require repairs at the end of every lap. So lift reduction is a real prospect, and genuine downforce may be achievable, depending on the precise shape of the car, its ground clearance, and the details of the spoiler and overall car design.

The effectiveness of a front spoiler working in this way can be increased by

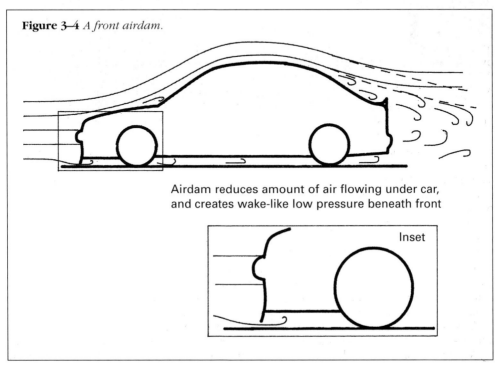

Figure 3–4 *A front airdam.*

Airdam reduces amount of air flowing under car, and creates wake-like low pressure beneath front

Inset

the use of side skirts, which help to seal the underside from flow entering along the lower sides of the car. Clearly, if the pressure has been reduced under the car, air passing down the sides will try to spill into this low pressure area, and if it was allowed to do so, it would raise the pressure again, which would reduce any benefit that might have been created. Go back to the extreme example again of the spoiler touching the ground, and it's easy to imagine that if the sides were also extended to touch the ground, then the conditions under the car would be exactly the same as in the wake. Lifting the skirts, if you'll pardon the expression, so that they don't quite touch the ground any more, obviously allows a gap through which air can spill into the reduced pressure region under the car, and the magnitude of the low pressure is reduced, which in turn reduces downforce. More of this in a later chapter, but it begins to be clear why the effect of an aerodynamic device at the front of a car may be affected by the shape and design of components or panels much further back.

So, the airdam spoiler creates lift reduction, or downforce if we are lucky, by blocking off the flow to the underside. What magnitude of effect can we expect? A study done on a road-going passenger car shape with a front ground clearance of 300mm (11.8in) showed that decreasing the car-to-ground gap with a simple flat sheet airdam spoiler reduced the front lift coefficient quite significantly, and also, initially at least, reduced the overall drag coefficient too. With a spoiler depth of just 90mm (3.5in), the ΔC_{Lf} value – that is, the change in front end lift coefficient – was around –0.21, and the drag had reduced to its minimum with a ΔC_D of about –0.04. This obviously represents an efficient change in aerodynamic performance. However, lift reduction continued at greater spoiler depths, and by 170mm (6.7in) the ΔC_{Lf} value had gone down to about –0.25, although drag had climbed back up to its original level again. Here at

least was a change which had no drag *penalty*. At spoiler depths greater than 170mm, the changes to the ΔC_{Lf} were tailing off, and had virtually levelled out at 250mm (9.8in) depth to around –0.27. Drag, however, continued to climb, although the increase even at 250mm depth was just +0.04, so the penalty was not huge (though its significance would depend on your competition arena, of course).

An interesting point shown in the data on this test was that the ΔC_{Lr} values actually *increased* as the ΔC_{Lf} decreased. In other words, in this test the lift coefficient at the rear got worse as the front got better. This may have been because the airflow to the rear had been modified by the airdam, or it may have been a mechanical cantilever effect due to the overhang of the airdam in front of the front axle. Either way, it is a further lesson in how changes at one end of the car can affect things at the other.

Anyway, we'll look at the front end in glorious isolation for a minute, knowing that it is potentially risky to do so, and put some numbers on these ΔC_{Lf} values. Once again we can tabulate actual forces for the levels of change to the front end lift coefficient that the study quoted above indicated were achieved. We'll use our typical family car dimensions of 25sq ft (2.32sq m) frontal reference area, and 100mph (160kmh) for the sake of example:

ΔC_{Lf}	Lift force
0.10	64lb (29kg)
0.15	96lb (43.6kg)
0.20	128lb (58.2kg)
0.25	160lb (72.7kg)

These values are obviously the same as those in the earlier table for the same change to the lift coefficient, only this time they apply to the front end. Furthermore, the same comments can be applied to the significance of these lift force values in relation to the static weight on the front axle of the car in question. Thus, 160lb (72.7kg) represents 14.5 per cent of the weight on the front axle of a 2,200 lb (1,000 kg) car with a 50/50 weight distribution, and if this much lift reduction is obtained, then the grip increase at this speed will be in direct proportion. And, if you recall, in Chapter 2 we said that typical production cars are said to produce around 160 to 180lb (72.7 to 81.2kg) of positive lift, overall, at 100mph. So an airdam front spoiler could be expected to not only cancel this level of positive lift, but if it was a reasonably deep and effective device, to generate some downforce as well, perhaps of the order of 80lb (36.4kg) or so at this speed. The danger here, though, is of over-generalising, and in reality the effect on any particular car will only be determined by wind-tunnel or track testing. But we have at least seen that the lift coefficient changes, front and rear, from the two types of spoiler looked at so far, can be of the same order, which means that it ought to be possible to reduce overall lift (or gain real down-force) *and* maintain an aerodynamic balance, which is extremely important.

There is a further important, related issue to keep firmly in mind when considering a front airdam for your racecar – cooling. And not just engine cooling, but brake and – particularly if the car is front-wheel drive – transmission cooling too. Interestingly, by creating a low pressure area below a car, the flow of cooling air through the engine compartment may actually be enhanced. At the risk of being thought slanderous, it always appears as if the designers of road vehicles include a nice big hole in the front of the car to channel air *to* a radiator matrix, but they then seem to forget about getting the air *from* the radiator. Somehow, the air is supposed to find its own way out, past the engine, and probably the transmission too, and into the turbulent, sluggish flow beneath the car. However, the fitting of an airdam, which we have seen causes a reduction in air pressure beneath the front of the car especially, can also create

some suction on the air in the engine compartment. The effect of this can be to encourage more cooling air away from the radiator, and the engine may run cooler as a result. This in turn may enable a smaller air intake for cooling air to be used, with a further positive influence on drag – but this would have to be the result of some cautious experimentation to avoid taking the notion to a reckless extreme, and causing overheating.

A front-engined car relies on a flow of air over its crankcase to facilitate some of the heat rejection, so care must be exercised when contemplating an airdam. At the very least, it may be necessary to provide an appropriately sited cut-out, ducted and radiused of course, to channel some air to where it is needed for this role. The same may apply to a front-wheel drive vehicle if the transmission requires cooling in this way, and, in the same vein, the airflow to auxiliary oil coolers must be maintained. Brake cooling will be ignored at your peril too, though the dependence on cool brakes will, of course, depend on the particular competition category. But as with the other aspects of cooling mentioned here, it is possible that installing an airdam will interfere with that part of the airflow which transports heat away from the front brakes (and possibly the rear brakes too, let's not forget). Once more, radiused ducts which channel air to the brakes may prove to be necessary. This whole topic of cooling is probably an area where track testing and actual competition will be the only way you will find out what the ultimate requirements are going to be.

Variations on the airdam theme
We have seen that the basic, simple airdam reduces under-car pressure by blocking off most, or some, of the flow under the car, which creates wake-like, low pressure conditions in that region. What an airdam will do in addition is locally accelerate the velocity of the air which does flow under the spoiler, in the

reduced car-to-ground gap, which will also create a locally reduced pressure. Now, on a lot of cars this is of no particular benefit because the area below and behind the airdam is just an empty cavity – beneath the radiator and ahead of the engine in the case of a front-engined passenger car, for example. As mentioned above, this local pressure reduction may enhance cooling efficiency, but unless we do something about exploiting it, no lift reducing benefits will be gained from this zone of low pressure. So how can it be exploited? Simple – to the airdam, add a horizontal return which extends rearwards. Or better still, incline the extension upwards towards the rear slightly, to form a kind of 'diffuser' (more on this terminology in a later chapter). See Figure 3–5.

What you have now is a device which accelerates the airflow, and reduces the pressure in the narrow gap between the airdam and the ground, and a surface on which this low pressure can act. The result is downforce acting on the horizontal, or near horizontal, surface which, providing the surface is rigidly fixed to the car, then pulls the front of the car down too. Current British Super Touring cars use this principle, though the regulations have seen to it that the flat surface cannot extend any further under the car than the front axle line. It follows that this kind of device would not work if the airdam reached right down to the ground and blocked off all flow here, and in fact, the principle probably requires rather more ground clearance than might be used with a simple airdam. If one looks at those Super Touring cars that exploit the effect, the central part of the front airdam is frequently higher above the ground than the outer portions. And similarly, some of the now extinct Class 1 International Touring Cars that ran in Europe up to the end of 1996, in particular the Opel and Mercedes cars, demonstrated complex, curved front airdams which were clearly shaped to encourage air to flow into these front 'venturi' sections.

The splitter

A further extension, literally speaking, which can be added to the airdam is the

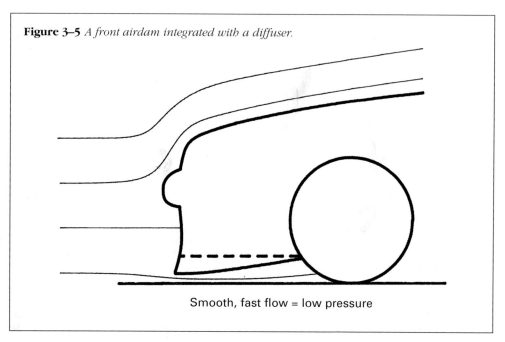

Figure 3–5 *A front airdam integrated with a diffuser.*

Smooth, fast flow = low pressure

Volvo S40 Super Touring car, with raised centre section in airdam. Compare with the Mondeo on page 40.

so called 'splitter'. This is a horizontal extension of the lower lip of an airdam which protrudes forwards. Simple, and even crude though the splitter may appear to be, it is actually an extremely efficient aerodynamic device which can create virtually drag-free downforce! How does it do that? In essence, by tapping into an area of high pressure. Most closed wheel cars, except the very streamlined, low drag type, have to some extent got a 'blunt' nose. As these cars move along, the air divides up and passes over, around, and under them. But immediately ahead of the blunt nose is what is known as a 'stagnation zone', where the air just kind of runs into the front of the car. Some of it is ducted into the cooling system from this area, which is logical because the air here is, relatively speaking, at a locally raised pressure, and so it will naturally follow any path which allows some relief to the high pressure. The stagnation zone can perhaps be thought of as a high pressure air bubble

stuck to the front of the car. Once again, therefore, we have a parcel of air that can be exploited, and again the technique is pretty simple – stick a flat plate out into it so that the high pressure exists above the plate, and the raised pressure presses down onto the plate, thus creating downforce (see Figure 3–6).

A splitter will also tend to assist with the original function of an airdam too, in that it is bound to restrict the amount of air that flows into the underside region of the car. Thus, in a sense, a splitter has the same effect as a deeper airdam, and as a result, yet more air is diverted around the sides of a car. This may help to account for the efficiency of the splitter as a downforce inducing device, in that very little if any extra drag seems to be incurred by a properly integrated splitter. (Indeed it was said that one Super Touring car in 1996, when fitted with just the front airdam/splitter kit, produced less drag than its standard production sister. The drag figure only got worse

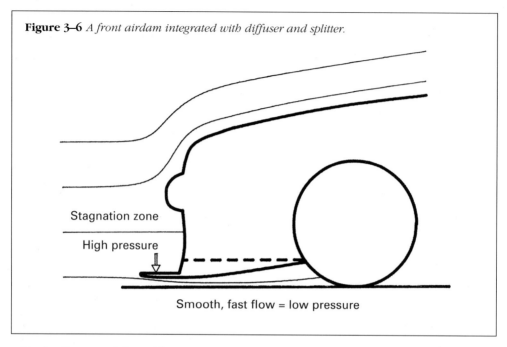

Figure 3–6 *A front airdam integrated with diffuser and splitter.*

Stagnation zone

High pressure

Smooth, fast flow = low pressure

with the fitment of the wider racing tyres and the rear aerofoil.) The amount of downforce created can be controlled by the length of the splitter, up to a point, and if the splitter is adjustable, then this provides a simple means of controlling the front-to-rear downforce balance. Some racing categories, of course, such as Super Touring cars, prohibit changes of this type, where aerodynamic packages have to be fixed for each entire season.

It is perhaps self-evident that it is only worth making a splitter of a certain length. If it protrudes beyond the high pressure stagnation region it will yield no additional benefit. It will also become a vulnerable liability dangling in front of the car! Equally apparent is that a splitter simply will not work at all on a car that has a sleek, low drag shape with a slender front end. The creation of the high pressure stagnation zone comes about because most cars have a blunt front end, and here a splitter can tap the high pressure area ahead of it. If your car has a sleek and finely tapered nose section, though, there may be no high pressure

area to tap, and you will have to pursue other routes to gain downforce.

One of the apparent problems with a splitter arrangement is that it can be very 'ground-clearance sensitive', or, if you prefer, 'ride height sensitive.' Changes to the ride height of a car, caused by a combination of dynamic suspension changes such as 'dive' under braking, and compression as the direct result of downforce, quite naturally alter the ground clearance of the whole of the body of a car. But airdams and splitters are already very close to the ground, and as we have seen, their very operation as aerodynamic devices is a function of their proximity to the ground. The nearer the ground they become, the more downforce they tend to create. So it is possible to envisage the situation where a car may produce very inconsistent amounts of downforce because its ride height is constantly fluctuating. One way of reducing this problem is to stiffen the car's suspension, which reduces the amount of suspension deflection for a given input load, be it mechanical or aerodynamic. This can have disadvantages, not only in terms of giving the driver a worse ride, but also potentially by reducing the ability of the car to grip the road, a condition which may make itself felt in slower corners where aerodynamics are not really helping. So the clever aerodynamicist will look for solutions which are less sensitive to changes in ride height, and which therefore allow the chassis engineers to retain a decent amount of suspension movement.

The previously mentioned variations on the airdam theme were designs intended to produce less sensitivity to ride height. By shaping the entry to the front under-splitter venturi channel as on the Opel Class 1 Touring cars of 1996, the possibility of 'blocking' the flow to the underside completely was eradicated, and more consistent downforce would ensue. But look closely at the design of these, and the Class 2 Super Tourers, and it can be seen that some of the front end devices are very much a combination of airdam, splitter, and venturi section. Naturally, the designers were looking for optimum efficiency, but consistency was high on the agenda too.

There is no doubt that splitters can produce significant downforce. In 1995, the McLaren F1 GTR sports racecar had been the recipient of very little aerodynamic development time, just one day having apparently been spent in the wind-tunnel prior to the date when designs had to be homologated and fixed for the season. It had a two-element rear wing, a rear underbody diffuser, and a simple nose section incorporating an airdam and a very small splitter. It understeered for most of the season, the front wheels creating a lot less grip than the rears. For 1996, a number of changes were made; the rules enforced a switch to a single-element rear wing, but also now permitted splitters extending up to 80mm further forwards. The car was refined during considerably more wind-tunnel testing than the previous year, and, Gordon Murray relates, downforce was up by an amazing 80 per cent on the previous year. It was also better balanced, with the previous year's understeer having been eradicated. Now whilst some of this improvement was due to other developments, the fitting of the front

The 80mm splitter extension helped eradicate understeer on the McLaren F1 GTR in 1996.

splitter did help the GTR to produce significantly more front end downforce.

It has been reported that a passenger-based closed wheel racecar produced a ΔC_{Lf} value of −0.20 for a ΔC_D of just +0.02 with the fitting of a full width splitter of unspecified dimensions. Clearly this is a very efficient gain in downforce, and if this can be added to the gains achieved from an airdam, it can be seen that the combined result might be as high as a ΔC_{Lf} of around −0.40 to −0.45. For our reference 'typical passenger car', of 25sq ft (2.32sq m) frontal area at 100mph (160kmh), this would create 256 to 288lb (116.4 to 130.9kg) of downforce to overcome natural lift and add to grip at speed.

Not just closed wheelers

Splitters may be thought of as devices whose use was limited to closed wheel racecars such as saloons/sedans and sports GT cars. But this is not so. Splitters have been used successfully in some single seater applications as well as the 'open wheel' sports racer in the form of the Clubmans car, which includes categories such as Formula 750 and Formula 1300 in the UK. In the late-1970s single seaters ran with what used to be rather vaguely called 'full width nose cones', as distinct from the narrow-nose-with-wings configuration, and cars like the March 782/783/793, Chevron B38/B40 and Formula 2 and Formula 3 racers of similar vintage were very successful with such noses installed. Most of them utilised some form of splitter, which was sometimes adjustable, and there would appear to have been no problem balancing the downforce from the rear wing with this set-up. Another form of adjustment applied to this nose type was the attachment of height-adjustable vertical plates mounted to the top lip of the nose, just ahead of the front wheels. Clearly these plates would act rather like a ridge spoiler on the rear of a car, and would have the effect of separating the flow locally, and creating small high pressure bubbles ahead of themselves. The additional downforce would not be great, but they provided a method of fine tuning.

Some Formula 750 cars use the wide nose with splitter arrangement.

This shape of nose continues to find favour amongst the competitors in some categories, and it may well be that on some cars it offers a lower drag, more efficient way of generating downforce. There is a school of thought amongst Formula 750 racers, who have very little horsepower to play with, and certainly none to waste, that the full width nose offers lower drag by diverting some of the airflow around the front tyres. It is equally certain, though, that cars in this formula with narrow noses and front wings are very successful. You pays yer money and takes yer choice.

Allan Staniforth, in *The Race and Rally Car Source Book*, relates the tale of observations made at hillclimb events, where he and some contemporaries were each driving their own full-width-nose-with-splitter equipped single seaters. Watching the cars through binoculars where speeds of 50 to 70mph (80 to 112kmh) were being attained, it was, apparently, evident that the front downforce being created was sufficient to compress the softly sprung machines' suspension quite signif-

icantly, and extra ground clearance had to be dialled in in the paddock between runs. He also adds a noteworthy caution – that the splitter needs to be parallel to the ground in the static condition, and of sufficiently robust construction and mounting. One of the above mentioned hillclimbers apparently did not have the centre of its splitter braced, and it could be seen to vibrate violently at speed. The car was also going noticeably light on its suspension too, proof, if it were needed, that the potential downforce was not being achieved. A small metal bracing strut cured this particular problem, but let this experience serve as a warning.

It may not be immediately evident, but today's crop of Formula 1 cars use a form of splitter, though not at the extreme front of the car. The regulations for Formula 1 demand that the cars have a flat underside between the rearmost tangent of the front wheels, and the front of the rear wheels. Most current Formula 1 cars also have the so called 'raised nose', with the underside of the nose signifi-cantly higher than the underside of the

The under-chassis 'splitter' on the Jordan 196 Formula 1 car. (Tracey Inglis)

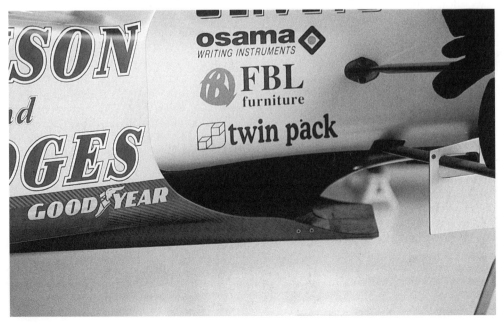

The 'tyre shelf splitter' on the Van Diemen RF97 Formula Renault Sport car.

central chassis. Thus, on most of the designs, the flat underside juts ahead of and below the rearward part of the nose underside, in much the same way as a splitter juts forward of an airdam. Consequently there is scope for a small stagnation zone to form above this 'splitter', and create a pressure differential which adds some downforce. And further back on Formula 1 cars (and many other current single seaters) there are flat extensions of the underside which stick out, to the maximum permitted body width, ahead of the rear wheels. Again, these panels exploit the stagnation zone that exists immediately ahead of the rear tyres to create a pressure differential above and below them, and add to the car's overall downforce. In each case, these panels need to be rigid enough to resist bending under the force applied, and to transmit that force to the chassis, and thence to the tyre contact patches.

Dive, dive, dive!

Another device which we will include in this chapter, since it doesn't neatly fall under any other heading, is the 'dive plate', or 'dive plane' if you prefer, so called because of its resemblance to the dive planes on submarines. In their simplest form they are flat plates, inclined downwards at the front, attached to the lower sides of the front ends of saloon/sedan and sports GT racers. Such an inclined plate will, of course, create some value of downforce, but it would not be expected to be very much, or very efficient. Again, they could be viewed as a means of fine tuning if they were adjustable or perhaps interchangeable. However, there have been cases where overall downforce figures have increased considerably simply with the fitting of dive plates, to levels that could not possibly arise directly from the dive plates themselves.

In these instances, there must have been some secondary influence on airflow which had a beneficial effect, and it is likely that the effect in these cases was to set up a vortex pattern down the sides of the cars, which had the result of sealing the underside from flow which otherwise would have leaked in from the sides. This in turn could lead to more

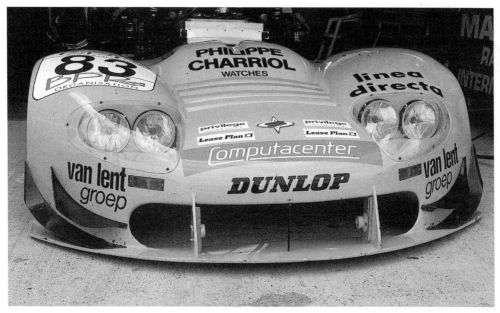

Dive plates on the front of this Marcos LM600 GT2 contender.

efficient downforce production from the underbody (more of which in a later chapter), and hey presto, lots more downforce, just by fitting little dive plates at the front! There is little likelihood that the amateur racer will strike lucky and get this kind of benefit from the fitting of dive plates – a few days in a wind-tunnel might just enable you to optimise their positioning and inclination – but as fine tuning devices, they obviously have a place. Dive plates have mutated into a variety of more complex forms, and in some cases it is immediately apparent that the designers were aiming to set up vortices down the sides of the car, whilst in others the devices appear to be there for fine tuning only.

Safety angles in NASCAR

Winston Cup stock-cars lap at very high speeds on ovals and Superspeedways, and as such, the aerodynamic forces which act upon them are pretty enormous. Downforce is held in check, with strict rules on airdams and rear spoilers, and bold efforts at aerodynamic parity between the different makes of cars are

also made by the regulators in an effort to ensure 'a good show' is put on, and everybody is competitive. But there is one problem which afflicted NASCAR which seems to have been particular to that category in terms of its frequency of occurrence. And the solutions just have to be unique in motorsport, even though they involved the use of spoilers.

The problem was that cars which were stable when being driven in the intended direction of travel, that is, forwards, actually became airborne when they went into a spin and started travelling almost backwards. Wind tunnel studies determined that at a yaw angle of around 140° – that is, running almost backwards – the profile of the upper surface of the car became very similar to a positive lift aerofoil. At speeds of around 160mph (257kmh), enough lift was generated for the car to leave the ground. Remember that these cars weigh 3,500lb (1,590kg), so a substantial amount of lift was being created. Various solutions were proposed and tried, but the combination of features finally settled upon exists nowhere else in the sport. The simple part of the solu-

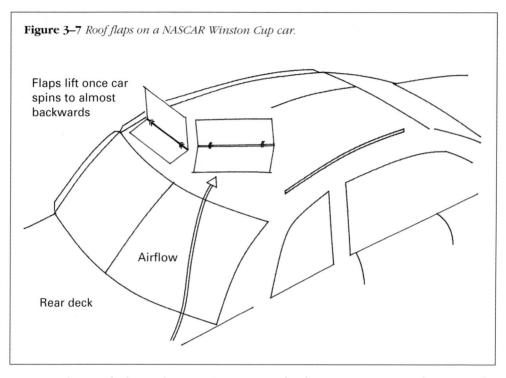

Figure 3–7 *Roof flaps on a NASCAR Winston Cup car.*

Flaps lift once car
spins to almost
backwards

Airflow

Rear deck

tion, tried out fairly early on during attempts to solve the problem, and still retained today, was to run half-inch (12.5mm) metal strips fore and aft down each side of the roof. At zero or small yaw angle, these strips would have little or no aerodynamic influence except, maybe, to enhance stability slightly. But at high yaw angles, specifically when travelling sideways, they would act as spoilers on the flow over the roof, and would tend to kill any lift forces that might start to build up. Further strips on the front and rear screens augment these roof strips, and small skirts on the bottom of the sills also contribute.

But this still didn't address the 'nearly backwards' situation. One attempted solution was to allow the entire boot/rear deck lid to hinge upwards under the influence of the air flowing in the 'wrong' direction, so that it became one huge spoiler. But in tests (using the Winston Cup corporate jet to supply a 200mph wind . . .) it was found that the forces

involved were so massive that even the retaining cables gave up and the lid blew completely off! Finally, the idea was refined so that roof mounted flaps, about 20 by 8in (510 by 205mm), hinged to flip up in the same way that the rear deck lid did, were fitted at the rear of the roof, where the lift at high yaw angles was greatest. One flap was orientated transversely, and another was located next to it, orientated at an angle perpendicular to the flow in the worst 140° yaw situation (see Figure 3–7). The flaps open under the influence of the enhanced low pressure which occurs when the car gets to that critical angle, but remain shut when the car goes about its business in the accepted direction. NASCAR now has some accumulated experience of the functioning of these safety enhancing spoilers, and the results seem to have been highly beneficial and successful. Very much a case of downforce – or at least, lift reduction – improving safety . . .

Chapter 4

Oh for the wings

ONCE IT BECAME clear that 'lift reduction' was only a part of what was possible with appropriately shaped and positioned aerodynamic attachments, the search was on for greater quantities of downforce to press racecars ever more firmly onto the track, and enable higher cornering speeds. Following Jim Hall's resurrection of the use of the inverted aerofoil, the downforce revolution turned really popular in the late 1960s, as Formula 1 cars sprouted wings front and rear, and we can now look back, 30 years later, to see where we've been (if only we could see where we're going as well . . .). The wing designs used in those days look pretty tame in comparison to the complex assemblages adorning each end of today's top level single seater racecars, and development continues at a furious pace at the sharp end of motorsport technology. Wings ain't what they used to be . . .

Definitions

Before we go anywhere, we have to start off with some background by way of terms and definitions, if only so that we know we're all referring to the same thing. It probably goes without saying that the terminology of wings, as well as some of the technology, comes from the world of aeronautics and aircraft, and the reference section at the end of this book gives a number of titles that the reader will gain far more detail and theoretical explanation from than will be included

here. Although the definitions start with 'A' they are not listed alphabetically, but rather as they came to mind. See also Figure 4–1.

Aerofoil, or airfoil if you prefer, is generally just regarded as another word for a *wing*, which is a body so shaped that its motion through the air creates lift, or, in our case, downforce, without causing excessive drag. An aerofoil is the cross section which defines the shape of a three-dimensional wing, and since wing shapes can be quite complex, it follows that a wing may have various sections along its length.

The *leading edge*, or LE, is rather obviously the front part of the wing, and is usually a more or less blunt, radiused shape. The *trailing edge*, or TE, is just as obviously the rearmost part of the wing, and is generally thin and tapered. The straight line joining the LE to the TE is the *chord line*, and the distance along this line from the LE to the TE is the chord dimension, denoted by the letter 'c'. The maximum *thickness* of the wing is denoted by the letter 't', and is expressed as a percentage or decimal fraction of the chord dimension. Thus if a wing has a chord dimension of 12in (305mm), and t = 0.18c, the maximum thickness is 12×0.18 = 2.16in (54.9mm). The maximum thickness position is also usually stated as a decimal fraction of the chord, measured from the LE, so if t_{max} is said to be at 0.3c, it will be 3.6in (91.4mm) from the LE of a 12in (305mm) chord wing.

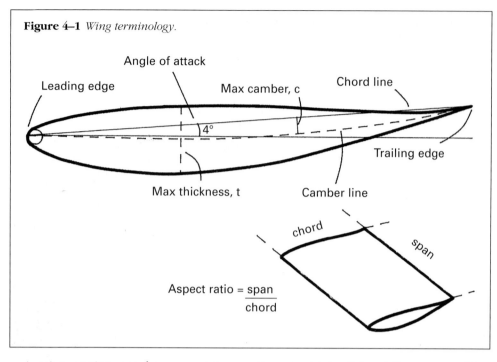

Figure 4–1 *Wing terminology.*

Angle of attack

Leading edge

Max camber, c

Chord line

4°

Trailing edge

Max thickness, t

Camber line

chord

span

Aspect ratio = span / chord

A wing section can be symmetric or asymmetric, and if it is the latter it is referred to as having *camber*, meaning that its lower surface (in a racecar context) is more curved than its upper surface. Race car wings generally possess camber these days, though early efforts were practically symmetrical. The line drawn through the mid-points of a wing, from the LE to the TE, is known as the *median line* or *camber line*. The amount of camber present is sometimes defined as the maximum distance between the camber line and the chord line, expressed once more as a decimal fraction of the chord dimension, c. The location of maximum camber is defined in the same way as maximum thickness, also as a fraction of c.

The width of a wing is known as its *span*, and the ratio of span to chord is the *aspect ratio*. Aircraft have high aspect ratios whilst racecars have very low aspect ratios. The *angle of attack*, or *angle of incidence*, of a wing is the angle between the approaching airflow and the wing's chord line. It is tempting some-

times to think of the airflow approaching a racecar wing as being horizontal, parallel to the ground. This may be true of front wings (though not necessarily), but is almost certainly never true of a rear wing. Race car wings are no longer allowed to have variable angle of attack whilst on the move – changes to angle may only be made in the pits or paddock. Jim Hall's Chaparral 2E and 2F of 1966 and 1967 had variable incidence angle rear wings, and were adjusted by the driver via a third pedal (the cars had auto transmission).

The point (or line) at which the forces on a wing appear to act, and at which there is no moment, is known as the *centre of pressure*. In reality this effect is the sum of the *pressure distribution* over the whole of the wing, both lower and upper surfaces, caused by the wing's influence on the local air velocities and the resultant local pressure changes. As we saw in Chapter 2, the effect of a wing is to reduce the local pressure below the *suction side* of the more cambered lower surface, and to raise the pressure of the

The Chaparral 2E and 2F (seen here) had driver-adjustable wing incidence angle.

air over the upper, *pressure side* of the wing (see Figure 4–2). The result of this is that both downforce and, unfortunately, drag are produced.

In the case of wings, downforce (or negative lift) and drag coefficients, $-C_L$ and C_D are quoted with reference to the *plan area* of the wing, that is, the span

Figure 4–2 *Generalised pressure distribution around a wing.*

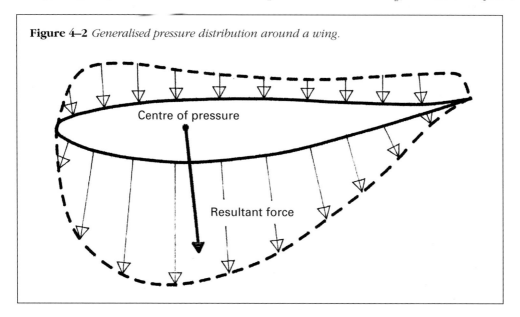

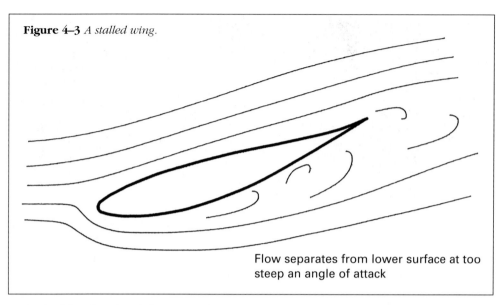

Figure 4–3 *A stalled wing.*

Flow separates from lower surface at too steep an angle of attack

multiplied by the chord for a simple rectangular wing, rather than the frontal area which is the reference area for a whole car. The *lift to drag* (L/D) *ratio* is once more used as a measure of aerodynamic efficiency. Downforce and drag both generally increase with larger angles of attack. However, there is a certain angle, and every wing has one, at which the airflow breaks down along the suction side of the wing, and instead of flowing smoothly it becomes very unsteady, and separates from the wing surface (see Figure 4–3). This is accompanied by a sudden drop in downforce, and an equally sudden increase in drag. The wing has *stalled*. This is an easy condition to remedy on a racecar, provided you know it has happened. With an aeroplane, the pilot will sense the instant it happens, but the consequences for him and his passengers are rather more drastic than for the racer!

Downforce and wing design criteria

Before we start to look in detail at the influence of wing design criteria, mention must first be made of the NACA wing profiles. The National Advisory Committee for Aeronautics (NACA) was an American body – the forerunner of the country's current aerospace agency, NASA – which developed a system of defining and cataloguing aerofoil shapes during the 1920s and 1930s, following on from earlier post-World War One work in Germany and elsewhere. The book by Abbott and von Doenhof (see Appendix 2) entitled *The Theory of Wing Sections* gives a great many of the NACA wing profiles, and this catalogue still serves as a valuable source of shapes that could be applied to motorsport. Yes, the profiles were created for aeronautical applications, and yes, the teams at the forefront of motorsport research may now have progressed beyond the need for this type of information. But that still leaves an awful lot of constructors and competitors, amateur and professional, who aren't in a position to design and test a wing by computer or refine it in a wind-tunnel, yet who would rather not make a completely blind guess about an appropriate profile. Such a reference book, however ancient and whatever its original application, is a godsend. Of course, the actual choice of profile still has to be made, but hopefully we can derive some guidelines here. Further sources of similar information are also given in the appendix.

Race car wings can be single-element,

Formula 750 cars run small wings because they cannot tolerate lots of drag.

dual-element or multi-element devices, depending on the racing category and the configurations its rules permit, as well as the demands imposed by the particular track and the tolerance of a given car to downforce and drag. Some cars run

Unlimited capacity British hillclimb cars don't worry about drag.

simple wings because they have to, like FIA GT cars, whilst others run them because they cannot tolerate large amounts of drag, such as Formula 750 cars in the UK. Other cars carry multi-element devices because their tolerance to drag is greater, and the need for large amounts of downforce is paramount – good examples of this category would be a Formula 1 car at a 'slow' track like Monaco, or an unlimited capacity British speed hillclimb car. One crucial point to remember is that the environment that a wing has to work in on a racecar is totally different to the environment in which an aeroplane wing has to work. So, although a lot of the basic information available on wings comes from the world of aircraft, keep in mind that things happen differently, and usually a lot less efficiently, on racecars (just why this is so will be picked up as we go through this chapter).

Single-element wings
The basics of lift, or downforce, creation start with the premise that, as was stated in the definitions above, downforce gets bigger with increasing angle of attack, up to a point known as the stall point, or stall angle. A symmetric single-element wing, not surprisingly, produces zero downforce at zero angle of incidence, but downforce increases more or less linearly with increases in angle, up to around the 14–16° angle, for a wing in 'free air' (see Figure 4–4 and Appendix 2). Note, though, that stall angle varies with wing section and flow conditions.

Thickness, t, affects downforce, and as the thickness increases up to around 0.12c, the stall angle occurs later, enabling greater downforce to be generated. For certain symmetrical wing profiles (such as the NACA 0006, 0009 and 0012, having zero camber, and thicknesses from 0.06c to 0.12c) the stall becomes more 'abrupt' as the stall angle is approached, whilst for others (eg the NACA 2412, 2415 and 2418, each having 2 per cent maximum camber at 0.4c, with thicknesses from 0.12c to 0.18c), increased thickness seems to lead to a more gentle stall (see Figure 4–5). If thickness is increased beyond 0.12c, the maximum $-C_L$ value actually tails off slightly again, and the implication of this is that if a wing is intended to remain as a single-element device, a maximum thickness of 0.12c could be construed as

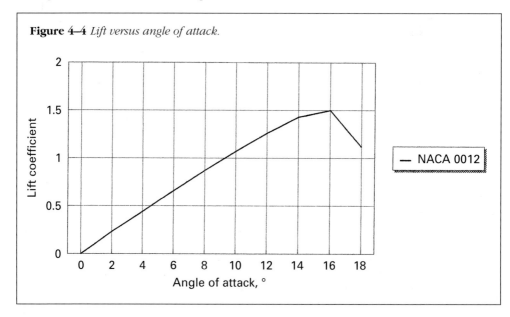

Figure 4–4 *Lift versus angle of attack.*

Figure 4–5 *Effect of thickness on lift curve.*

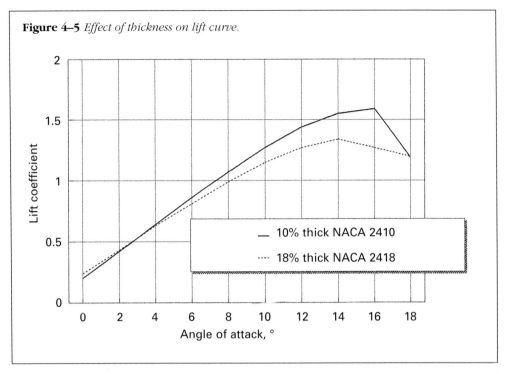

10% thick NACA 2410

18% thick NACA 2418

a design parameter. However, very thin wing profiles seem to be associated with an abrupt stall, caused by leading edge separation. In contrast to this data from Abbott & von Doenhof, McCormick (see Appendix 2) shows that at Reynolds Numbers of two million and less, increasing thickness over 12 per cent has little effect on $-C_{Lmax}$, and this has significance for a great many competition categories, except, perhaps, the very fastest.

The effect of changing camber is rather different to changing thickness. Putting camber into a wing profile enables more downforce to be generated at a given angle of attack. In fact, cambered wings create downforce even when their angle of attack is 0°, or less. The zero downforce angle may be a significantly negative angle of incidence (see Figure 4–6). Camber with a rearward bias, that is, maximum camber at, say, 0.6c instead of 0.4c, has a larger effect on downforce generation, and produces a more gradual stall than forward biased camber. But forward biased camber may be more applic-

able to a low drag wing set up at a low angle of attack. By changing the geometry of the rearward sections of a wing profile, the downforce characteristics can be altered, and this is most easily done with adjustable flaps, of which more later. A cambered wing may actually stall at a lower angle than a symmetrical wing.

Leading edge radius is another parameter on which contradictory references may be found. It may be that a sharp leading edge, especially on a thin wing section, can cause leading edge separation, creating an abrupt stall to occur at the stall angle. However, at a shallow angle of attack, it may also be the case that a sharp leading edge helps to maintain a thinner boundary layer over the first part of a wing, leading to improved efficiency, as determined by the lift/drag ratio. Both effects may occur on the same wing at different angles of attack. Furthermore, in the case of high downforce, multi-element wings, the increase in suction is so pronounced that the air is caused to flow significantly faster

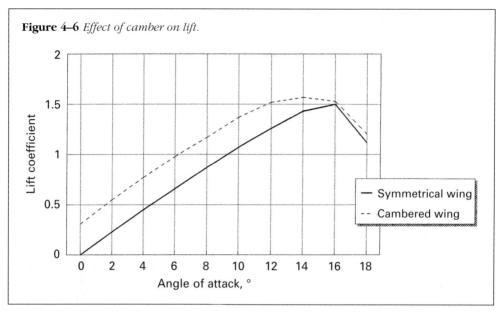

Figure 4–6 *Effect of camber on lift.*

around the leading edge too. In order to prevent early leading edge flow separation, a change to the leading edge shape may be required, such as a sharper, more cambered profile. Historically, leading edge profiles in the major single seater formulae around the world have changed from blunt, large radius designs to much sharper shapes, perhaps of the order of 1–3 per cent of chord. Thus, a 300mm (11.8in) chord wing might have a leading edge of 3 to 9mm (1/8 to 1/4in) radius.

So, for a single-element wing, the selection parameters include:

1. Low angle of attack for low downforce and low drag, high angle of attack – up to a maximum of around 14–16° *relative to the airflow* for greater downforce, with inherent drag penalty.
2. Thin section thickness for low downforce, low drag, up to about 0.12c thick for greater downforce, though in most lower speed regimes, thickness is much less critical.
3. Small amounts of camber, say at 0.3c, for low downforce, and greater camber, perhaps in the 0.05c to 0.15c region, for more downforce, together

with a rearward bias, possibly as far back as 0.5c or 0.6c.
4. Leading edge radius probably in the range 1–3 per cent of chord.

There is still an endless choice of thickness and camber distributions to pick from, but this general four point plan may help to draw up a short list of candidate profiles to suit a particular competition category, and the venues visited – it may not be possible to pick *one* profile that suits all the venues due to be visited, but the decision on whether to compromise on just one wing, or to have a selection available, is yours. Various practical considerations should also be applied to the decision process, such as is (are) the wing(s) going to be bought or made? Either way, the precise shape(s) that it is possible to obtain will in part be governed by influences such as availability, or perhaps by the presence or otherwise of the necessary tools (and, dare it be said, the skills) to create the desired shape. But more of that in a later chapter.

So how much downforce can be created by a single-element wing? This obviously depends in part on the plan area of the wing, so for the purpose of the exam-

Single-element rear wing on the 1996 McLaren F1 GTR.

ples to be used in this chapter, we will refer to a rear wing of fixed dimensions (unless otherwise stated) of span 3ft by chord 1ft (0.91 by 0.305m), giving a plan area of 3.0sq ft (0.28m²). The other factors that govern how much downforce is created are the speed, which we will fix at 100mph again (160kmh), and the lift coefficient, which is the bit we're really interested in here.

The aeronautical data given in Abbott and von Doenhof suggests that the maximum lift coefficients of single-element wings range from about 1.2 to 1.6 just before they get to the stall angle, and a typical value for a medium thickness (say 0.12c), moderately cambered wing (say 4 per cent camber at 0.4c), such as the NACA 4412, is a maximum C_L of about 1.5 at 13°. Just in passing, it is interesting to note that this wing also has a C_L of 0.4 at 0°, and 1.2 at 8°. However, all of these C_L values are at Reynolds Numbers of Re = 3 million, or 3×10^6), and stall angles tend to reduce at lower Reynolds Numbers, leading to lower C_L values. In the case we are using for our example here, the wing has a chord of 1ft, and a

speed, in feet per second now, of 146.67ft/sec. Going back to Chapter 2 briefly, we said that the Reynolds Number could be calculated thus:

Re = 6,300 × speed × 'length', which in this case is the chord dimension. Thus, our Reynolds Number here is 6,300 × 146.67 × 1.0, which comes out to 924,000, or 9.24×10^5. This is a lot lower than the value at which the above lift coefficients are quoted, and we can safely assume, therefore, that the lift coefficient at this lower value will also be lower, maybe in the order of 1.3 to 1.4 at the maximum angle of around 12 to 13°.

Other factors will also conspire to produce a lower C_L than we might desire, such as turbulence from the rest of the car ahead of the rear wing, and the fact that the wing has a small aspect ratio (dealt with in more detail later). But let's not get too pessimistic! To make the sums easy in this instance, we'll just assume that the effective C_L has declined by around 25 per cent, and is going to be exactly 1.0. So we can now calculate the downforce that our single-element wing might produce at 100mph:

downforce, lb = $1/2\rho A\ C_L v^2$
= $1/2 \times 0.00238 \times 3 \times 1 \times (146.67 \times 146.67)$
= 76.8lb (34.9kg)

So even if the wing is operating in 'dirty' air at the back of the car, and due allowance is made for the loss of achievable downforce as a result of this, around 75 to 80lb of downforce could be expected from this size single-element wing running at close to its maximum angle at 100mph. This could be regarded as a more realistic estimate than might be calculated by using the theoretical maximum C_L value directly from a source such as Abbott and von Doenhof.

Dual-element wings

If greater downforce is required than can be obtained from a single-element wing, and the tolerance to the extra drag that will be generated exists, then a move to a more complex aerofoil assemblage may be desirable. From the basic equation for downforce, where we saw that downforce = $1/2\rho A\ C_L v^2$, it is evident that at any given speed, downforce can be increased by increasing A, the area of the wing, or C_L, the lift coefficient of the wing. In most competition categories, regulations define the maximum size of aerofoils, and it makes sense to exploit the degrees of freedom available at least as far as possible, so long as wing efficiency is not compromised significantly. So, for example, a wing should certainly have as big a span as the rules allow. But

if the chord dimension is not specified in the rules, should the wing have as big a chord as can be fitted onto the car? Not necessarily, because a low aspect ratio (span divided by chord) makes for a less efficient wing in terms of lift and drag (though curiously it can help by delaying stall to a steeper angle than on a high aspect ratio version). A more efficient route to greater downforce might be to maintain a moderate aspect ratio but go for an increase in C_L, and this might be achieved either by employing a single-element profile with more camber, or, if considerably more downforce is required, by using a multi-element wing.

The simplest multi-element design is, of course, the dual-element wing, where the *mainplane* is supplemented by a *flap* (see Figure 4–7). If a flap is added to an existing single-element wing in the appropriate position, a number of things happen. Firstly, the plan area is increased, which, as we have seen, enables the creation of more downforce. Secondly, the effective camber of the dual-element device is increased, which again will supplement downforce at a given angle of attack. And thirdly, the crucial interaction between the mainplane and the flap brought about by their positions relative to each other assists in the creation of more downforce by modifying the airflow on the suction side of the wing.

There are two common dual-element wing geometries used in motorsport

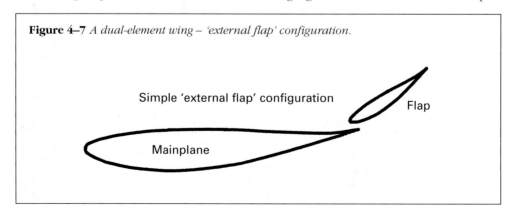

Figure 4–7 *A dual-element wing – 'external flap' configuration.*

Simple 'external flap' configuration

Flap

Mainplane

Figure 4–8 *A dual-element wing – 'slotted flap' or 'Fowler flap' arrangement.*

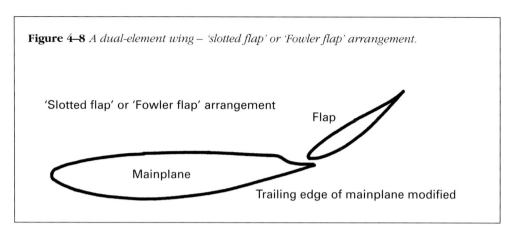

'Slotted flap' or 'Fowler flap' arrangement

Flap

Mainplane

Trailing edge of mainplane modified

applications, and these are referred to as the 'external flap' arrangement (as in Figure 4–7), and the 'slotted flap', also known as the 'Fowler flap' arrangement (see Figure 4–8). The slotted flap, more complex in form, and therefore more complex to manufacture, would seem to derive from aeronautical applications, wherein the flap is a movable device which can be deployed and retracted, as well as rotated. The shape of the mainplane is dictated as much by the ability to 'nest' the flap within the overall mainplane profile when it is not deployed, in low drag 'cruising mode', as it is by considerations of the airflow when the flap is extended. The external flap utilises a simpler mainplane shape, and is arguably simpler to make. There would not appear to be any particular advantages in motorsport applications for one configuration over the other, although there have been claims of improved $-C_L$ and C_D values with the Fowler configuration, and the

Dual-element wing on a Van Diemen RF97 Formula Renault Sport car.

tendency these days is for external flap arrangements to be more common.

There are, however, a number of criteria relating to the flap size and, especially, position which *are* important. The size of the flap – that is, the flap chord dimension – is generally of the order of 25 to 30 per cent of the *overall* (mainplane plus flap) chord, C. Bigger flap chords of 30 to 40 per cent C are used, and can produce higher increments in downforce coefficient. The actual shape of the flap is frequently a scaled down version of the mainplane, but may just be a simple NACA profile and still function effectively. Practical considerations may dictate that it is relatively somewhat thicker than the mainplane, relative to its own chord dimension, in order that it can be made stiff enough.

The most important consideration with a dual-element wing, however, is the positioning of the flap in relation to the mainplane. The key here is that a narrow slot is formed between the mainplane trailing edge and the flap leading edge. This necessitates an overlap between the two elements, with the flap being positioned above the mainplane trailing edge in a downforce-inducing application. The size of the gap between the mainplane and the flap is generally thought to be best at around 1–2 per cent c, and the overlap between the flap leading edge and mainplane trailing edge, though not critical, is usually of the order of 1–4 per cent c. The most critical criterion, however, is that the shape of the slot must be convergent – that is, narrowing from its opening to its exit. The only way to optimise the geometry of a wing and flap is to do lots of testing, preferably in a windtunnel. But the figures above will get you in the ball park.

It is frequently said that the function of a flap is to not only add area (possibly) and camber to increase downforce, but 'to allow some air from the upper, pressure side of the wing to bleed through the slot into the suction side. By forcing this air to pass through a convergent slot,

it is accelerated, and as such enters the flow on the suction side with increased energy, and lower pressure. This helps to control the boundary layer, and delay flow separation, which in turn ought to enable a higher angle of attack to be used before stall occurs'. However, the record can now be put straight on this popular misconception, because this is *not* the fundamental mechanism by which a flap augments lift. The effect of fitting a flap is too large for this to be a primary lift-enhancing mechanism.

The reality is that, not surprisingly, a number of interactions occur. The flap actually induces a rise in air velocity over both the pressure and suction sides of the main element, and in the case of the suction side this helps by reducing the severity of the adverse pressure gradient, which helps to prevent separation. Further, the additional velocity imparted at the trailing edge increases the 'upwash', effectively increasing the angle of attack. So the combination of additional area (maybe), increased camber, and the beneficial modification of the flow field around the mainplane, all add up to produce a very significant increment of extra downforce.

What, then, are the general design criteria that should be employed for a two-element wing? Well, some of the basic criteria for a single-element wing will still be applicable to the mainplane design. However, thicker mainplane sections can work better with flaps, and if the flap chord is at the higher end of the preferred range, say 30 to 40 per cent c, then a mainplane thickness as high as 0.20c is said to give a significant increase in downforce compared to a mainplane of around 0.10c thickness. The amount of camber in the mainplane will depend on the application, and is likely to be in the range of 5–15 per cent c, possibly more for high downforce applications, positioned perhaps slightly forward of or around halfway along the chord. The adjustment to the angle of the flap will have the effect of altering the rearward bias of the camber of the overall wing.

As for the flap itself, as has already been stated, the flap chord will most likely be around 30 per cent c, and the flap thickness may need to be, relatively speaking, slightly greater than the mainplane thickness. The position of the flap's maximum thickness is often fairly well forward, say at around 0.20c – this can help to create the converging slot shape between the flap and the mainplane by producing fairly rapid curvature from the flap's leading edge onto its lower surface. The flap profile does not seem to be critical for it to perform a useful function. But logic dictates that the same criteria that apply to a single-element mainplane as regards its shape and performance ought to be applicable to the shape of a flap and *its* performance. So it would seem to be a reasonable assumption that a more cambered flap will help to generate more downforce than a less cambered one. Furthermore, the use of a flap with more camber can make it easier to achieve the convergent slot shape than if the flap has a flatter profile. Similarly, if there is an optimum thickness for a main element – which, as we have seen, may be thicker in the case of a two-element wing than a

single-element one – then the same should be true of the flap, with the qualification already mentioned that the flap will almost certainly end up thicker in relative terms in order to make it strong enough. The maximum angle of inclination of the flap relative to the mainplane chord line, will be determined by testing, but will probably not exceed 40°. Whilst downforce will increase with steeper flap angles, the increments become smaller, whilst the increases in drag become larger, so efficiency drops off. In aeronautical terms, the overall angle of attack that can be used is not as steep as can be used with a single-element wing, though what is possible on any specific racecar may well fly in the face of generalised aeronautical experience and practice! The only way for this to be satisfactorily determined is to do some form of testing, either in a wind-tunnel, or more likely – for the vast majority of competitors – out on the track. But as a start point, maybe it would be wise to assume a maximum angle of attack, overall, of about 12°, and at least stalling will be avoided. Angles considerably greater than this will, in all probability, be tolerable on your competition car.

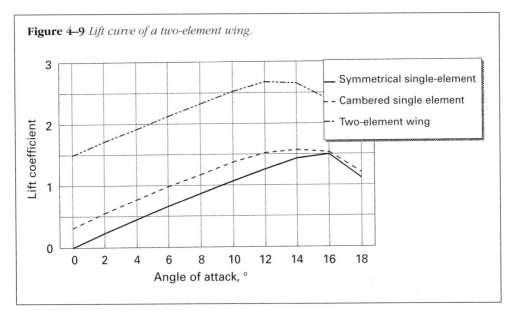

Figure 4–9 *Lift curve of a two-element wing.*

The increases in available $-C_L$ values using a dual-element wing are considerable, and it is possible that the maximum $-C_L$ could almost double (see Figure 4–9 and Appendix 1). As was noted earlier, though, stall may actually occur at a slightly lower angle of attack with a flapped wing, this stall angle decreasing with increasing flap deflection. Nevertheless a substantial gain in downforce, in direct proportion to the increase in $-C_L$ value, should be achievable. The flap also provides a simpler means of wing adjustment for fine tuning the aerodynamic balance of a car.

Multi-element wings – more flaps, and slats

Still greater $-C_L$ values are attainable if further flap sections are added. The 'double slotted flap' arrangement, where two flaps are positioned above the mainplane trailing edge, is a logical extension of the single flap set up, and effectively increases the wing camber even more (see Figure 4–10). The geometries of the two flaps are often shown in aeronautical texts as being quite different from each other, with the first flap perhaps being smaller and thicker than the second, and some racecars adopt this principle. However, the all-important slot gap shape between all the wing elements still matters, and double flap set ups on racecars are just as likely to be made up with similar if not identical shapes and sizes for the two flaps. The size of the slot gap between the mainplane and the foremost flap, and between the fore flap and the secondary flap, may be similar, or the former may be bigger than the latter. Aeronautical data gives a mixture of information here, but this may be because the geometry of deployed flaps on aircraft can be altered in flight, and the gaps will be different at different deployed flap angles. On a racecar however, the flaps must remain fixed once the car leaves the confines of the pit-lane or paddock, and the flap positions and gaps must therefore be chosen beforehand for each adjustable angle that can be set. However, this actually gives better scope for slot gap optimisation than on aircraft, which have practicalities like 'nesting' the flaps to consider. Frequently it can be seen that the second slot gap is smaller than the first. The best arrangement will only be ascertained by comprehensive testing, though unless some means of measuring results is available, such as a wind-tunnel or suitable data acquisition can provide, all that can really be done is to make a best first estimate. To this end, and in the absence of any better information, setting both slot gaps to the same as that suggested for a single flap wing would appear to be a fair starting point.

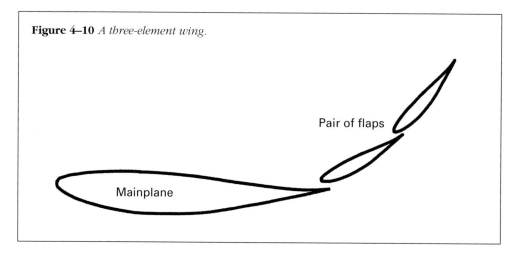

Figure 4–10 *A three-element wing.*

Pair of flaps

Mainplane

Three-element wing on a Gould-Ralt GR37 hillclimb car.

The combined chord dimension of the two flaps would appear from the aeronautical texts to be ideally set in the range 30 to 40 per cent of the overall wing chord, so in relative terms, the flaps here are individually smaller than in the dual-element case, where the single flap was of approximately 30 per cent of overall chord. However, one only has to look at different racing categories to see that the respective rules governing each formula have a marked effect on the designs that have evolved. Formula 1 cars have very short mainplane chords relative to the flap chords, and this results from the tight restriction on overall chord. Indycars have a different set of rules (actually, different *sets* of rules, for the various circuit types on which they race), and in this category, mainplanes for the short ovals and road courses have a much deeper chord. This suggests that as long as you are prepared to optimise a set up for the circumstances in which it is to be used, there aren't really any hard and fast rules. Once again there is evidence that a thicker section mainplane produces better results when working

with double flaps than a thinner one, and thickness values tending towards 18 per cent c are associated with a gradual increase in $-C_L$.

In terms of performance gains, the addition of a second flap adds a further substantial increment to the $-C_L$ value that can be achieved, and figures of well over $-C_L = 3.0$ are frequently cited for this kind of arrangement. But in general terms, smaller additional downforce increments are added by additional flaps. The aeronautical texts indicate that stall angles are not as steep as for single-element wings. However, racecar wings can frequently be seen with *overall* angles of attack (mainplane and flap considered) well in excess of 20°. Angles of flap inclination might be in the region of 25 to 30° for the fore flap, and between 30 and 70° for the secondary flap, all angles measured relative to the mainplane chord line. Some configurations leave the fore flap fixed, with only the secondary flap being adjustable, whilst others allow both flaps to be adjusted as a pair – the flaps remaining fixed relative to each other, however. In both cases, this means that only one of the two slots is altered, and if nothing else, this makes engineering the attachment and pivot points for the flaps a lot easier! Figure 4–11 shows the magnitude of C_Ls achievable versus angle of attack for an aeronautical double flap set up (see also Appendix 1).

For more downforce, yet more flaps can be added, and an extreme case, known as the 'Venetian blind' flap arrangement, is variously reported with three of even four flaps in addition to the mainplane. Clearly, optimising such a set up will be a time consuming task, there being rather a large number of possible configurations to consider. Such a wing is probably best left to the professionals to sort out! As an indication of what is possible, though, in some pre-1997 rules Indycar configurations the rearmost flap has been inclined at an angle steeper than 90°, with the trailing edge actually pointing towards the front of the car! This was a 'maximum lift, don't worry about the drag' configuration if ever there was one (see Figure 4–12). The rather peculiar general profile was the result of the dimensional restrictions in the rules, which said that, in side view, the wing

had to fit a 28 × 10in (711 × 254mm) box. Thus the main element was rather flat, with a low leading edge to give the steepest possible overall angle of attack, and the camber was heavily biased to the rear with the three flaps.

It was mentioned earlier that high downforce wings can suffer from leading edge separation, and that a change to the forward geometry of the wing may be required to prevent this from happening. One way this can be achieved, which precludes the need for altering the mainplane profile itself, is to use a leading edge *slat* (see Figure 4–13). This is a device which is rather similar to a flap, but which is located, as its name suggests, at the opposite end of the mainplane, actually below the leading edge. It has the effect of adding 'downwash' to the front of the wing, which reduces the velocity under the front part of the suction side, and this reduces the likelihood of leading edge separation such as might be prone to occur with heavy rearward camber bias and steep angles of attack. The slat also adds an increment of lift of its own (see Figure 4–14). The benefit of a slat only starts to take effect at steeper

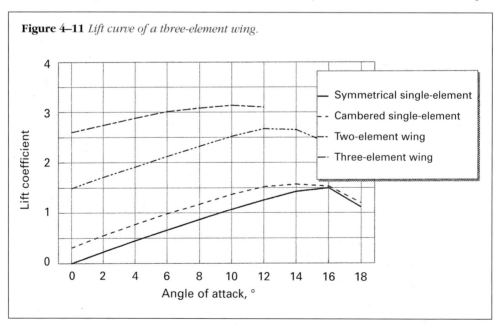

Figure 4–11 *Lift curve of a three-element wing.*

— Symmetrical single-element

- - Cambered single-element

-- Two-element wing

-·- Three-element wing

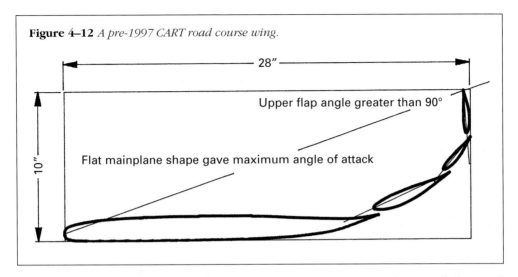

Figure 4–12 *A pre-1997 CART road course wing.*

28"

10"

Upper flap angle greater than 90°

Flat mainplane shape gave maximum angle of attack

angles, and stall may be delayed until a much steeper angle than normal is reached. Thus, the device enables a higher $-C_L$ to be created before the dreaded stall occurs, and a substantial increase in downforce can be obtained.

Data on the $-C_L$ values that are obtainable with these extreme wings is rather sparse, as might be expected, given that the development of such devices is confined largely to the motorsport arena, a notoriously secretive industry. Somewhat

theoretical sounding figures of 4, 5 and even 6 are mentioned, but perhaps a more realistic value can be obtained indirectly from a paper which was actually about the structural loadings imposed on the chassis of a Formula 1 car, in this case a Williams. The maximum loading from the rear wing was said to be in excess of 6,000 Newtons (612kg, or 1,346lb), and putting this figure into the lift equation, together with an assumed maximum speed of 200mph, and an

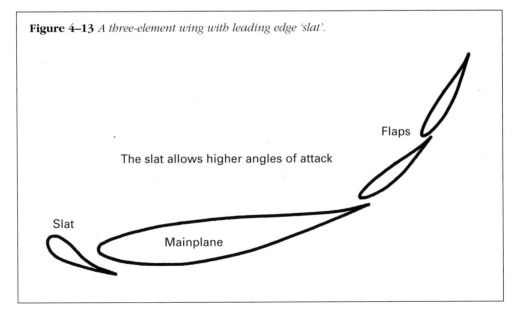

Figure 4–13 *A three-element wing with leading edge 'slat'.*

Flaps

The slat allows higher angles of attack

Slat

Mainplane

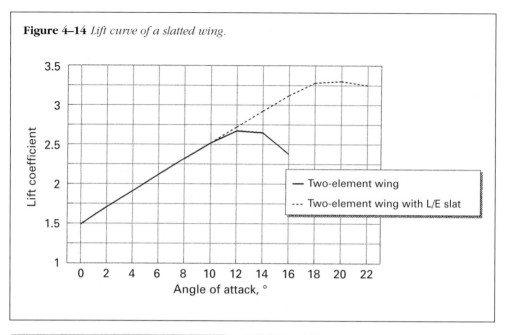

Figure 4–14 *Lift curve of a slatted wing.*

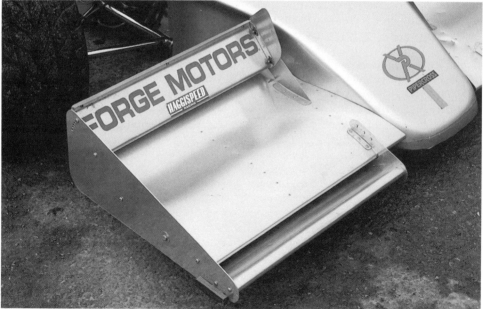

Front wing with flap and leading edge slat.

approximate area of 3.28×0.98ft (1.0×0.3m), produces a $-C_L$ value of 3.7. So we can safely assume that rear wing lift coefficients in excess of 3.5, and maybe as high as 4.0, are actually achieved from the multi-element, multi-tier devices seen in that category.

Multi-tier wings

This brings us nicely on to the subject of

Two-tier rear wing on the Benetton B197 Formula 1 car.

multi-tier wings. The first powered aircraft to actually fly was a biplane, so the multi-tier concept is not exactly new. The apparent benefit of increased wing area is the obvious reason for using a biplane or multi-tier configuration, especially when there are limited locations in which the wings can be attached. But there is a distinct disadvantage that arises from such an arrangement. Consider that the upper tier produces low pressure beneath its undersurface. Now envisage what happens when another wing is located beneath the upper tier. The low pressure area beneath the upper tier acts upon the upper surface of the lower tier, and this is about as rewarding as trying to lift yourself off the ground by pulling up on your boot laces! So why do some racecars persist with multi-tier wings? Because it's not as bad as that. There *is* interference between the tiers, and the net result is that you don't get twice as much downforce from two tiers as you do from one when they are relatively close together. However, the combined effect can still be of net benefit, with more downforce

being achieved than with just one tier. Indeed, with a vertical separation equal to the chord dimension, the suggestion is that two identical tiers will produce at least half as much downforce again as one tier alone. But there are other possible benefits from a multi-tier arrangement. The first is that, although wing efficiency – determined by the downforce to drag ratio – may become unfavourable with three or four tiers, the effect on the airflow is such that an increase in the overall angle of attack may become tolerable, allowing more downforce to be generated before the wing stalls. And secondly, the lower tier(s) may be positioned so that it (they) interact(s) favourably with the underbody airflow, assisting and augmenting the production of low pressure in the underbody region. Thus, a large gain in overall downforce may be achieved through careful design and development of this aspect.

Bolt-on bits: end plates and Gurneys
There are two virtually ubiquitous devices that are bolted to wings which have a

profound effect on the wing perfor-mance, and which cannot be passed over here: end plates, and Gurney flaps (or wickers). End plates are not just there to hide the precise shape of the wing profile you are using from your competitors, or to put a sponsor's name on. They serve an extremely valuable purpose, which is to increase a wing's downforce consider-ably, perhaps by around 30 per cent, over the value that would be achieved if they were not present. Without end plates, or 'spill plates' as they are some-times more usefully known, the differ-ence in air pressure between the lower and upper surfaces of a wing prompts the air on the high pressure side to try to migrate to the low pressure side, and it spills off the wing tips in a diagonal motion (creating the characteristic vortex pattern). This causes a loss of downforce. Fitting end plates reduces or prevents this motion occurring over the wing surface, and helps to maintain the pressure differ-ential above and below the wing (see Figure 4–15). End plates do need to be reasonably large to be effective, although generally there is not much scope to have too much end plate above a rear wing if the wing itself is already as high at its trailing edge as the rules allow (and it certainly should be). However, that gen-erally leaves plenty of room for end plates to extend below the wing, and often the end plates actually constitute the primary wing mounts, or at least the secondary, stabilising supports. Front wings tend not to allow much end plate below the lower surface because of ground proximity.

The Gurney flap is a small right-angled strip bolted to the trailing edge of the rearmost element of a wing. The device, first used by American Dan Gurney – who reportedly told competitors who asked that it 'served only a structural pur-pose', in a hopeless attempt to avoid giving the game away – is a means of adding downforce for surprisingly little drag penalty, in spite of its apparent crudeness. Recent research has now shown that the Gurney forms a pair of

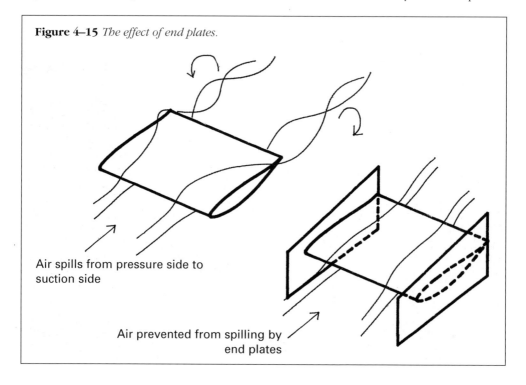

Figure 4–15 *The effect of end plates.*

Air spills from pressure side to suction side

Air prevented from spilling by end plates

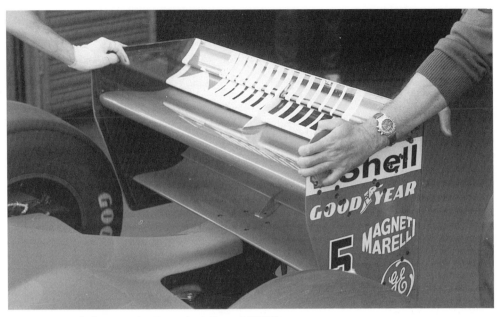

Rear wing end plates on the Formula 1 Ferrari F310B.

counter-rotating vortices behind itself (see Figure 4–16), which has the effect of adding a vertical component to the velocity at the trailing edge. This deflects the flow upwards, and increases the downforce. The effect is the same as adding

Front wing end plates on the Formula 1 Arrows A18.

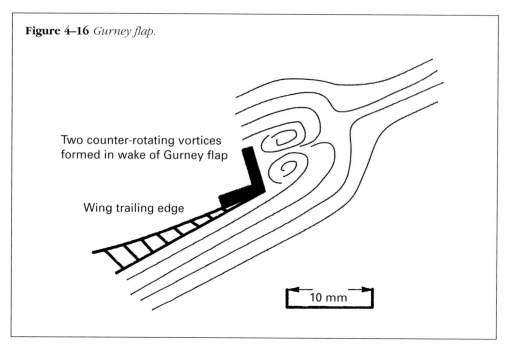

Figure 4–16 *Gurney flap.*

Two counter-rotating vortices
formed in wake of Gurney flap

Wing trailing edge

10 mm

more camber to a wing. One of the main practical advantages of the Gurney is that it is easily fitted and removed, or replaced with one of a different size, and it is thus an important part of the fine tuning kit that racers take to the track.

Small Gurney flaps give rise to quite substantial increases in downforce for a

Gurney flap on the McLaren MP4/12 front wing flap.

small extra drag component, whilst larger Gurneys add smaller extra amounts of downforce, but bigger chunks of drag. Thus there are sensible limits to work to here, and Gurneys are usually less than 5 per cent of chord in height. Smaller sizes than this will be most efficient, and a Gurney of around 2 per cent of chord can add as much as 0.30 to the C_L with a very small additional drag increment. An experiment by the author with a 20in (500mm) chord three-element rear wing on a hillclimb single seater in the MIRA full scale wind-tunnel showed that a 3/8in (9mm) Gurney gave an extra 8.2 per cent downforce for only 2.8 per cent extra drag.

The operating environment
Wings on competition cars have to function in less than ideal conditions compared to an aircraft, the wings of which can be thought of as operating in 'clean' air. Even front wings on a racecar, though in a far better site than the rear wing, are affected adversely by the presence of rotating wheels nearby, suspension mem-

bers, and the nose itself. The rear wing has to work with air that has been stirred up by all the protuberances ahead of it which form the rest of the car, including the wheels, the bodywork and mirrors, the driver's head, the roll-over structure, and the engine cover. In the case of the saloon racer, the rear wing is all but masked off by the passenger compartment canopy, and the quality of the flow to the wing will depend very much on the roof and rear screen shape. The complex shapes, viewed in front or rear elevation, of some Super Touring car rear wings demonstrates how the designers have tried to deal with the variations in the quality of the airflow to different parts of the span of the wings.

Ground effect and front wings
Many of the above influences on wing performance are essentially negative, and detract from the downforce that a wing actually creates, as distinct from the theoretical downforce that it should produce. But there are influences which have a marked positive effect on the downforce

Complex shape of the Renault Laguna Super Touring car rear wing.

produced by front wings, one of which is 'ground effect'. The downforce produced by a wing well clear of the ground actually increases as the wing is brought nearer to the ground. The cause can perhaps be explained by thinking of the wing-ground system as being analogous to a venturi tube – the pressure reduction becomes more marked between the wing and the ground than it would have been below the wing in 'mainstream' air. The effect becomes more marked the nearer it gets, until, at a point when it is only just above the ground, the effect reverses and downforce declines again, this happening as the boundary layer interferes with the ground and effectively starts to block off the flow under the wing (see Figure 4–17).

To try to put some numbers on this effect, a wing operating in the region of 2in (50mm) ground clearance could be expected to produce up to double the downforce that it would produce in 'mainstream' air, that is, at very large ground clearances greater than the chord dimension in magnitude. This becomes very relevant when selecting a front wing profile to balance a rear wing, as we shall see in a later section. A further interesting comparison is that the C_L value at 2in clearance may be as much as 50–60 per cent greater than that produced at 6in (152mm) ground clearance. This demonstrates the sensitivity of the C_L to proximity to the ground, and naturally leads onto a brief look at 'pitch sensitivity' with respect to front wings.

In a dynamic situation, a car is constantly rolling, pitching, and yawing on its suspension in response to the mechanical loads being fed through it, and as its speed rises and falls, the downforce it produces also goes up and down. These effects combine to produce changes in ride height, and pitch attitude (nose up or down), which can have a marked influence on the actual proximity of the front wing to the ground, and its angle of attack. This in turn creates varying amounts of downforce, and the net result is that a car can become unpredictable, and even unstable, as the generation of inconsistent levels of downforce serves to

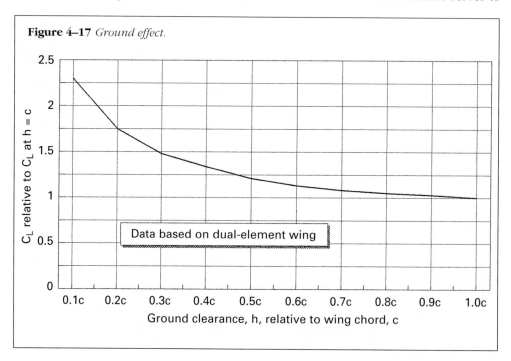

Figure 4–17 *Ground effect.*

Data based on dual-element wing

C_L relative to C_L at h = c

Ground clearance, h, relative to wing chord, c

confuse the driver and dent his confidence in the car. There is a further, even worse manifestation of pitch sensitivity, which can occur when the front wings are run too close to the ground. In this situation, the wings are running in what might be termed extreme ground effect. In circumstances which then conspire to cause an excessive reduction in the front wing ground clearance, the wing can get into the area where the boundary layer interacts with the ground, and blocks off the flow beneath the wing. This then causes the downforce to fall off rapidly, so that the front of the car rises up again, only to allow the airflow back underneath, which creates more downforce which sucks the nose down again . . . This strange oscillation is known as 'porpoising', and it was a particular problem in the era of 'underbody ground effect' generated downforce in Formula 1 in the 1980s. Thus, pitch sensitivity and methods of lessening its effects – using active suspension systems and, nowadays, damping systems which enable the inde-

Spanwise curvature on the Prost JS45 Formula 1 car's beautiful front wing.

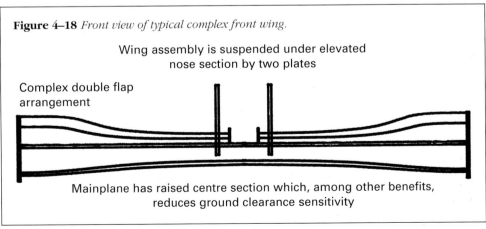

Figure 4–18 *Front view of typical complex front wing.*

Wing assembly is suspended under elevated nose section by two plates

Complex double flap arrangement

Mainplane has raised centre section which, among other benefits, reduces ground clearance sensitivity

pendent adjustment of high and low damper piston speeds so as to isolate and control the slower vehicle attitude changes from the faster wheel movements – are often right at the top of designers' priority lists.

Further improvements in pitch sensitivity reduction have also arisen from the use of complex spanwise front wing shapes. Many front wings on top flight single seaters have a degree of either curved or angular 'anhedral' built into them (see Figure 4–18). In part this is tied up with managing the airflow to the car's underside and to the radiators within the sidepod ducts. But a further benefit is that pitch sensitivity is reduced because the wing-to-ground gap is variable across the span of the wing. Therefore the situation where the flow beneath the wing gets completely blocked at very low ground clearance cannot arise. Such a wing will probably not produce quite as much downforce as one with constant, very low ground clearance, but it should be more consistent, and provide the driver with a more confidence-inspiring car – an often overlooked but vital element in getting a car around a track as quickly as possible.

How to select
and design a wing set up
What follows may look mathematical, but don't let that fool you! It is, in all honesty, highly empirical, and just happens to contain a few calculations that might make it look more complicated on first glance than it really is. But for the competitor who wants to fit wings to his or her car for the first time, or who perhaps wants to try to figure out if the set up already fitted to their pride and joy is somewhere in the right ballpark, the principles outlined here – full of assumptions and estimates though they are – will hopefully provide a better first approximation than blind guesswork on its own. The basis of the scheme is that you have to figure out how much drag you are prepared to accept from a wing set up, and

having once determined that, you can then select the appropriate wings. The scheme is outlined here for a single seater racecar, but could also be applied to other categories, at least in part.

The eight point plan to a first approximation of a wing set up is as follows:

1. Calculate the theoretical top speed *without wings* – this needs values for the frontal area, the power at the wheels, and the C_D.
2. Decide how much you are prepared to knock off that top speed by the addition of wings. An implicit assumption here, based on experience and hard measurements, is that the front wings do not add any significant drag. Only the rear wing contributes tangibly to a car's drag.
3. Calculate the difference in power absorption figures between the top speed without wings and the top speed you are prepared to accept with wings.
4. The difference between these two power absorption figures is what you are going to 'donate' to the rear wing in the quest for downforce.
5. Calculate the maximum wing C_D value that this represents. This requires values for the wing span and chord dimensions to work out the *plan* area of the wing.
6. Using an estimated value for the lift to drag ratio, work out what C_L figure corresponds with the C_D value, and then consult the wing catalogues to seek out first a basic configuration (that is, single, dual, or possibly multi-element), then a specific profile that will provide this C_L value, and at what approximate angle of attack. A few wing configurations and profiles and their lift characteristics are provided in Appendix 1 at the end of this book, but the choice is from a vast range of possibilities.
7. Calculate the theoretical downforce figure that the rear wing will give, then calculate the downforce required at the front to balance this value. The front wing dimensions will be needed here,

as will the wings' ground clearance, so that ground effect can be allowed for in determining the requisite $C_{L(front)}$ figure.

8. Consult the wing catalogues again to determine a suitable configuration, profile, and approximate angle of attack for the front wings.

Perhaps one surprise here is the statement that the front wings do not generate significant drag. The previously mentioned tests on the hillclimb single seater in the MIRA full scale wind-tunnel demonstrated this fact, and even large changes to angle of attack – which produced large changes in front end downforce – did not alter the overall car drag by more than a percentage point or so. However, relatively small changes to the rear wing configuration not only altered the downforce but also made big differences to the car's drag figure. This situation is typical and representative of single seaters in general.

The guesstimate as to what you are prepared to drop your maximum top speed by is going to have to be based on the best knowledge you have got about the speed regimes of the tracks you compete on. For example, you will probably have a good idea of the maximum speed you achieve on each track. You will also be able to at least estimate the time you spend at various speeds, and if your car is equipped even with just a rudimentary data acquisition system such as a rev counter with a memory, you will be able to work out exactly how long you spend in the various speed brackets. With a more sophisticated data acquisition system, you will be able to let a computer work these things out for you, and plot out how long you spend in each sector of the track too. All of this will facilitate a reasonable judgement to be made as to how critical top speed is at a given track. Further analysis, objective wherever possible (but subjective will do if data isn't available), has to take into account how much time is spent accelerating, braking and cornering, and at what speeds. This will all help, firstly, to cause lots of confusion (!), but secondly, to get a handle on the nature of each track, and to help decide whether it's a 'downforce track' or not. Naturally there are no black and white decisions here. Even the pros, equipped with lap time simulation software on powerful computers, are actually working on assumptions and guesstimates at least as much as hard data and past experience. So get to it and start analysing!

Perhaps the hardest thing of all to take into account is that the rear wing will not give you as much downforce as you hope it will from this method. Without the benefit of wind-tunnel testing, or actual measurements on the real car, it's impossible to say just how much the rear wing is going to suffer from the mess that the rest of the car makes of the airflow. All that can be said is that whatever this approximation throws up as a solution will be hard pressed to achieve the theoretical results predicted, and you may need a steeper angle of attack, or perhaps even an additional wing element if the results suggest fitting something which is marginal between, say, a single-element and a dual-element wing. Anyway, it's instructive as well as fun to attempt a numerical solution to this vexing problem, so let's work through an example to see what comes out.

Wing configuration calculation

Taking the aforementioned hillclimb single seater with which the author has intimate experience, having co-assembled and developed it, the frontal area without wings is 12.6sq ft (1.17m²), the wingless C_D is 0.65. Power at the flywheel is around 295bhp, making about 260bhp left to overcome aerodynamic drag (the 12 per cent or so deduction is intended to account for powertrain losses and rolling resistance for a car of this nature with its normal footwear of wide, but cool, tyres). This power figure will correspond exactly to the power absorbed at the vehicle's maximum speed in this wingless state, which would be:

$$v_{max} = 3\sqrt{[(260 \times 146{,}600)/(0.65 \times 12.6)]}$$
$$= 167.0mph\ (268.4kmh)$$

This is way in excess of the maximum speed on any track visited. The fastest speed recorded at any hillclimb venue the car has been driven on is 118mph. Therefore, for the sake of the example, let's assume that we decide that a maximum speed of, say, 135mph was going to be more than enough to leave some top end acceleration at the fastest part of the fastest course visited. How much power would be absorbed at 135mph (217kmh)?

$$bhp\ absorbed = \frac{0.65 \times 12.6 \times (135)^3}{146{,}600} = 137.5bhp$$

The difference between this and the 260bhp absorbed at the absolute maximum speed is the value that we are going to 'donate' to the rear wing drag, = 260 − 137.5 = 122.5bhp. So what wing C_D does this correspond to? To figure this out, we need to know the wing dimensions, and in this case they are 42.1 × 21.7in (1.07 × 0.55m), or 6.34sq ft (0.5885 m²). Using the re-arranged power absorption equation again, we can say that the maximum wing C_D will be

$$C_{Dmax} = \frac{122.5 \times 146{,}600}{6.34 \times (135)^3} = 1.15$$

So what kind of wing will have a C_D of 1.15? Unfortunately we can't just look this up in the wing catalogues. The texts that list wing data tell us what the wing 'profile drag' or 'section drag' coefficients are, but this is only a part of the drag caused by a wing. Induced drag is also created by a wing producing downforce, and gets worse with increased downforce generation, and decreased aspect ratio. Consequently a racecar wing is an inefficient device, in terms of lift to drag ratio. So a short cut to finding out what sort of wing will correspond to a particu-

lar C_D is to use a lift to drag ratio – based on real data on wings trawled from the literature – to determine the likely C_L that this will correspond to, and then use the catalogues (listed in Appendix 2) to seek out a configuration and possible profile that would produce this C_L. It *is* possible to work this out from theory, but, somehow, hard data just has a more secure feel to it . . .

The plot in Figure 4–19 shows a tentative correlation based on published data points of lift to drag ratio versus C_D, and Figure 4–20 shows the C_L values, versus C_D figures, derived from this. Once again, this should get you in roughly the right area. In our example, a C_D of 1.15 should correspond to a C_L of about 2.95 (the lift to drag ratio is therefore around 2.57:1).

Consulting even the few example wing data charts in Appendix 1, we can see that this would correspond to a three-element wing. A two-element design could perhaps achieve this C_L value, but a three-element, double flap arrangement could be set at a low angle, or with low flap deflection, to achieve a lower downforce level, or with a higher angle to obtain a higher coefficient, so providing more options. Thus, the likely best first estimate of a rear wing configuration to suit this car, on the basis of the assumptions made here, is a three plane rear wing. Curiously, this is what it currently sports. However, there has been some suggestion that the car might be losing out by carrying too much wing, and a possible development route is to install a two-element wing built to the maximum span allowed of 55in (1.4m), and with a smaller chord to achieve a higher aspect ratio, but similar plan area, to the original wing. As with all amateur racers who do not have the luxury of a wind-tunnel to try out these ideas on a scale model first, or even to measure the effects under controlled conditions, the only option for this team is to build the wing, fit it, and see if it helps performance in absolute terms (against the clock) or relative terms (against the opposition).

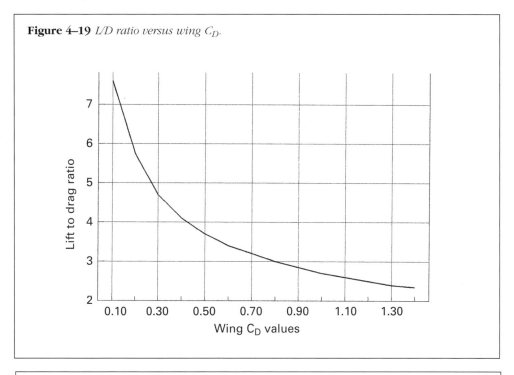

Figure 4–19 *L/D ratio versus wing C_D.*

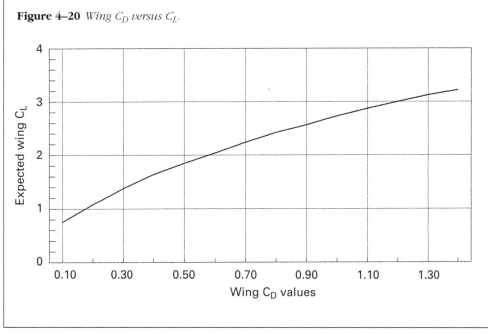

Figure 4–20 *Wing C_D versus C_L.*

But we have yet to work out the front wing configuration that should, theoretically, balance this rear wing. To do this. we will assume equal cantilever effect front and rear (they aren't equal, but it makes the calculations easier, and anyway, this book is not about mechanical leverages!), and an aerodynamic balance that is to be in proportion to the weight distribution, which, with driver aboard, is about 38:62 front:rear. Front wing area is about 4.34sq ft (0.4 m²). Thus we can say that the downforce at the front needs to be 38/62 times the downforce at the rear, which, putting in the relevant values for area, means we can say the following, using the basic downforce calculation:

$$\text{downforce}_{rear} \times 38/62 = \text{downforce front}$$

so

$$0.5\rho A_{rear}C_{Lrear}v^2 \times 38/62 = 0.5\rho A_{front}C_{Lfront}v^2$$

The 0.5ρ and v^2 on both sides of the equation cancel each other out, which means

$$A_{rear} \times C_{Lrear} \times 38/62 = A_{front} \times C_{Lfront}$$

so

$$C_{Lfront} = \frac{A_{rear} \times C_{Lrear}}{A_{front}} \times 38/62$$

Put in the value for the C_{Lrear} of 2.95, together with the figures for the front and rear areas, and the answer is that the C_{Lfront} needs to be 2.67.

But we have yet to take into account ground effect, which, by making the front wings produce more downforce by being close to the ground, means we don't need a section with this high a C_L value in order to achieve the level of necessary downforce. Figure 4–17 showed how downforce increases as a wing gets closer to the ground. Let's assume that the front wings are going to be about 5in (12.5cm) clear of the ground. The wing chord is 13.75in (35cm), so the ground clearance is about 0.36c relative to the chord. Figure 4–17 tells us that we can perhaps expect an increase in C_L, relative to the wing in 'mainstream' air (that is, well away from the influence of the ground), of about 1.37, or 37 per cent. So, we only need to use a wing configuration that

produces a C_L of 2.67/1.37, or 1.95. This corresponds to a two-element wing, perhaps at low to medium overall angle of attack, with a moderate flap deflection of, say, 30°, although there are other two-element set-ups that will fit the same criteria, of course. The important thing is that we have determined that this car could run with a three-element rear wing, which would be balanced with a pair of two-element front wings. Precise installation angles would have to be determined by testing. Interestingly, the car in this example is balanced with a pair of two-element front wings, although the angle of attack at the front is somewhat steeper than the calculations suggest. This may be because the car has a fairly narrow front track, with reasonably wide tyres not far behind the trailing edge of the front wing flaps. This would tend to reduce the effective working area of the front wings, and require a steeper angle of attack to make the effective portion work that much harder in order to balance the rear wing.

What none of this takes into account, of course, is the downforce that might be generated by the underside of the car. *If,* and it's a big *if,* the underside happens to produce its downforce with a convenient front to rear split matching the weight distribution (there or thereabouts), then the wing configuration calculations here will still be valid with regard to working out a balanced set-up. But, if the underside produces, say, rear biased downforce, then the implications are that the rear wing may not have to produce as much downforce, and also that the front wing(s) may have to work harder to balance the rear. This would appear to be the case with the current crop of Formula 3 cars, for example; with their tiny regulation rear wings and apparently relatively large front wings, it has to be concluded that the rear underbody and diffuser must be making a significant contribution to rear downforce. Furthermore, the interaction between rear wings – especially of the multi-tier type – and the rear diffuser cannot be taken into account by the empirical approach. This is something that can only really be solved with wind-tunnel and track testing

Wing mountings

No mention has so far been made of some of the practicalities involved with choosing a wing set-up. The manner of attachment of front and rear wings can have an effect on their efficiency. For example, at the front of a single seater, a pair of wings either side of a nose cone will have a plan area limited by the maximum width permitted, minus the width of the nose. Consequently the narrower the nose is, the bigger will be the available plan area, and the larger will be the aspect ratio, which combine to produce more downforce more efficiently. It is even better if the front wing is a single device, with a span dimension equal to the full width permitted, creating the maximum possible aspect ratio. This can be achieved either by mounting the wing above the nose, or below it. Mounting

above the nose doesn't really help a great deal, because the central portion of the wing will lose effectiveness by virtue of the proximity of the nose cover, and the whole wing will, most probably, be so far above the ground that it will lose the benefit of ground effect. But mounting the wing below the nose puts the whole underside of the wing into ground effect, and utilises the wing's width to the maximum. Thus the current phase of under-slung wings in so many single seater formulae at present is exploiting these advantages to the full.

Rear wings have two options for attachment, which are sometimes combined: the 'centre post' and 'end plate' mount variations are both used across a wide range of racing categories. With either method, it is important to consider the effect that the mounting structure can have on the flow on the all-important underside of the wing. If the mounting is to be of the centre post type, then the post – or twin plates, as are sometimes used – should be shaped and faired so as

The underslung front wing of the Van Diemen FR97 Formula Renault Sport.

Centre post rear wing mounting on a Jedi hillclimber.

to interfere as little as possible with the wing's airflow. In the case of the end plate mounting, since the thickness of the end plates has a controlling influence on their rigidity, it follows that they are likely to eat into some of the available wing area (if span is restricted by regulations, which it usually is), and also exert an

End plate rear wing mounting, clearly exploited for additional aerodynamic effect on the Jordan 197.

effect on the airflow at the outer edges of the wing. Again, the leading edges (at least) of the end plates should be shaped so as to disturb the airflow onto the wing as little as possible. Structural considerations will be discussed in Chapter 7.

Aspect ratios again

It has already been mentioned in passing that a larger aspect ratio makes for a more efficient wing. Figure 4–21 shows in general how the lift coefficient versus angle of attack alters with aspect ratio. It is clear that a very low aspect ratio yields a lower lift coefficient. But, on the positive side, the stall angle is delayed, and stall becomes less abrupt, making a low AR wing a less sensitive device. But this is not a good reason for selecting a low AR wing! Better to maximise the span in order to achieve the best aspect ratio possible. Referring back to the sample calculations on the rear wing of the hillclimb car, the maximum span allowed in this competition category is 1.4m, and there really is no good technical reason for *not* having a wing of this span, so as to maximise the possible AR. There is a formula

used for estimating the lift coefficient of an (elliptical) aerofoil, which in simplified form tells us that

$$C_L \text{ is proportional to} \quad \frac{1}{1 + (2/AR)}$$

where AR is the aspect ratio. This means that increasing the aspect ratio does indeed lead to an increase in the lift coefficient at a given angle of attack. Feeding some AR values into this formula over the typical range of competition car aspect ratios, and plotting them on a graph, relative to the lift at AR = 1, yields the plot shown in Figure 4–22. If the wing on the hillclimb car in the example had its 1.07m × 0.55m (AR = 1.95) replaced with one of 1.40m × 0.42m (AR = 3.33, with the same plan area), then this graph suggests that its lift coefficient will increase by over 25 per cent, if all other things remain equal. But the news gets even better! There is also an approximation for calculating the induced drag component of the total drag caused by a wing. As we have seen, the induced drag gets greater with increased downforce. But it is also affected benefi-

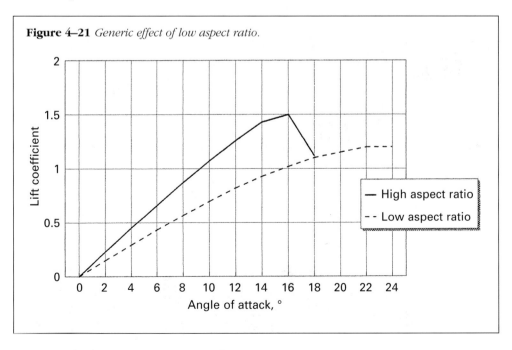

Figure 4–21 *Generic effect of low aspect ratio.*

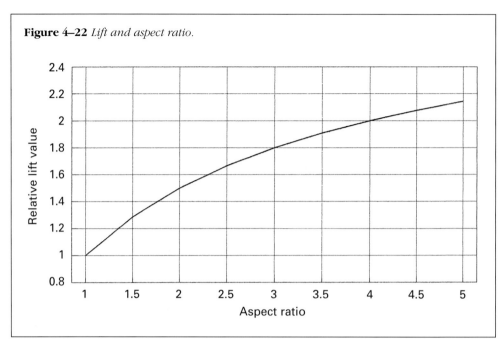

Figure 4–22 *Lift and aspect ratio.*

cially by an increased aspect ratio, and a formula for approximating a value for induced drag is

$$C_{Di} = \frac{K.C_{L}^{2}}{\pi AR} \quad (\pi = \text{Greek letter pi, K} = 1.2 \text{ approx})$$

If we look at the two configurations for the hillclimb rear wing, one with AR = 1.95, producing a C_L of 2.80, and the other with AR = 3.33, which theoretically will create a C_L 25 per cent greater – that is, 3.50 – then the induced drag coefficients work out at 1.54 for the former, and 1.41 for the latter. Thus, not only has the theoretical lift increased, but the theoretical induced drag has reduced in spite of the extra lift! This is too good a bonus not to be exploited. It also indicates that the earlier correlation put forward for

deriving C_L values from lift to drag ratios, which was based on reported data, can only really be applied with any confidence to the aspect ratios of the wings that the data were measured on, which were in the range 1.5 to 2.0. Larger AR wings will perform better.

Wings are the most obvious manifestation of the use of downforce to improve competition car performance. Perhaps it is because of this that they are under attack as the cause of what is seen as reduced overtaking and a decline in 'proper' racing in a range of racing categories around the world. Whether or not you agree with this, it is indisputable that wings have, and will probably continue to have, an important role to play in motorsport – even if it's only to carry the sponsors' names!

Chapter 5

Undercurrents

A bit of history

If wings enabled a step forward to be taken in competition car performance, then the exploitation of underbody airflow to generate downforce facilitated the proverbial giant leap. It had long been realised that the airflow under a car was affected by the close proximity of the ground, but only the disadvantages seemed to be noticed at first, and effort was put into reducing the airflow beneath the car in order to reduce drag; early examples of this approach include the MG speed record attempt vehicles in the 1950s. However, during the heated debate on the wings of Formula 1 cars during 1968–69, when it looked likely that wings would be banned for evermore, BRM did some work on designing a car body that used its own 'wetted' surfaces to create downforce. Peter Wright, working under Tony Rudd, had been running some tests during 1969 in the Imperial College, London, wind-tunnel, and the results were sufficiently good for BRM to set about very secretively building a car to exploit the new-found effects. Sadly, perhaps, the legendary BRM politics intervened, and the car never reached a race track. Rudd and Wright departed, Wright to Specialised Mouldings, where he designed the very simple inverted wing-shaped sidepods for the March 701 Formula 1 car, which, whilst using the inverted wing principle to create a modicum of downforce, were not really exploiting ground proximity.

Around this time, that famous American racer/innovator, Texan Jim Hall, burst into the limelight again, producing the latest variation on the Chaparral sports racer theme, the 2J. This had a supplementary motor – actually a snowmobile engine – powering two large fans which sucked away at the underbody region in order to reduce the pressure there. To maximise the effect, virtually the entire under-car region was sealed by flexible Lexan plastic rubbing strips, so that the car became a hovercraft in reverse, so to speak. Estimates of the downforce that the car achieved vary from 1,300 to 2,000lb (590 to 910kg), substantial enough to make the rather heavy (2,000lb/910kg) car extremely competitive – in the skilled hands of Vic Elford – against the all-conquering McLarens in the CanAm series of 1970, although the unreliability of the auxiliary engine kept the 2J from being consistently effective. The special thing about the fan car concept, of course, is that its downforce was not speed dependant – it could develop as much downforce at rest as it could at race speeds, so the Chaparral's starts and slow corner performance were said to be nothing short of devastating.

But the storm of protest over the fan car concept led to its being banned by the governing body, and to this day the 'movable aerodynamic device' rule has been used to prevent, or, at least, to *attempt* to prevent, any such concept from reappearing – more of this shortly.

The way forward from here was a little time in coming, and once more Peter Wright and Tony Rudd, now at Team Lotus, in Norfolk, England, were intimately involved when the next stage of development began in 1975: Rudd had been presented with a list of crucial questions by Colin Chapman, and since most were aerodynamic in nature, Peter Wright was brought in.

Wright and his team were again using 1/4 scale models in the Imperial College wind-tunnel, which was equipped with a 'moving ground' conveyor belt to simulate the car moving over the road. They noticed that the sidepods, designed to carry radiators and fuel, were sagging on the model, and producing inconsistent results. So, after wiring them up more securely, they also sealed the bottom edges of the sidepods with 'skirts', and then started to get some unbelievable results. In fact, they repeated the tests several times to convince themselves of what was happening. Chapman wanted to know what would happen if the sidepods were shaped like inverted wings, whereupon Wright produced his photos of the never-raced 1969 BRM 'wing car'. In fairly short order a new Lotus Formula 1 car was drawn, a model made, and during the latter part of 1976 Mario Andretti tested what had been designated the Lotus Type 78. The car was immediately two seconds a lap faster than the admittedly tardy type 77, and Andretti's scarcely contained enthusiasm was picked up by sponsors John Player, who apparently insisted on the car being renamed the JPS Mark III. At the car's glitzy press launch, the designers were sworn to say only that they had found 'something for nothing', a reference to the substantial gain in downforce for little or no drag penalty; and thus was made the biggest single leap in racecar performance – *ever*.

The Lotus 78 won races during 1977, but Wright and the R&D team spent all year perfecting a reliable sliding 'skirt', which sealed the underbody from unwanted sideways migration of air into the low pressure region, the function of the skirt being crucial to the underbody's effectiveness. The lessons from the 78 were carried over onto the superb type 79, which was effectively the first no-compromise ground effect car, and this proceeded to dominate the World Championships for Drivers *and* Constructors during 1978. However, there was one small hiccup for Lotus that year – the Brabham 'fan car'. Earlier attempts at regulating against the use of fans to create suction beneath the car had reckoned without the ingenuity of Gordon Murray, then Brabham's Chief Designer. His current charge, the Alfa Romeo flat-12 powered BT46, needed a new cooling system to replace the unsuccessful surface cooling concept tried in early-1978. Murray decided on a large air/water heat exchanger mounted above the engine, fed by cool air from a large fan – which happened to draw its air supply from the Brabham's underbody area. And the car just happened to have two transverse and two longitudinal skirts sealing the underbody region, so that the fan sucked the car down onto the road surface very firmly indeed. The car won its first race in Sweden, with Niki Lauda at the helm, but the protests from the other teams led the governing body to ban any further use of fans for creating downforce. They allowed the win to stand, however, perhaps by way of apology for giving the idea tacit approval at the concept stage! There are still some sporting categories where fan induced downforce has *not* been banned, but most formulae and classes no longer allow this kind of downforce generation.

However, the development of ground effect 'tunnels', as the underbody channels became known, continued, despite various attempts by the regulators to contain the incredible cornering speeds that resulted. Major single seater and sports racing categories all around the world were affected at all levels of motorsport. Come 1982–83, the FISA had had enough, and banned profiled undersides in Formula 1 (and subsequently other categories), and the next phase of development was concentrated on the 'flat floors'. In the United States, the Indycar World Series (now CART), amongst others, continued with tunnels, though year by year their effect has been mollified by dimensional changes in order to contain cornering speeds to 'safe' levels. Tunnels also came and went in top level sports racing categories, and they now generally adopt the 'flat floor between the front and rear wheels' rule. And that's pretty much how things stand today – most racing categories insist on a 'flat floor', though there are some which still allow tunnels. However, even where flat floors have to be used, there is still a degree of freedom with respect to undertray shape ahead of the front wheels, and behind the rear wheels, and, as we shall see, this is significant.

The rather lengthy, if incomplete, historical prelude to this chapter is quite deliberate, because there is no question that the development of underbody aerodynamics has been the most significant as far as downforce production and performance gains are concerned. Once the Lotus 78 had paved the way, *all* competition car categories had to at least look at the concept to see if there was benefit to be gained, and although many formulae now severely restrict design freedom in this area, the exploitation of 'ground effect' is not going to go away as long as competition cars run in close proximity to the ground.

Back to basics

All cars, by definition, operate in 'ground effect'. This means that there *will be* interference with the airflow underneath the car arising from the proximity of the car and the ground. This has a large bearing on the overall behaviour of the airflow over and around a car, and, as such, the influence on performance can be considerable. Interestingly, though, the effects may be beneficial or adverse, depending

on the exact nature and design of a car. We saw in Chapter 4 that the downforce produced by a wing in ground effect was greater than that produced by the same wing in freestream air, and the effect increased the closer to the ground the wing was moved, until, at a certain, close distance, the boundary layer around the wing interfered with the ground, and blocked off the flow, so reducing the downforce again. Similarly, the development of the boundary layer under a car is central to the ability of the underbody airflow to produce downforce.

A typical passenger car has a very rough underside, with such items as the exhaust system, suspension, transmission, drivetrain, and fuel tank all protruding into the underside region, and cavities such as those around the engine and transmission and wheel wells, adding to the 'roughness'. Chapter 3 discussed how this roughness contributes to drag; what happens is that this type of underside creates a thick boundary layer, which tends to haul the air below the car along with it. Thus, the boundary layer will extend right to the ground, and at the rear of the vehicle, it merges with the wake, which will now also reach the ground. The flow along the underside is slow and turbulent, if not blocked off altogether by this interference, and the effect on the pressure distribution is to create just what we don't want, a *high* pressure region under the car. Added to the usual generation of low pressure over a passenger car, the enhancement of positive lift is not welcome (see Figure 5–1). So pretty obviously, anything that can be done to improve the airflow under the car is going to be very beneficial in this dire situation.

There are three main factors here to be considered for a given car: the ground clearance; the underside 'roughness'; and the shape of the underside. The impact that each of these factors has is related to each of the others. For example, if a car has a very rough underside, then one method of decreasing the positive lift that

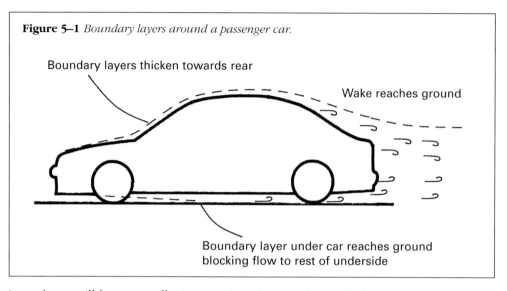

Figure 5–1 *Boundary layers around a passenger car.*

Boundary layers thicken towards rear

Wake reaches ground

Boundary layer under car reaches ground blocking flow to rest of underside

it produces will be to actually *increase* its ground clearance. Conversely, reducing the ground clearance in an effort to lower a car's centre of gravity for competition use – a basic and essential aim to improve cornering and handling – may actually make the positive lift worse if the car's underside is rough. The corollary of this is that rough undersides are not good! In fact, it is pretty self-evident that fitting a smooth underpanel is bound to enable the air to move faster along the underside, and it is equally obvious that drag will be reduced as well if the lumps and bumps can no longer interfere with the smooth passage of the air. Studies on the effect on the lift coefficient of fitting a smooth underpanel to conventional cars of 'average underside roughness' have shown that a typical reduction in C_L of around 20 per cent could be achieved, and this is likely to be exceeded with a car running closer to the ground than average. A couple of other practical benefits to arise are that the car will require less cleaning after use, especially if it was of open spaceframe construction; and if the underpanel extends under any liquid-containment areas, then spillages or leaks are unlikely to affect fellow competitors and get you black flagged! Take note, though, that special arrangements may

have to be made for cooling if the installation of an undertray blocks off the passage of cooling air to any sensitive components.

The shape of the underside has a marked influence on the under-car airflow too. If the pressure under the car is positive, which may still be the case even with a smooth undertray fitted, then the airflow can be improved by shaping the undertray. If some lateral curvature is incorporated, involving the rounding of the sill areas, then any high pressure air under the car will be encouraged to bleed out sideways into the fast, unobstructed, low pressure flow passing down the sides of the car, which will help to relieve the high pressure under the car. But this would be a rather unimaginative remedy, treating the symptom but not curing the cause of the problem. It would be better to create a lower pressure region under the car, in which event the flow is likely to want to migrate from the sides into the low pressure region under the car, and this is to be actively *discouraged!*

In order to create a low pressure region under the car, it is necessary to start thinking in terms of longitudinal shaping of the underside. By raising the front portion of the undertray in a gentle

The front undertray on this Mercedes ITC car was curved to accelerate air into the underbody region.

curve, and doing the same with the rear section too, we can ease the airflow under the car in a smoother, more regular way, with delayed boundary layer formation, and a higher speed, thus producing a lower pressure. The car becomes more like the aerofoil running close to the ground, with a venturi section formed between the car and the ground, and the possibility for downforce production now exists. Raising the rear section of the undertray allows the low pressure which exists in the car's wake to exert an influence on the underbody flow, and help to maintain low pressure under the rear of the car (Figure 5–2).

The precise ground clearance that a particular car should run at in order to create beneficial ground effect conditions is specific to any one vehicle and it is impossible to generalise. But to start to get a feel for things, we can look at some

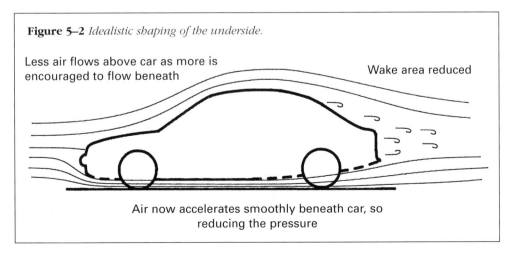

Figure 5–2 *Idealistic shaping of the underside.*

Less air flows above car as more is encouraged to flow beneath

Wake area reduced

Air now accelerates smoothly beneath car, so reducing the pressure figures based on experiments done on road vehicles of average underbody roughness. Scibor-Rylski (see Appendix 2) tells us that at ground clearances of between 0.125 and 0.600 times the wheelbase, 'conventional' cars produced negative lift coefficients, as the 'venturi effect' assisted the underbody flow; but at ground clearances of less than 0.125 times the wheelbase, the lift coefficients became decidedly positive. Consider that an average ground clearance to wheelbase ratio will be of the order of 0.05, and we can see why conventional cars with rough undersides are operating in a highly unsatisfactory *positive* lift regime. The conclusion to be drawn once again is that it is imperative to fit a smooth underpanel if positive under-car pressure is to be avoided, and that this panel should be shaped to encourage a fast, smooth flow under the car.

Clearly, if common practice is anything to go by, competition cars are able to run close to the ground without generating the positive pressure that the conventional, rough underbodied vehicles referred to above apparently developed. A further reference, Katz (see Appendix 2) gives some hope here, and suggests that a 1/5 scale model with a smooth underbody produced a minimum lift coefficient at 1.38in (35mm) ground clearance, which corresponds to 6.9in (175mm) at full scale. However, the tests that gave this result were measured over a fixed ground plane, and it is likely that the result over a moving ground plane would have produced the minimum C_L at a smaller ground clearance. So this is getting nearer the order of ground clearance that might be seen on typical competition cars, which is quite useful, and means we can start to think about the *benefits* of running close to the ground, rather than any possible disadvantages. Clearly, during the early 1990s extremely small ground clearances were in common use in some of the FIA's single seater categories, Formula 1 included, and though logic might tend to suggest that the

ground clearances were impossibly small to allow significant, smooth, fast flow along the underbody, this patently was not the case. But the underbody and diffuser solutions in these categories were derived in the large majority of cases from wind-tunnel development in moving ground test facilities, where the criticality of running so close to the ground could be evaluated under carefully controlled conditions. Consequently the designers were able to run their cars at the absolute minimum ground clearances in order to generate maximum downforce. They almost universally seemed to push into the background that this also made the cars incredibly sensitive to changes in ground clearance and pitch attitude, which in turn made them inconsistent and unpredictable for the drivers – yet another example of the poor driver being made too small a component in the design equation, an incomprehensible approach considering that racecars are not yet piloted by radio control from the pit wall . . . Anyway, we will return to the topic of ground clearance anon.

From here there are two possible routes that could be followed in the search for low under-car pressure. The first was dealt with in Chapter 3, in the section on front airdams and spoilers. The principle involved blocking off some of the airflow beneath the car, and is a valid technique, particularly where regulations or matters of practicality prevent much underbody smoothing or profiling. The second, though, requires that the airflow under the car is encouraged, and at the same time carefully controlled so as to develop not just low pressure, but low pressure in the right place, if at all possible. If low pressure can be produced over a large planform area, it can be seen that only modest pressure reduction will lead to large downforce.

Flat floors

Looking first at the simplest configuration of underbody, with a flat and, we will now assume, smooth underside, then as

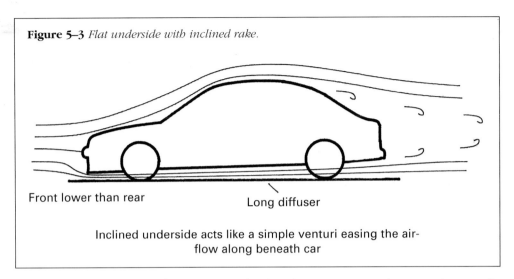

Figure 5–3 *Flat underside with inclined rake.*

Front lower than rear   Long diffuser

Inclined underside acts like a simple venturi easing the airflow along beneath car

well as ground clearance being a critical parameter, shape is also crucial too. Whilst 'flat' and 'shape' might seem to be mutually exclusive terms, there is one very important and simple way in which a flat undertray may be 'shaped', and that is by ensuring that it has a negative incidence angle, or rake. In other words, the front of the undertray *must* be lower than the rear (see Figure 5–3). This is common sense really, and it is blindingly obvious, hopefully, that if the reverse was true, and the front was higher than the rear, then air would pack under the car at speed and give it a very unhealthy, and very unsafe, upwards lift. Ensuring a car

has this negative incidence angle is vitally important.

At the very least, a significant reduction in a vehicle's (positive) lift coefficient can be expected from a correctly raked underpanel, and references suggest that only a small angle of 1 or 2° is enough to make a big difference. How does this produce a benefit? In essence, the entire underside of the car has now become a simple venturi section. There is a narrow throat under the front of the car, through which the air will be accelerated, producing low pressure there, and the rest of the underbody has become a long diffuser, which, being smooth, allows the air

Better to keep the front lower than the rear under all conditions if possible!

to continue flowing rapidly – though gradually decelerating – towards the rear. Here, the upwards rake of the under-panel will allow some interaction between the wake and the underbody flow, which will help to ensure that the pressure remains relatively low below the back of the car.

But remember that rake and front ground clearance are inextricably related, and there will be an angle at which the front of the car is low enough for bound-ary layer interference to block off the underbody flow altogether, which we are trying to avoid, and this is why only a small rake angle is sufficient. The rake must be adequate, though, to ensure that it does not become positive – that is, rear-down – during normal suspension movement, and preferably under any other circumstances such as cresting a rise at speed. Thankfully, tales of cars flipping over are few and far between these days, in large part because down-force keeps them pressed firmly onto the track, and it is usually only when freak circumstances launch a car's nose high into the air that the dreaded 'back-flip' occurs.

Diffusers

We'll ignore the chronological sequence in which under-car aerodynamic develop-ment took place, and pass on to a config-uration more common currently, which is the flat floor augmented by the diffuser. A diffuser will be defined in this context as a region of the underbody, generally towards the rear, incorporating an increase in rake angle compared to the forward part of the underbody. In essence, it is that part of the venturi which is divergent, as distinct from the convergent forward part, and the narrow-est part, the throat of the venturi (see Figure 5–4). Though the common usage of the word 'diffuser' within motorsport is only as old as the exploitation of under-body ground effects, the practical appli-cation of diffusers on cars, perhaps surprisingly, goes back to the 1960s, for example on the Jaguar E-type. The

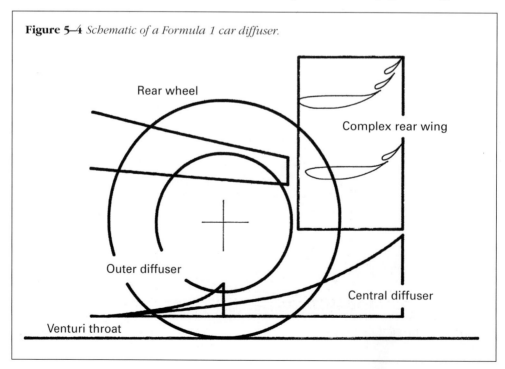

Figure 5–4 *Schematic of a Formula 1 car diffuser.*

Rear wheel

Complex rear wing

Outer diffuser

Central diffuser

Venturi throat

smooth lower rear panel of this curvaceous sports roadster was shaped very
much like a diffuser panel on much later
competition cars (except it did not have
side 'walls'), curving gradually upwards
throughout a relatively long rear overhang.

The purpose of the diffuser is, in part,
to open up the rear area of the underside
flow to the influence of the low pressure
within the wake. But just as the vacuum
created by the induction stroke of an
engine compels air to accelerate through
a carburettor venturi, so the forward
motion of a car provides the impetus for
air to accelerate around, over, and under
it. A divergent, upswept diffuser has an
expanding volume which *must* be filled
with air as the car travels along – the diffuser cannot defy nature and become an
airless void – and so air accelerates
through the throat of the venturi, creating
reduced pressure in that region, before
entering the diffuser and gradually returning back to, more or less, the original,
ambient velocity at which it joins the
wake (see Figure 5–5).

So the diffuser, in effect, compels the
air ahead of it, under the flat underside of
the car, to accelerate, so creating low

pressure, and hence downforce. It also
serves to return the velocity of the mass
of air flowing through the throat back to
the original velocity it had prior to entering the convergent part of the venturi. It
does so in a controlled, progressive way
that deals with the adverse pressure gradient, and the associated risks of flow
separation. In other words, the diffuser
has to have a gradual change of angle so
as not to cause the flow to separate from
the 'roof' or the sides. It will not have
escaped the attention of the observant
reader that all diagrammatic representations of venturi tubes, including the
highly schematic one in Figure 2–2, show
the convergent part to have a steeper
convergence angle than the diffuser section divergence. This is not just a representation, but a compliance with the laws
of nature, which dictate that there must
be a *gradual* increase in pressure along
the venturi diffuser, and it is just as
applicable to a car's underbody diffuser.
However, a car which is required to have
a flat centre section to its underbody,
extending as far back as the rear wheels,
may not have very much room for a
gently sloping diffuser, and clearly some
Formula 1 diffusers, which are very short

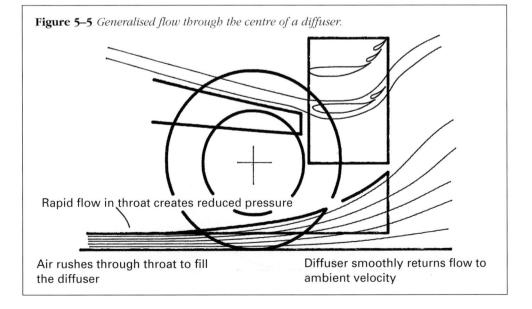

Figure 5–5 *Generalised flow through the centre of a diffuser.*

Rapid flow in throat creates reduced pressure

Air rushes through throat to fill
the diffuser

Diffuser smoothly returns flow to
ambient velocity

This Minardi M197 underbody illustrates the sharp angular change which occurs at the outer diffuser especially.

because of regulations, seem to have out-rageously steep divergence. The influence and interaction of the rear wing, which will be looked at shortly, has a major role to play here in explaining this apparent anomaly.

The flat floor and underbody configuration is prevalent in many competition

Side plates prevent unwanted sideways ingress of air into the diffuser, as on this Porsche 911 GTR.

car categories, and has been developed to a level where, for example, Formula 1 cars are able to generate almost as much downforce as when they were permitted to use 'tunnels', which are discussed below. Various estimates put the amount of downforce attributable to the underbody alone on a Formula 1 car at around 330 to 420lb (150 to 190kg) at 100mph (160kmh), or very roughly one third of the total downforce of the car. By way of an interesting comparison, the late lamented (by the author at least) FIA Class 1 International Touring Cars of the mid-1990s, which were said to produce between 200 and 400lb (90 to 180kg) *total* downforce at 100mph (160kmh) were also claimed to only produce about 5 per cent of this total from their flat underbodies and diffusers. The stated reason for this seemingly low proportion was the protuberances of the rear differential (four-wheel drive was permitted) and exhaust system interfering with the airflow under the cars. One suspects, though, that this 5 per cent was something of a 'modest underestimate' designed more to confuse opponents than to be informative. The complexity of shape, and obvious development that had quite plainly gone into the diffusers, told a rather different story, and one strongly suspects that the actual proportion of downforce from the underbodies was more than this figure suggests.

In general, the greater the angle of slant of the diffuser the greater will be the lift reduction, or downforce production. Katz (see Appendix 2) shows a simplistic and generalised case of a passenger-car based experiment with an inclined but flat diffuser panel. Lift reductions were very marked over the 0 to 4° range of angles, and became actual downforce values (negative C_{LRS}) at angles steeper than 4°, though with the benefit gradually tailing off. However, gains were still measured up to the steepest angle shown, of 11°, and elsewhere it is said that diffuser angles are usually less than 15°. Fitting side plates to the diffuser

creates an even greater benefit, and large downforce values can be attained in this way, the side plates preventing the ingress of sideways flow. This configuration, which is in effect a venturi tunnel, leads us neatly into the next section.

Tunnel visions

The precursor to the flat underbody-with-diffuser configuration was the ground effect 'tunnel' design, which, in later refined forms, produced the largest downforce figures ever seen in motorsport. Instigated, as we have seen, by Team Lotus in what looks now to have been the relatively simplistic Lotus 78, tunnels swept through motorsport and caused a step change in lap times the world over. That first ground effect car (ignoring ones with auxiliary power that preceded it) used inverted wing section sidepods, attached to the chassis between the front and rear wheels, to generate its underbody downforce. The proximity of the wing sections to the ground was seen to enhance their beneficial effect, and their very low aspect ratio – which would ordinarily lead to low efficiency – ceased to be a problem when 'end plates' that reached to the ground almost totally sealed the underbody from deleterious sideways migration of airflow to the underside. To accommodate vertical movement of the car on its suspension, the lower parts of these end plates were allowed to slide up and down within the outer side panels of the wing sections, so that they maintained contact with the road surface (see Figure 5–6). These devices became known as sliding skirts, and in general were not fondly remembered. They massively increased the available downforce when they slid up and down freely, but an equally massive reduction in downforce occurred when they stuck in the 'up' position. They were far from 100 per cent reliable, and many a wide-eyed driver had to walk back to the pits when the sudden loss of grip from a stuck skirt pitched his car off the track. Skirts were eventually banned on

Figure 5–6 *Sliding skirt on early ground effect car.*

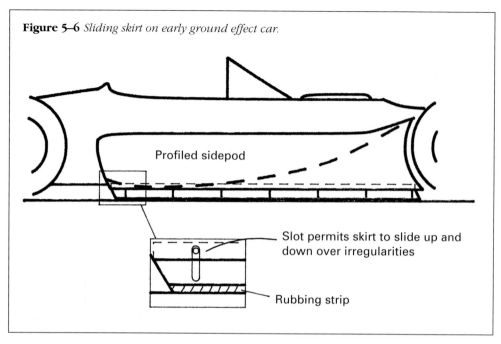

Profiled sidepod

Slot permits skirt to slide up and down over irregularities

Rubbing strip

safety grounds, but not before several years had passed.

The Lotus 79 that followed on from the trend-setting 78 was a superb refinement of the basic wing car idea, and was the first true, no-compromise, ground effect car. All other detail aspects of the car's design, except perhaps the basic place-

Rocker arm front suspension cleaned up the entry to the Lotus 79's tunnels.

ment of the engine, gearbox, wheels, and driver were secondary to the effectiveness of the tunnels. The whole concept of ground effect was refined on this car, and its success on the track is testimony to its superiority over the opposition at the time. Lotus had truly found Chapman's desired 'unfair advantage'.

The concept of twin venturi tunnels either side of the centre section was dictated by the positioning of the engine and gearbox behind the driver in mid-engined single seater and sports proto-type and GT cars (Figure 5–7). Clearly a front-engined, front-wheel drive car could, if permitted, utilise a single tunnel virtually the whole width and length of the car (Figure 5–8). But whatever the configuration of the car, the basic design parameters for the venturi tunnels were the same: the profile had to consist of a short convergent section, followed by a narrow throat which led into a divergent diffuser section. The overall shape, in three dimensions, was determined on the one part by the ground, and on the other by the specific packaging of the funda-mental components of the car. The con-

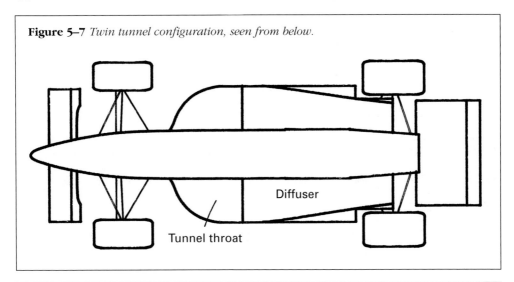

Figure 5–7 *Twin tunnel configuration, seen from below.*

Diffuser

Tunnel throat

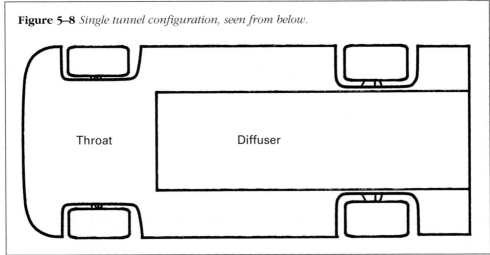

Figure 5–8 *Single tunnel configuration, seen from below.*

Throat

Diffuser

Left-hand tunnel diffuser on the 1986 Jaguar XJR-6 sports prototype routes neatly past engine, transmission and wheel.

vergent and throat sections were generally fairly easy to shape and position, and a wide front track ensured that the front wheels were as far out of the way as possible. But the diffuser sections had to be routed through to the rear of the car, past the engine and its ancillary components and exhausts, preferably without impinging on the adverse effects of the rear wheels.

The importance of the expanding diffuser sections of the tunnels can be gathered from the lengths that designers went to try to attain as uncluttered and clean a shape in this region of the car as possible. Gearboxes were made especially narrow, exhausts were re-routed, engine ancillary components such as fuel and oil pumps were re-located, and in one particularly famous example – that of the Porsche-built TAG turbo engine destined for John Barnard's McLaren MP4/2 in 1984 – the shape of the engine was designed from the outset, to Barnard's specific criteria, to enable the fullest opti-

misation of the rear of the tunnels. The governing body pulled the carpet out from under the feet of this project when it banned profiled undersides in Formula 1, but in all probability the careful packaging exercise that was done allowed aerodynamic advantages even on the flat bottomed car that the engine ultimately powered.

Peter Wright, the man responsible for the design and development of the early Lotus ground effect cars, wrote a paper in 1983 (see Appendix 2) in which he presented graphically the effect on downforce levels of ground clearance, pitch angle, and skirt-to-ground gap. He found that the greatest downforce, and the best lift to drag ratio, were achieved at 2.56in (65mm) ground clearance, with a nose-down angle of around 0.7 to 0.9°. Lift coefficient, with respect to frontal area, was about −2.25, with a lift to drag ratio of 3.3:1, representing a drag coefficient of 0.68; but these are whole car figures and include the contribution of front and rear wings. The underbody was said to contribute 80 per cent of the 3,600lb (1,636kg) total downforce at 180mph (290kmh). The effect of the skirt-to-ground gap was interesting, with a 0.4in (10mm) gap creating a 26 per cent reduction in downforce, and a 0.8in (20mm) gap almost halving the whole car's downforce. Obviously these numbers applied only to the car from which the data was derived, but they must have been fairly representative of late-1970s ground effect cars in Formula 1.

Ground effect tunnels between the front and rear axles create a centre of pressure which is fairly well forward on a car, and the business of attaining a front to rear aerodynamic balance is rather different to the flat bottom-with-diffuser case. Indeed, as a rather obvious generalisation, the further forward the throat of the venturi, the further forward will be the centre of pressure. This had the advantage that in order to attain a front to rear balance, very little and sometimes *no* front wing needed to be run, which in turn meant that the airflow into the tunnels was cleaner. This situation seemed to last as long as sliding skirts, but with the overall reduction in downforce brought

about by the banning of sliding skirts, front wings reappeared and grew larger again. However, it was still crucial that the front wings did not impede the airflow into the tunnels, or, for that matter, into the cooling matrices, which were now generally housed in, and fed by ducts in the leading edge of, the sidepods (Figure 5–9). Current 'tunnel' cars benefit from the use of asymmetric front wings, so that the portion of the front wing or flap ahead of the tunnel entrance/sidepod duct is less extreme than the outer portions.

Rear wings never disappeared from ground effect cars, and this can be put down to two factors: firstly, the rear wing provided a means to balance the aerodynamics, and if front wings were absent it was the *only* method of doing that, since tunnels were non-adjustable; and secondly, the interaction between the rear wing and the flow through the tunnels was to augment the pressure reduction in the tunnels, so the effect of the rear wing reached well forwards of its location. This will be looked at in more detail later.

A well-designed tunnel was very much a three-dimensional device, and not just a two-dimensional venturi shape in side

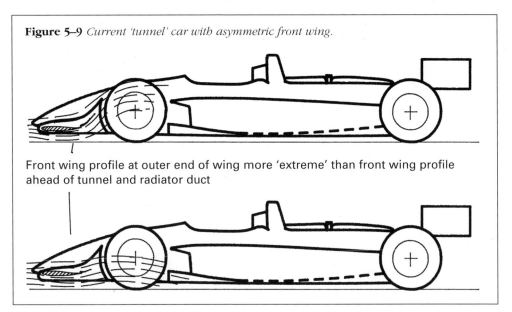

Figure 5–9 *Current 'tunnel' car with asymmetric front wing.*

Front wing profile at outer end of wing more 'extreme' than front wing profile ahead of tunnel and radiator duct

elevation. Although consisting of a 'roof' which was at right angles to the 'walls', in order to maximise the cross-sectional area of the tunnel and hence the mass flow of air through it, the roof-to-wall joins needed to be generously radiused so as to prevent the likelihood of flow separation in these regions. Conversely, in the case of skirt-less tunnels, the lower joins from the bottom of the tunnel wall to the outer portion of the floor were beneficially left sharp. This had the effect of creating a vortex within the diffuser as the inevitable sideways flow migrated into the tunnel, which actually assisted with maintaining attached flow (Figure 5–10).

The tunnels were rarely straight from front to rear, but instead angled inwards to direct the airflow inboard of the rear wheels. Allowing the airflow to impinge on the rear wheels would have caused major turbulence in the diffuser, which would have seriously affected the efficiency of the tunnels. All the transitions within the tunnel had to be gradual, with no sharp changes of shape that might create flow separation. And the leading edge of the inlet to the underbody region was radiused to ease the air into this region of accelerating flow.

It was found to be imperative that the tunnels be made as rigid as possible, so that the quite large pressure differentials did not distort the structure and give inconsistent downforce. Obviously the mounting structures needed to be adequate to carry the very large downloads too. Just as important as it was to attempt to seal the outboard edges of the tunnels from the flow beyond, so it was to seal the inboard edges against the chassis – the low pressure in the tunnels could just as easily pull air in from around the engine bay, for example, if such leakage was allowed.

As we have seen, the lowest pressures occurred in the throat of the tunnels, and by using a longer throat, more downforce could be achieved. The downside of this was greater sensitivity to ride height and rake angle. This is a similar story to the front wing running in ground effect, described in Chapter 4, and once again it was a case of the designers trying to find a compromise that the drivers could live with. However, this did not stop a ludicrous phase in development that saw spring stiffnesses climb to almost unbearable (for the driver) levels in order to maintain a consistent aerodynamic platform. Whilst the aerodynamics might have benefited from incredibly stiffly sprung racecars, the drivers certainly did not.

Once skirts were banned and a mini-

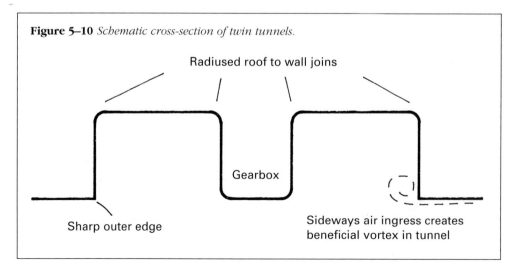

Figure 5–10 *Schematic cross-section of twin tunnels.*

Radiused roof to wall joins

Gearbox

Sharp outer edge

Sideways air ingress creates beneficial vortex in tunnel

mum ground clearance was specified, there was a drop-off in downforce levels for a time, but various ploys were tried in order to win back the losses. Some were patently silly, such as the short-lived fashion for driver-controlled devices that altered ride height, allowing cars to run right down on the deck out on the track, but on the way back to the pits they would be reset to a legal level again. How the authorities permitted this state of affairs to even exist, let alone persist for a while, is a mystery! But there were more clever, subtle, and legal ideas tried, such as the shaping of the outer, lower edges of the sidepods to create a 'rolling vortex' down the length of the sidepod, the principle behind which was to prevent the ingress of air into the underbody region, and so recover some of the losses caused by the removal of skirts (Figure 5–11).

All of the above has been written in the past tense, but of course applies to those categories that still permit tunnels. The USA's premier single seater category, once more known as CART, allows tunnels, but in much-reduced and emascu-

lated form nowadays, as the championship regulators respond to constant development and try to keep performance in check. Whilst it is not too surprising that the finger always seems to be pointed at aerodynamics as the cause of performance increases, the fact is that competition between engine suppliers and tyre suppliers in CART and in Formula 1 are the most recent contributors to reduced lap times. Undoubtedly aerodynamic gains continue to be found, but with tight restrictions imposed these days in the premier categories, the gains are small increments only, rather than the quantum leaps produced by the advent of wings, or more particularly the subject of this chapter, ground effect.

Vortex generators, turning vanes, and exhaust blowing

Other devices which work in conjunction with ground effect aerodynamics, be they tunnels or flat bottoms with diffusers, include vortex generators and turning vanes. Vortex generators can be seen on current CART cars, and are the saw-tooth

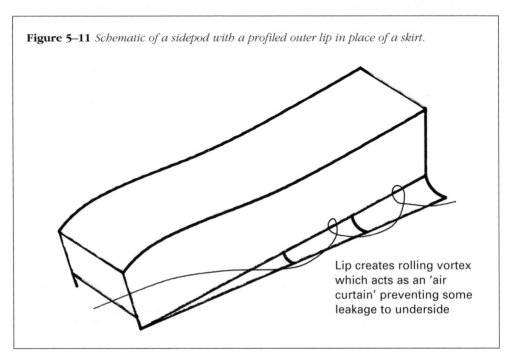

Figure 5–11 *Schematic of a sidepod with a profiled outer lip in place of a skirt.*

Lip creates rolling vortex which acts as an 'air curtain' preventing some leakage to underside

shaped plates attached to the side of the chassis just ahead of the entrance to the tunnels. Their function is to induce a strong vortex at the tunnel entrance in order to regain any lost momentum in the airflow as the result of its passing under the front wing and around the nose section of the car. Curious though this may seem, the effect is to increase downforce, which suggests that the effect persists fur-

ther along the tunnel, augmenting that effect created by the sharp outer-floor-to-tunnel-wall joins mentioned earlier.

Turning vanes can be seen in the majority of diffusers. Their purpose is to smooth and control the lateral element to the airflow that inevitably exists in the throat-to-diffuser region, especially where that region is located at or near the rear axle line (it is in line with the front of the

Turning vanes in the outer diffusers can be seen in this rear view of the Jordan 197 . . . whilst this snapshot of the underside shows them from below.

rear wheels where FIA rules stipulate flat undersides). Because the low pressure in this underbody region sucks air in from the sides, and because the air also has to funnel in between the rear wheels, there is bound to be a convergence in the flow in this area. Turning vanes, vertically mounted in the diffuser, are positioned so as to channel this lateral flow back in line with the long axis of the car, so maintaining the desired smooth flow in the diffuser (Figure 5–12).

Exhaust blowing refers to the practice of routing the engine exhaust outlets into the rear diffuser. The principle here is that the high speed gas emerging from the exhausts is 'injected' into the flow in the diffuser, and increases the suction in this region (Figure 5–13). The exhaust jet actually creates a vortex in the diffuser which may help to delay separation. This all sounds like a good use of energy that would otherwise go to waste, until you remember that the effect varies with throttle opening and engine rpm. The benefit is therefore not consistent, being at its greatest when the engine is at high rpm with the driver pressing the throttle firmly, a set of circumstances not always coincident with travelling around a corner, and certainly not when braking hard. However, some drivers learned to exploit the effect better than others, developing a technique of left foot braking, which enabled them to keep the right foot on the throttle, and so keep the flow of exhaust gas into the diffuser at or near its maximum. Two-pedal layouts and hand clutches made their appearance in Formula 1 to assist with this aspect of driving, though it would seem to be at some cost to clutch control from a standing start, sometimes turning a hard won grid position into a first lap disaster. The gain in downforce from exhaust blowing is said to be relatively small, but some Formula 1 cars still have exhaust outlets routed so as to create some benefit.

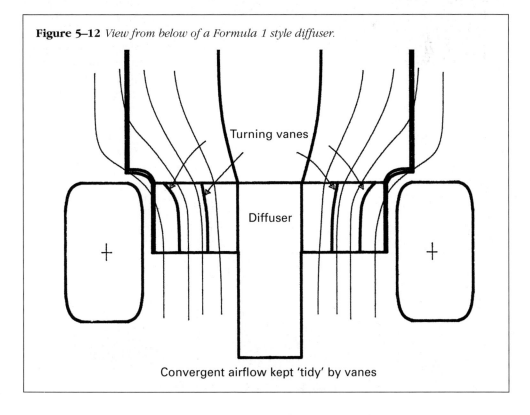

Figure 5–12 *View from below of a Formula 1 style diffuser.*

Turning vanes

Diffuser

Convergent airflow kept 'tidy' by vanes

Figure 5–13 *Exhaust outlets positioned in the diffuser.*

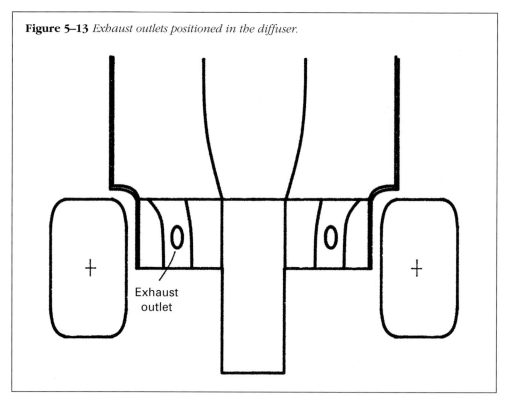

Exhaust
outlet

Wing interactions

Wing and underbody interactions have been alluded to several times now, and clearly can be adverse or beneficial. The effect of an ill-designed or badly deployed front wing can be very negative, not just on the underbody flow, but on the flow over the whole car. However, the impact can be minimised with care, and the attention to detail paid by the top professionals is an object lesson for all. Front wings are not made complex just to give the pattern makers and laminators an interesting time at work!

The most obvious thing that a front wing must not do is stall. If so much front downforce is needed that the front wing is anywhere near stall, then it is better to balance the car by using *less* front wing and taking off rear wing, because the disturbance caused by a front wing working this hard is likely to be to the detriment of not only the underbody flow, but also the flow to the radiators, and quite prob-

ably to the rear wing too. An alternative, and perhaps longer-term, fix would be to use a larger chord front wing, or to make the car's nose narrower and make larger span front wings, each of these changes adding wing area, and hence downforce, all other things being equal, or giving equivalent downforce at a smaller, and less flow-disturbing angle of attack. Secondary front wing elements on top racecars are often steeper at their outer extremities than at the inner part of their span. This again allows a better flow to the radiators, but also to the first part of the underbody. An easier, more practical solution is to use a simple profile flap, but only part span, and mount it on the outer part of the main element.

Top level front wings have still more complex detail integrated into their shapes. They are usually curved spanwise, so that the leading edge in the centre is higher than at the outer ends. This trend was initiated in rather extreme

Part-span, asymmetric flaps allow improved flow to side radiators and to the underbody.

form by the Tyrrell Formula 1 team with the 'anhedral' front wing design on the type 019, connected to the first of the now almost ubiquitous 'raised nose' configurations. The aim was, and is, to improve the flow to the underbody. It

Formula 1 front wings are shaped to channel air to the radiators and the underbody.

also made the front wing, and indeed the whole car, less sensitive to changes of ride height and pitch, because the flow beneath the wing did not get blocked off if the car's nose dipped ground-wards. Formula 1 cars nowadays have their front wings suspended by plates from a high nose, which maximises the working span of the wing, and allows the nose to be shaped so as to channel the air to the required destinations downstream, such as the radiators, and the underbody.

The rear wing has a marked impact on the performance of the underbody region too. Generally speaking, rear wings do not overhang the back end of competition cars by very much (one exception is British Speed Hillclimbing, where a 59in [1.5m] overhang, measured from the rear axle line, is permitted), this aspect being usually dictated by regulations. There is, therefore, an interaction between the low pressure created under the suction side of the rear wing, and the airflow in the diffuser(s) at the back of the underbody. This effect applies to just about any category you care to think of that uses a rear

wing, and where attempts are made to keep the underbody flow at the very least tidy, if not controlled, so as to reduce under-car pressure.

Katz (see Appendix 2) again gives examples of a variety of vehicle types, from passenger-car based racers to single seaters, on which pressure distribution plots were carried out with and without rear wings. In all cases the rear wing had a profound beneficial effect on the under-car pressure, and the effect extended well forward in each case, so that, integrated over the underbody area, the enhancement of total downforce was very significant indeed. The effect is clearly similar to the positioning of a flap at the appropriate place to augment the effect of a single element aerofoil – in that case, the flow around the flap, and through the slot between the flap and the main element, enabled more downforce to be created by the combined wing structure. In the case of car plus wing, the scale is different, but the wing's suction effect amplifies the underbody's pressure reduction.

The rear wing 'drives' the diffuser.

It is possible to see the designers' efforts at exploiting this interaction if one studies the relative position and shape of the rear wings and diffusers of current Formula 1 cars. The fore and aft positions of the wing and diffuser are effectively defined by the regulations, but the vertical positioning offers more freedom. Here the lower tier of the sometimes multi-tier wings is very close to the extended central portion of the diffuser. As was stated earlier in this chapter, the upsweep on this part of the diffuser is often very extreme, and the only reason this configuration can be used is because the lower wing tier helps to keep the flow attached to the diffuser roof. In fact one Formula 1 aerodynamicist has stated that the rear wing actually 'drives' the diffuser. Thus, in spite of the regulation-restricted length of the diffuser, its cross section can be expanded to quite a large area, which has the effect of increasing the velocity of the flow of air through the throat upstream, and thus more downforce is created. The incredible complexity of shape of current Formula 1 diffusers reflects the search for fractions of a per cent gain here and there in the endless battle for a slight advantage over the opposition.

Some numbers

As with previous chapters, let's pause a while to look at some numbers, via, in this case, some very simplistic sums. It was implied earlier that the underbody of a Lotus Formula 1 car, complete with tunnels and skirts, produced around 2,880lb (1,309kg or 12.8kN) of downforce at 180mph (290kmh). For the sake of comparison with earlier calculations, we'll work out what this would be at 100mph (160kmh), using the usual 'downforce is proportional to the square of speed' rule. So at 100mph this car would have generated about 890lb (404kg or 3.95kN) from its underbody region.

From an estimate of the plan area of the 'active' region of the underbody (assumed to be the rectangle whose four sides were defined by the skirts, and the front and rear extents of the sidepods – see Figure 5–14), which was around the 5,205sq in mark (3.36m²) in the case of the Lotus. This allows us to work out what the average pressure drop over the entire underbody was, by dividing the downforce by the area. This comes out to 0.17lb/sq in, or 1.18kPa (1kPa = 1kN/m²). Clearly the *average* pressure drop does not describe the actual pressure drops over the underbody – the absolute minimum pressure would be much lower than this, and would be located in the tunnel throat areas, whilst the central, unprofiled region would show much less

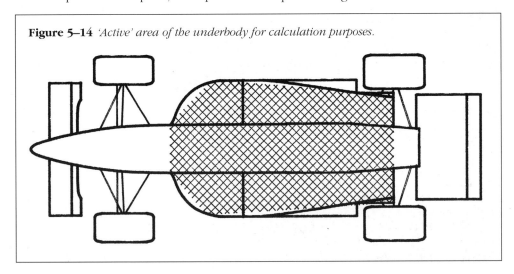

Figure 5–14 *'Active' area of the underbody for calculation purposes.*

pressure drop. But nevertheless, this calculation does illustrate how a seemingly modest pressure, when integrated over a large area, mounts up to a lot of downforce.

Peter Wright's 1983 paper showed how the Lotus's ability to generate downforce dropped off with increasing skirt-to-ground gap. For the sake of illustration, it is interesting to look at the drop-off at a skirt gap of 1.57in (40mm), a value imposed as a minimum ground clearance in many UK competition categories nowadays. According to Wright, the negative lift coefficient at 40mm skirt gap was about 20 per cent of the value at zero skirt gap, implying that only 20 per cent of the underbody downforce would be available with this size gap. This would equate to around 177lb (80.5kg or 793N) at 100mph (290kmh), a much more modest, but nevertheless potentially useful, figure.

The underbody area of recent Formula 1 cars is about 4,648sq in (3m²), and, as was stated earlier, reported downforce values attributable to the underbody alone are in the region of 330 to 420lb (150 to 191kg, or 1,471.5 to 1,872.8N) at 100mph (160kmh). Thus, average pressure drops are of the order of 0.07 to 0.09lb/sq in, or 0.49 to 0.62kPa. This pressure drop is considerably greater than that obtained with the Lotus Formula 1 car with a 40mm skirt gap, but about half the value produced by the skirted car that actually raced. Nevertheless, the progress made at clawing back this much of the downforce lost by, first, the banning of skirts, and then the banning of tunnels altogether in Formula 1, is considerable, and reflects the time, effort, and ingenuity that has been directed at the task.

Low drag

As mentioned earlier, when Lotus announced the type 78 to the world they used the phrase 'we've found something for nothing'. The importance of the implications of this comment cannot be overstated, although it has to be said that Lotus did *not* manage to break the laws of Nature here! What they had done was to manage the airflow around the car in a much more efficient way, so that the large increase in downforce was achieved at very modest drag penalty. By creating a means for the air to flow smoothly underneath the car, in order to maintain high flow velocity, and hence low pressure, they also created a low drag regime too, with little turbulence where there had once been aerodynamic mayhem! And further, by raising the underbody towards the rear of the car, and maintaining the smooth flow right back to the rear of the diffusers, the effective base area of the car was reduced, and so the area in which flow separation occurred was also reduced. In other words, the size of the wake was made smaller, and the form drag was cut as a result. However, there would have been some increase in the induced drag as the result of creating the downforce, but overall the gains were at very small cost in terms of drag. So 'something for nothing' was overstating it a bit, and, however appealing that notion is, you *never* get something for nothing. The illusion came from making the aerodynamics work much more efficiently.

Whilst ground effect tunnels were banned from Formula 1 from the start of 1983, the FISA, as it then was, did permit the use of tunnels to continue in 'Group C' sports prototypes, up until that category's demise in 1992. A rule requiring a compulsory 39.4 × 31.5in (1,000mm × 800mm) flat plate beneath the driver/passenger compartment was intended to limit the effectiveness of the underbody, but beyond that, tunnels were permitted. The basic configuration of the sports prototype, which also includes cars built to Professional Sports Car Racing Inc (formerly IMSA) rules in the United States (even though these have flat bottoms), permits a very large underbody area, and the enclosed wheel nature of the cars also permits low drag, streamlined designs to be built. Thus it was in this general sports prototype group that the most efficient downforce producing designs *ever* were made. Cars like the Jaguar XJR series, the Porsche 956 to 962, the Peugeot 905, the Nissan P35, and the Mazda RX7-792 were developed to such a degree that $-C_L$ values approaching 4.0 were quoted, with C_Ds of around 0.7, lift/drag ratios therefore approaching 6! These figures, of course, are in relation to frontal area, and reflect that downforce was being produced, in large part, by the big plan area of the cars.

We have seen that the underbody of a vehicle can be shaped or modified to produce a large amount of downforce, and that the components upstream and downstream of the underbody region can have a marked influence on the efficiency of the underbody aerodynamics.

Other than general guidelines, however, there is a lack of specific information that serves to help the amateur competitor, who, if he or she wants to build or improve tunnels, or a rear diffuser, is once more constrained to lengthy trial and error development out on the track and back in the race-shop. The professionals, meanwhile, have computational fluid dynamics to model their ideas on before they ever become solid reality even in scale model form, and then wind-tunnels in which to test out myriad configurations in order to home in on an optimum solution. The next chapter will look in more detail at the tools that are used by the pros, and also at those that can assist the amateur in the search for an aerodynamic solution to going faster.

Chapter 6

Removing the guesswork

VEHICLE AERODYNAMICS MIGHT be a branch of engineering, but that doesn't stop it from being an art form at the same time. If it was simply a precise engineering discipline, the chances are that all cars would be virtually identical in appearance, and quite possibly in performance too. Thankfully that is not the case, and there is still scope for individualism. This goes on to mean that the amateur aerodynamic stylist has just as much chance of making his or her ideas work as not, but in order to increase the likelihood of success, it does help to be able to determine what is going on in the air moving around your creation, and what the actual effects on the vehicle are. There are various ways of doing this, some more precise than others, and there are some that the amateur competitor can only admire from the comfort of the armchair. Nevertheless, with careful observations and perhaps some prudent investment, even the amateur can divine a surprising amount of aerodynamic data to help design and develop a competition car.

Flow visualisation

When asked to explain why he lived in New York City, comedian Woody Allen apparently once said 'I never trust air I can't see'. He probably didn't realise it at the time, but he had hit upon one of the problems faced by amateur and professional aerodynamicists alike – they cannot see the medium they are dealing with until they contaminate it with some-

thing, or use some means of revealing the direction it is flowing in and the state it is in – that is, smooth or turbulent.

It is sometimes possible to catch brief glimpses of evidence of flow patterns around cars from the sidelines or even on television. For example, on particularly humid days Formula 1 and CART/IRL cars can sometimes generate visible rear wing-tip vortices. The vortices are always there, of course, when the car is in motion, but the special nature of the humid atmospheric conditions means that the low pressure in the core of the vortex causes the water vapour to condense and become temporarily visible. In wet conditions, the extraordinarily high 'upwash' from rear wings can be seen as tall rooster tails of spray. Other occasions when more general flow patterns show up occur, for example, when one of these cars blows an engine in a cloud of oily smoke. The engine owner's loss is our gain, as the smoke gets caught up in the larger scale circulatory patterns created by the car, and rather than just being able to see the core of the rear wing tip vortices, the whole rotating flow at the rear is, again briefly, visible. A car's influence on dust, leaves, and other detritus may also make certain aspects of the airflow around it temporarily visible, but all of these instances, fascinating though they are, are transient, and not much use for serious study. More controlled methods of revealing airflow patterns are needed.

Flow visualisation is not really a primary technique used by professional aerodynamicists in the world of motor sport, but it does tend to be used as a means of checking out the cause of a particularly interesting or crucial result arising from a change or a modification. For example, during a set of wind-tunnel trials, gradually increasing a wing angle may yield positive gains in downforce up to a point at which drag continues increasing, but the downforce gains start to tail off. The obvious assumption is that the wing has stalled, but maybe only part of it has actually stalled. Using a means of flow visualisation around the wing in question could help in determining whether just a part of the wing has in fact stalled. And if that proved to be the case, the spanwise wing profile could be altered so that the flow across the entire span remains attached for longer, allowing more downforce to be generated before stall occurs.

However, for the amateur and clubman aerodynamicist, being able to see what is happening to the air around one's competition car – and in particular around and near crucial areas like wings, spoilers, and diffusers, as well as cooling intakes and outlets and so forth – can help greatly in understanding what is going on. It can also provide much food for thought, and pointers for areas to improve and develop in order to make a more aerodynamically efficient vehicle. There are various ways of doing this, which for the most part can be used out on the track, either during testing, or in competition if test time is hard to come by.

The best known and perhaps most often used means of showing up the flow patterns near a car's surfaces is the 'wool tuft' method. Pieces of wool yarn about 2 to 3in (50 to 75mm) long are stuck to the 'wetted surfaces' of the vehicle – that is, the bodywork, wings, spoilers, and all the parts of interest (including the driver's crash helmet possibly) – with self-adhesive tape (make sure the tape is stuck down flush with the body) so that they can trail backwards in the expected direction of flow. The car is then driven along, perhaps at a set of pre-determined speeds, whilst observers look on and take photographs. This might be done from the track-side, or from another car running alongside the car under test, assuming the venue and occasion will permit such liberties! However, care must be exercised to ensure that the 'chase car' does not get so close that it affects the airflow over the test car. The images yielded by this exercise can be somewhat startling, with the flows over and around parts of the car being rather different from what might have been imagined! For example, the flow coming off a single seater front wing can be seen to be very non-uniform, especially if the span of the wing extends in front of the front wheels. Similarly, the flow over the bonnet area of a passenger-based car can be seen to be remarkably complex. This is where this kind of study can begin to really help in the understanding of what air does as it passes around, over, and under a competition car – the general effects and influences can actually be seen, and gathering this information is perhaps the first step on the way to being able to direct and manage the flow in a way that eases its passage past your vehicle in the most efficient and productive way – or should that be 'in the least damaging and performance sapping way'?

Wool tufts can show up the flow directions near important details like the trailing edges of rear wings, or over the rear deck ahead of a rear spoiler, and near cooling inlets or NACA ducts which feed air perhaps to an oil cooler or the engine inlet system. It is also possible to see whether the flow is smooth or sometimes unsteady. If the car is being watched, it will be seen that some of the wool tufts trail back smoothly in the direction of flow, whilst others are flailing wildly about, possibly lifting above the surface instead of lying back along it. In photographs, the tufts in smooth flow regions will show up just as they are seen, whilst those that were flailing about are likely to appear as fan shaped blurs, providing the camera shutter speed is not too fast (perhaps no faster than, say, 1/60th of a second). Clearly these are indicators of very disturbed and separated flow in the regions concerned – it may or may not be possible or even desirable to do something about it, but at least you'll know the situation exists.

It has been suggested that an ordinary workshop compressor airline can be used to provide the airflow for static wool tuft tests, by directing the nozzle along the bodywork surface to simulate the local flow. Whilst this could be useful for assessing some qualitative aspects, an inherent problem with this method is that it is hard to know whether the air is being squirted from the right direction. And air emerging from such a nozzle does so in a broad cone shape, quite unlike any flow that might pass over a car in reality. Another possibility for a source of airflow, though I have never tried it, nor heard of its being tried, might be a leaf blower, one of those devices for blowing fallen leaves into your neighbour's back yard. In all probability the emerging air will be too turbulent to be any use, but it might be worth a try, especially if the flow can be straightened out with, for example, a matrix of vanes such as might be found on a domestic extractor fan.

Wool tuft testing does have its shortcomings. For one thing, in common with some other flow visualisation techniques, only the flow immediately adjacent to the surfaces is shown up, which means that a mental picture still has to be built up of the three-dimensional flow above the surfaces; but at least this will be a bit easier once the surface flows have been visualised. For another, it is, of course, impossible under normal circumstances to see what's happening underneath wings, splitters, and the entire underbody. However, one can imagine that with some ingenuity it would be possible to fix a remotely triggered camera – via a secure mounting to, say, the rear wing mounts – in order to photograph the wing underside, or perhaps the flow at the rear of the diffuser. More determined efforts, aided by a little technology, could probably provide images of underbody flow too, providing the image capture device wasn't so big that it affected the flow along the underbody!

Another method of visualising the flow directions over a car's surfaces is to look at the streak marks left by liquids which land, either by design or otherwise, on your car. This can happen on a wet and dirty day, when rain and dust combine to leave muddy streak marks over parts of the body, or when one car has been following another which is losing fluid, such as oil, and depositing it on the car behind, whereupon it too leaves tell-tale marks all over the bodywork. On these occasions it is most instructive to take a

Wool-tuft pictures can be taken from the track-side. (Tracey Inglis)

close look at these marks when the car returns to the paddock, and even to make sketches and take photos. As an example of the kind of thing that can be seen, Figure 6–1 shows how the influence of the centre post mounting of the rear wing on one of the author's shared hillclimb cars, a Delta T82, was spotted on one such miserable day. The post was neatly faired with an aerofoil shaped alu-

minium shroud for all but the last inch or so (25 to 30mm) immediately adjacent to the wing, which on the evidence of the streak marks was the bit that mattered! Other experiments have shown where parts of the upper flap section of wings have been running stalled, evidenced by flow separation over parts of the span of the rear flap (Fig 6–2), a situation which had not been picked up as having

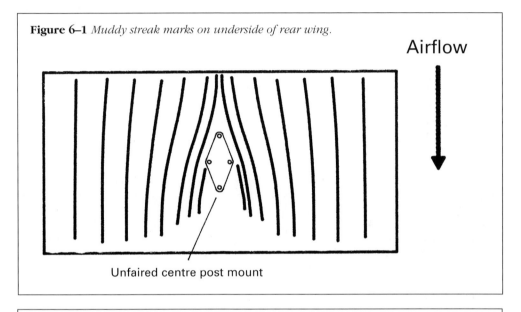

Figure 6–1 *Muddy streak marks on underside of rear wing.*

Airflow

Unfaired centre post mount

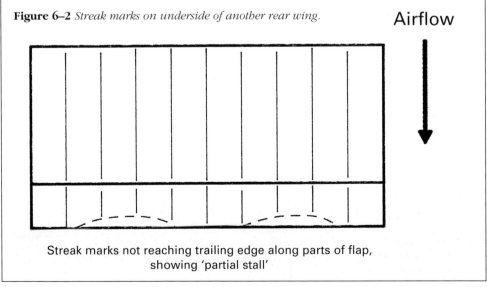

Figure 6–2 *Streak marks on underside of another rear wing.*

Airflow

Streak marks not reaching trailing edge along parts of flap, showing 'partial stall'

affected performance at all, but which may well have been adding unnecessarily to drag with no benefit to downforce. By trimming back the flap slightly, a more efficient setting was established.

It isn't necessary, of course, to wait for a wet day, or for an unfortunate fellow competitor running ahead of you to start losing oil. You can apply droplets of suitable liquid to areas of interest prior to going out on track, and then take a look at the results on returning to the paddock. Fluids that can be used for this exercise need to be relatively low viscosity and not so volatile that they evaporate too quickly, and paraffin (kerosene), diesel engine fuel, and thin lubricating oil have all been found excellent for this purpose. Don't for goodness sake use anything corrosive towards paint or any of the other surface finishes on your car! In order for the streak marks to show up, some form of colouring such as poster-paint powder needs to be added, although often there is enough dust around to adhere to the oily marks. The idea is that the liquid will actually evaporate during the test run, so leaving behind

a kind of printed record of the flow pattern. If the liquid is insufficiently volatile, it may not evaporate, and will run back down to the low points of surfaces once the car slows or stops, thereby confusing or even obliterating the faithful record of what happened at speed. It may be that the application of a little ingenuity could see the rigging up of a pump, a fluid reservoir and some piping, so that the driver could release the fluid, over the chosen parts of the vehicle, once up to a pre-selected speed. If the run speed was then maintained for a few moments whilst the fluid dried out, leaving behind the coloured dye, the streak patterns left would be a record of that particular speed.

As mentioned previously, this general form of flow visualisation is used by professional race teams during wind-tunnel test programmes, when checking out a particularly interesting condition or configuration. Having spent some time with a top single seater team in a scale wind-tunnel, it was fascinating to watch the methodical collection of downforce and drag data as increasing increments of

Poster paint streak marks provide food for thought on the flow beneath this front wing. (Tracey Inglis)

front wing angle were worked through. At a reasonably steep angle of front wing incidence, the downforce gains started tailing off, and so the technicians applied their own particular liquid brew (diesel fuel-based) to the front wings, dashed out of the tunnel, and wound up the wind speed again. After the run, they then slid a large mirror beneath the car to examine the flow patterns on the lower surface of the wings, and further back in the under-body region. The information that they garnered resulted in a phone call to the production department to see if the wings could be made with a modified amount of spanwise twist. And this highlights two of the special advantages of using fluid markers for flow visualisation: an observable two dimensional record is left on the car, which can be studied, sketched, and photographed; and because of this, it is relatively easy to study flow patterns on the under surfaces of components and the main body. Some wind-tunnel technicians have even used fluorescent dyes in the test fluid, so that under ultra-violet illumination the streak marks show up particularly vividly.

Still, though, with the exception of those transient cases mentioned at the beginning of this section, it has only been possible so far to examine the flow at the surfaces of a car. But there is one technique that enables the flow in regions *off* the body of a car to be examined – smoke plume flow visualisation. The major shortcoming of this technique, at least as far as the amateur is concerned, is that you really need a wind-tunnel in which to carry out the trials, and probably a full-scale one at that, since a scale model is unlikely to be available to most amateurs. But, as we shall see in a later section, the luxury of a full scale wind-tunnel may not be totally unattainable.

The generation of a smoke plume is done by heating a suitable oil like paraffin, and passing the smoke down a tube to a probe, which can be positioned so as to direct the smoke plume in the airstream at any area of interest. A mobile probe can be used for rapid visualisation of the flow all around the car, or multiple probes can be used for simultaneous study of the flow at various positions. This form of flow visualisation makes the

Smoke plume testing allows three-dimensional flow visualisation, but requires a wind-tunnel. (MIRA)

Details like wing tip vortices can be visualised with smoke, as on the Pilbeam MP82. (MIRA)

three-dimensional nature of the passage of the air around a car much easier to comprehend and envision. It becomes all too easy – especially when looking at two-dimensional photographs and drawings – to allow the mind to restrict itself to thinking in just two dimensions, but that would be a dangerous habit to get into. With a smoke plume, it is possible to see how far above or beyond the car's surface changes of shape and contour exert an influence on the airflow, whereas the previous two visualisation methods only show what is happening at the very surfaces themselves. Such things as vortex formation, for example, can be seen at the trailing edge tips of a rear wing, or down the sides of sculpted sidepods. Airflow turning under the lower edge of ground effect sidepods; the marked influence of the front wings on the airflow to the rear of the car; and flow separation zones over rear screens and ahead of spoilers – all of these can be seen. This helps one get a better three-dimensional perspective on what actually happens to the air around a car, and can assist in determining the existence of specific effects such as wing stall.

Maybe that's overdoing it a bit on the smoke!

One final word of caution on flow visualisation. The medium being used to show up the flow can itself affect the flow pattern . . .

Nobody said this would be easy!

Data gathering

One aspect of competition car technology that has grown and developed rapidly in recent years is data acquisition. It is now possible for the well-heeled amateur to buy much the same kind of data logging electronic wizardry that professional race teams use, and amass mountains of information about chassis (and engine) related parameters. But gathering useful data need not be expensive. The important thing is to make careful observations, and equally careful records of everything relevant that you *can* measure. If your budget stretches only to the ubiquitous stop-watch, then just make sure you get all the really relevant times – total elapsed as well as split times in critical parts of the tracks – that you can. If improving cornering speeds by adding downforce is what you are interested in, then time your car through corners where that is going to make a difference; if it's drag that you are worried about, look at straight line segments. And then relate those values to elapsed times to check out the overall impact of the tests you are running. This kind of thorough, disciplined approach does not need huge expenditure, and yields some very useful information.

Supplementing records of stop-watch times with objective visual observations can often prove very helpful. A trustworthy team member who knows what he or she is looking for, positioned at important parts of a track, can come back with invaluable feedback on car behaviour, and can relate that to other cars in your class or category too. So if your new 'barn door' rear wing allows you to go faster through a particular corner, that much might be evident from split timing, but it will be even more useful also to know the split times of your competitors through the same section. If, then, that knowledge is supplemented by your observer's remark that the car 'looked really planted through Turn 2 compared to all the others', then that all helps in the interpretation of your development progress.

Detailed observations can sometimes provide surprises, and not always welcome ones. Photographs of your car on track taken with a telephoto lens can provide all sorts of information. For example, one such photo of the Pilbeam hillclimb car that the author has driven, taken at Prescott Hill Climb, Gloucestershire, England, shows the car on the fastest part of the tight, twisty course, just about to enter the fastest corner on the course. It is very evident that the car's suspension has been compressed through a fair proportion of its available travel, and since the track is reasonably smooth, and there is little cornering load yet developed, the conclusion must be that the suspension has been compressed by aerodynamic downforce. It is small wonder that the following corner, which has a change of camber running across it just after the apex, was frequently the scene of a disconcerting sideways lurch in this car. The chances are that the combination of downforce compression, coupled to cornering load, and with a bump thrown in, used up all the available suspension travel, and thrust the car onto its bump stops. The car now has stiffer springs fitted. But it could be that without the photographic evidence, we'd have spent longer trying to find a solution to that particular problem.

Driver feel and feedback is vital too, and comments need to be recorded alongside all the objective information that you can collect. Whilst the stop-watch will tell you the impact of an aerodynamic change on speed, unless the car is equipped with the very best of data logging gear only the driver will be able to tell you how, or whether, the change affected the car's behaviour. Now that so much information can be logged objectively whilst a car is performing, the much maligned driver seems to have come in for an even harder time from race engineers and team directors. This should not be the case, because without the driver, the team has *no way* of knowing what's really going on. It is up to the engineers and the driver to learn how to communicate effectively with each other so that the hard data and the subjective feedback can be put together to give a complete picture. This particular difficulty doesn't occur, of course, if you're a one-man band who engineers, prepares, drives, and develops the car, so chances are you'll have less arguments! But that doesn't mean you shouldn't try to measure everything you can and record it all alongside your remarks about subjective feel.

If yours *is* a one-person team – or at least, one with a small complement – you will probably benefit greatly from some form of data logging, given that there may not be any spare people to go out and do split times and the like. Once again, though, this does not mean spend-

ing huge sums of money so long as you are prudent, and prepared to spend some of your spare time at the track, and at home between events, squeezing as much information from a simple data logger as you can. Don't be misled into thinking that unless you can monitor speed, lateral G forces, longitudinal G forces, steering angle, and throttle position that you won't be able to learn anything of value. It is actually possible to learn a great deal from a simple rpm versus time graph, such as is provided by one of the proprietary recording tachometers otherwise known as intelligent rev counters. These devices can play back on the tacho dial the recorded revs during a run or a lap, but to be of real value the information needs to be downloaded to a computer, to be analysed and studied with the software that the manufacturer will sell you for that express purpose. You therefore need to be reasonably familiar with computers, though you do not need to be an expert. However, you do *need* a computer, quite probably a portable one so that you can

A simple rpm data logger reveals much useful information.

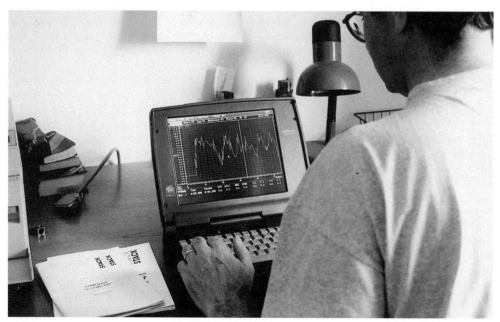

download runs at the track. So the cost of attaining this capability may be somewhat more than the relatively modest outlay for the recording tacho and the software if you don't already own a computer. But once you've bought the kit, the information you can obtain and build up *never wears out*, which just has to be a unique achievement in motorsport!

The surprisingly varied information that can be gleaned from just a trace of rpm versus time, and which can be used for assessing aerodynamic aspects of performance, includes corner and straight speeds (calculated from the speed per 1,000rpm in each gear), the elapsed time of a run (if other forms of timing are not available), the split times between various sections of the track, braking deceleration rates (calculated from the rate of change of speed in a braking zone), and, if some corner radii are known – or can be measured – then lateral G forces could even be calculated. Thus, all other things being equal, it becomes possible to measure gains in corner speed from increasing downforce, perhaps with a related drop off in straight line speed, and this can be set against overall elapsed time as a measure of net gain or loss. And lift coefficients can even be worked out, albeit approximately, if braking or cornering G-forces can be calculated, and the tyre friction coefficients can be ascertained from the supplier. Simplistic though this type of analysis might be, it has to be better than just stop-watch timing, and furthermore, a permanent printed record of each and every lap or run you ever do can be kept for more thorough inspection, if you ever get the time.

More sophisticated data acquisition systems will be able to provide more easily interpreted plots of what has been going on, and, with their ability to monitor many more 'channels', can offer the opportunity to measure directly some aerodynamically influenced parameters such as dynamic suspension movement and ride height changes, suspension loads, and even aerodynamic pressure changes around the car in specific locations. Monitoring ride height can be used to determine the downforce produced by the body of a car if constant speed straight line runs are executed. The suspension compression can obviously be related to the amount of downforce being generated if there are no cornering forces, and if the effect of transient changes as the wheels pass over bumps is 'filtered out'. This interpretation can also be made of measurements of suspension loads if the same type of tests are performed. This will allow real data on downforce at the two axles to be measured, but it cannot be equated to downforce at the tyre contact patches because the inherent lift generated by the wheels and tyres is isolated from this measurement. However, it will provide very good comparative data on differing aerodynamic set-ups, and will be invaluable in attempting to establish a front to rear aerodynamic balance. Reasonably good approximations of lift coefficients will also be possible with the information gathered in this way. Professional teams are able to take this kind of instrumentation several stages further, and have been known to stuff a car full of pressure tapping equipment to monitor and log the local static pressures at numerous locations around the car during running, which, by comparison with the dynamic pressure – determined by a sensor measuring the off-car pressure some distance above the body – then allows them to build up three-dimensional pressure maps of the air in the immediate vicinity of the car. So the gathering of relevant data can range from simple measurements of parameters indirectly related to aerodynamics, to the highly complex direct measurement of air pressure around the car.

Wind-tunnels

It is a measure of the importance of efficient aerodynamics that so many competition car manufacturers making cars for motorsport categories from Formula 1 down to Formula Ford use wind-tunnel testing as a part of their design and development process. The amount of testing that can be done is, naturally, budget related, and in the case of the very best funded teams, nothing less than their own wind-tunnels – allowing constant access and a continuous test programme – will do. Less well funded teams must use a tunnel available for commercial hire, and several Formula 1 and CART/IRL manufacturers, for example, hire large blocks of time at wind-tunnel facilities such as Southampton University, MIRA, or Imperial College (London) in the UK, or the Swift tunnel in the United States.

It would be reasonable to assume, then, that wind-tunnel time does not come cheap, and that most likely it was well beyond the reach of the small manufacturer, let alone the amateur *garagiste* or clubman competitor. Fortunately, this is not necessarily the case. It *is* possible, in the UK at least, to hire a wind-tunnel on a day or even part-day basis, enabling a reasonable number of tests to be carried out, and to gain a basic picture of the aerodynamics of your particular competition car. The tunnel in question in the UK is the full scale wind-tunnel at the Motor Industry Research Association (MIRA), in Warwickshire, England, and time can be booked on a highly flexible basis that caters for a wide range of budgets. It is even possible for a small group of people to book the tunnel for a day between them, and take three or four cars along, spending a part of the session on each car. Providing the team is organised and has made sensible preparations, it should be possible to test several different configurations on each car, depending on the time taken to change from one configuration to the next. Obviously, incremental changes to aerofoil angles are quick alterations, whereas fitting a different underbody probably would not be. Nevertheless, a programme of highly informative tests can be carried out, and it would certainly be possible to gain

hard facts such as lift and drag coefficients, front and rear proportions of lift (hopefully of the negative variety), and the impact on the lift distribution made by altering front and rear downforce inducing devices, be they splitters, spoilers, dive plates, skirts, or wings.

It has to be said that full-scale tunnels have one principle inherent disadvantage – they normally have fixed floors, which means that a boundary layer develops along the floor of the tunnel, and as such, the airflow conditions underneath and along the lower regions of a car are not the same as out on the track. So the results obtained in a fixed floor tunnel tend to give low estimates for overall downforce, especially if a car runs a low ground clearance and a profiled underbody in order to create downforce. The downforce values for front wings tend to be underestimated too, since they are usually operating in ground proximity. Thus, overall downforce values are on the low side, with a rearward bias from this type of wind-tunnel.

But why should a full-scale wind-tunnel have a fixed floor? Because it isn't all that practical a proposition to run a moving ground 'conveyor belt' of the size required and at the relevant speeds. There would, however, appear to be three wind-tunnels that are the exception to prove the rule: Lockheed, the US aerospace giant, has a wind-tunnel with a very similar cross sectional area to MIRA's, capable of producing air velocities some three times greater from a power supply nearly seven times bigger – and the MIRA full-scale tunnel has a *megawatt* of power available to supply it's air moving fans; and there are full-scale moving ground tunnels at DNW in Holland, and Pininfarina in Italy. MIRA also has plans to introduce a moving ground belt in its full-scale tunnel.

The most obvious advantage to using a full-scale tunnel is that you can put a full-scale car more or less straight in and test it. It is only necessary for the wind-tunnel technicians to set up the pads that each wheel sits on to cater for the specific track and wheel-base of each car, so that the loads on the wheels are transmitted to the load cells beneath, and thence to the data processing computer in the control room. There are, again rather obviously, no problems related to scale and the mystical Reynolds Numbers when dealing with full-size vehicles – scale models do present problems here, as will be discussed below – although relatively low air speeds still can't fully simulate high speed competition conditions. But things like imperfections of body panel fit, rain channels, and window seals, all difficult to mimic in scale models, are all there, at life size, to trip up the airflow and produce realistic results and influences. So in spite of their disadvantages, for the purposes of generating basic aerodynamic data, perhaps where none existed before or where comparison with previous configurations is required, a full-scale fixed floor wind-tunnel is still a very useful weapon. The fact that pro-race teams use them proves that.

The author was fortunate enough to be able to spend a half-day in the MIRA facility a few years ago, and a number of different configurations were tested on the Pilbeam hillclimb car shared with my co-owning brother, giving us, for the first time, some hard aerodynamic data. This session led to some beneficial developments and modifications, and provided a much clearer understanding of the aerodynamics of this particular car, and single seaters in general. The types of test that we were able to carry out ranged from the establishment of a baseline, which was the configuration as developed and balanced on track; various front and rear wing angles and configurations; wings with and without Gurneys front and rear; flat floor versus tunnels; add-ons like strakes and vortex generators to influence flow in the tunnels; a hoped-for low drag shape modification to the rear of the sidepods that actually gave the same drag but more rear downforce (!); and the effect of the driver's weight, which altered ride

height and pitch angle, on downforce and its distribution. In all, 22 different tests were carried out during a busy four-hour period. We had prepared with some thought for the session, making bits and pieces that could be easily removed or added. For example, the sidepod shape modification was made up of pieces of wood and cardboard taped in place before the session, so that we actually ran that test first. It was obviously faster to remove the wood and cardboard on the day than to add it, so this saved precious time. Other components had also been made up in advance, such as the flat floor panels that were taped over the tunnel diffusers prior to coming to the wind-tunnel; this configuration was also run at the beginning of the session.

Having learned so much in the space of just four hours, it has been a constant frustration since that we have been unable, through lack of funds and time, to continue with a test programme But the data obtained and the principles established by that short session are ours, and we are infinitely better off having got them. There was even time to take some photographs. Such a test session can only be recommended – it may at first appear to be expensive at roughly the equivalent cost of a couple of sets of new slick tyres, but it will almost certainly be money well spent.

Scale-model testing
If it becomes imperative to implement an on-going aerodynamic test programme, a team will need to invest in the resources and facilities required to enable wind-tunnel testing of scale models of their competition cars. The reasons for testing scale models rather than at full size are that it is a lot easier, considerably more rapid, and much cheaper to build a scale model than a full-size test vehicle. Making new shaped sections to modify the model is also cheaper than working at full scale, and so the through-life costs of a particular model are relatively low too, until such time as the designer dic-

tates that a whole new shape is needed.

There are 'economies of scale' with respect to the size of wind-tunnel needed to test scale models as well. Clearly a tunnel that only has to accommodate a 40 per cent size model will be smaller than one which has to take full-size test vehicles. This in turn means that less air has to be moved, so the power requirements of the fan(s), and their running costs, will be a lot less. But perhaps the most useful advantage is that it becomes feasible to use a moving ground belt on the floor of the tunnel at scales of up to about 50 per cent (the biggest scale using moving ground technology currently in use in motorsport); and it has been said that it is pointless testing models of competition cars with small ground clearances without a moving ground plane. Hence, the top race teams like Williams have their own 50 per cent scale moving ground tunnel, Benetton and Ferrari are building similar facilities, and other major teams either use their own 40 per cent tunnels, or rent

time in commercial 40 per cent tunnels such as the R. J. Mitchell tunnel at Southampton University or MIRA's upgraded model tunnel in the UK (see Figures 6–3 and 6–4), or the relatively new Swift facility in California.

In essence, all wind-tunnels fulfil the same basic functions – air is sucked through a contracting aperture that accelerates the flow velocity, and is drawn towards the model, which is usually suspended, but in contact with the floor, from a vertical strut, or 'sting'. The floor is actually a rubberised fabric conveyor belt, driven at a speed which exactly matches the air speed. In order to prevent any boundary layer from reaching the belt (a boundary layer will have developed on the fixed part of the tunnel floor prior to the moving floor of the test section), suction is applied through the floor, just ahead of the moving ground belt, and the boundary layer is carefully sucked away. The controlled and boundary layer-free (at ground level) flow of air is then

MIRA's new 'open jet' 40 per cent wind-tunnel facility. (MIRA)

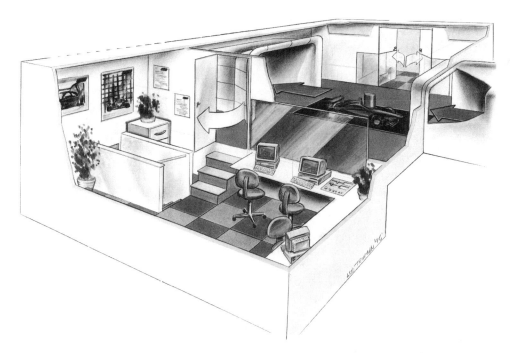

Figure 6–3 *Cutaway drawing of MIRA's 40 per cent wind-tunnel facility.* (MIRA)

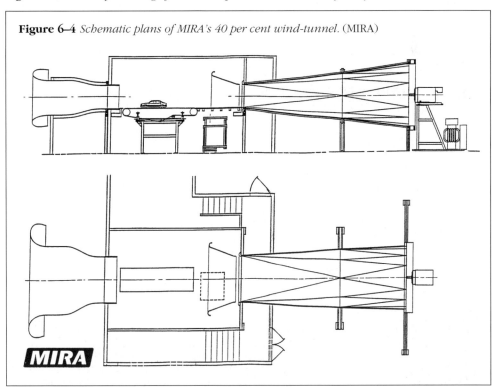

Figure 6–4 *Schematic plans of MIRA's 40 per cent wind-tunnel.* (MIRA)

passed over the model, and drawn out of the tunnel by one or more fans, depending on the power requirement. Usually the air is recirculated through a return loop.

This all sounds pretty simple in principle, but the effort needed to get things just right, and to produce repeatable results that can be correlated with full-scale reality, is considerable. For example, in order that the moving ground belt remains absolutely flat beneath the car, the belt must run over a perforated plate, and suction must be applied from underneath to hold the belt flat against the plate. Remember that the underside of low mounted wings, and the underbody of a great many competition cars, will be doing their best to suck the floor upwards as they create low pressure between themselves and the 'ground', so this is crucial. The belt running at high speed, over and around its drive rollers and over the suction plate, creates a lot of heat through friction, and some form of liquid cooling system is usually employed. Belt life is partly governed by the physical wear from this friction, but mainly by the friction from test model tyres, which tend to run in the same grooves the whole time and concentrate the wear in two narrow bands.

Maintaining consistency and repeatability is absolutely essential in a development field that is often looking for small percentage improvements. Thus, it is imperative that the model is attached to the support in as rigid a manner as possible, and that it resumes every test, after alterations to settings or configuration, in precisely the same position and attitude. Ride height and pitch angle are usually adjustable from the control room by adjusting stepper motors in the sting, whilst roll and yaw angles tend to be set manually. As a further aid to repeatability, temperature control is desirable. Both the viscosity and density of air alter with temperature, and dramatic shifts in these values would have an effect on results. Aerodynamic parameters are measured by load cells or strain gauges in the sting, and passed electronically to a data acquisition computer in the control room. Pressure logging may also be carried out, via tiny holes drilled in the model surface, connected with small bore tubing to a multi-port pressure transducer, which then sends its data to the computer.

The main drawback of testing scale models is precisely to do with their small size. We saw in Chapter 2 how boundary layers developed, getting thicker the further along a body the air travelled. If a boundary layer got excessively thick and turbulent, the airflow could be tripped into separating at the merest hint of an adverse pressure gradient. And that's the crux of the problem of testing at reduced scale – if a model is 40 per cent of the size of the real thing, the boundary layers that develop around it and the components hanging off it, will not be the same as on the full size vehicle, and so the overall airflow will not precisely simulate the full sized version. In the worst case, the flows on critical parts of the model remain attached, but separate on the real thing, causing much anguish, fretting, and hair pulling in the aerodynamics department.

So how is this potential trap avoided? Essentially by running the airflow as fast as possible so as to achieve a Reynolds Number which is as close to the real thing as it can be. We saw in Chapter 2 that the Reynolds Number was proportional to the length of the body multiplied by the airspeed. So if a model is 40 per cent of the size of the real thing, then the Reynolds Number – and hence the airflow behaviour – would be the same if the air speed was multiplied by 2.5 times. This sounds like an obvious solution, but propelling air at speeds of up to 500 mph isn't really a practical proposition, in terms of the energy required actually getting it to that speed, and then having a model that could survive the super-hurricane onslaught! Furthermore, at such high speeds, air becomes a compressible fluid, and starts behaving very differently.

So a practical compromise that gets as close as possible to a situation that can be confidently correlated with reality is the best that can be achieved. At present, most scale wind-tunnels can test at maximum speeds in the 80 to 110mph range (130 to 175kmh), though the Californian-based Swift facility can achieve 140mph (225kmh).

Other critical factors in testing scale models include the accuracy of details. It is important that all aspects of the model are true to scale, including suspension arms, brake ducts, wing to flap gaps, end plate thickness, and so on. The wheels must be made to rotate at the same speed as the air and the ground belt are moving, and must be in firm contact with the latter. Internal cooling flows must be faithful to life-size, together with realistic back pressures. And perhaps most difficult of all to achieve, surface roughness must also be to scale. Perfection in all of these areas is impossible to achieve, but the closer to true scale everything is made, the more meaningful will be the results.

The cost of time in a scale model wind-tunnel was in the region of £2,000 ($3,200) a day in the UK in 1997. The chances are that you would have to book a minimum of a week to make it worthwhile setting up your model. Finding an available week might be hard, with teams already booking large blocks of time well in advance at most commercial tunnels. And then, of course, you would have to build your superbly detailed model capable of being mated up to the tunnel's support structure and data acquisition equipment. But, by the time you've saved up the £10,000 ($16,000) for your week's testing, and managed to book a free week, you'll probably have had the time to build the model!

Computer modelling

If model wind-tunnel testing seems a little out of the reach of the vast majority of competitors, then the computer simulation of fluid flows, and the capabilities offered to generate virtual models of cars and their aerodynamic characteristics, are somewhere out beyond Jupiter in terms of accessibility. But the experts say this will not be the case for long. It is already possible to model simple cases on what might be termed a leading edge home computer (in other words, a pretty powerful one), but the problem is that at present, a thorough technical understanding of the mathematical principles involved is required to get the best out of the software. This is another way of saying that a lot more development is needed on the software in order that you and I can buy it from our local computer superstore and get good results from it. So this section will just take a brief tour around the topic in order to marvel at the possibilities.

Computational fluid dynamics, or CFD, is the use of a computer to solve the complex equations that have been developed to mathematically model what goes on in fluid flows. If you consider that it would take quite a while with pen, paper, and calculator to solve the equations to define the airflow around a given point on a body, then it is clear that solving the case for the whole surface of that body would be a very large task indeed. This is where number crunching computers come in handy. But, as anyone who has suffered the frustrations of dealing with computer generated gibberish knows, what comes out is a direct result of what's put in. So the key to producing worthwhile and meaningful computer generated predictions of air flow, or any other fluid flow, is defining the problem and the problem solving techniques.

There are various aspects of fluid flow that a 'CFD code', or program, has to deal with. Equations involving the mass of fluid and its velocity, together with the forces that the fluid exerts, are central to the problem. But, in order to model things accurately, viscous flow equations are also needed, which is where the process gets more complicated. Solving problems relating to laminar flow would appear to be not too troublesome, but where the flow is turbulent and separated, the mathematics becomes very complex, and incredibly time-consuming. In order to cope with the complexity, the software is written so that a given problem can be worked on by lots of computers simultaneously, or 'running parallel' to use the jargon. Even so, a large-scale problem, such as solving the flow around a substantial portion of a single seat racecar, may need to be left to run on a cluster of computers for several hours. So you can see why the home computer won't do yet. But computing power is forever increasing, and it may not be many years before this kind of problem can be run on a single machine.

CFD is now just about capable of modelling whole car problems, but it is a very time-consuming process at this stage in its development. So the top teams that use it, such as the Benetton Formula 1 team – who use Fluent CFD software in a partnership that both companies have benefited from, both technically and commercially – tend to model parts of the car at any one time. But, as we have seen in this book, it is crucial that components that interact are studied together; so when, for example, Benetton wish to examine a new rear diffuser configuration, then they do so in conjunction with the rear wing assembly, and with a 'generic front end' of a Benetton to provide a realistic virtual flow pattern to the new component. Similarly, when a new front wing is studied, the problem is solved with the front suspension and front wheels and tyres integrated into the model too. And the software even accounts for the rotation of the wheels . . .

So how does CFD fit into the design process at a manufacturer like Benetton? In essence, CFD is a complementary tool to the wind-tunnel, but it is possible to build and test models on computer rather faster than real solid ones. Thus, a larger number of basic configurations can be examined using CFD in a given time than is possible with wind-tunnel testing. So why wind-tunnel test at all? Because the

computer predictions need validating, and this can only be done using real flow over solid models. But conversely, if an interesting result is found from some demon tweak in the wind-tunnel, then the computer may well be used to examine the case in detail to work out why. So the two approaches are used together, often in parallel as it were, to look for efficient aerodynamic solutions.

CFD works basically by firstly creating a shape, which is the component or part of the car to be studied, using computer aided draughting (CAD). Alternatively, an existing CAD drawing may be imported from another program, if the designers are using a stand-alone CAD system to design their cars on (the top ones do). The fluid dynamicist then uses the CFD software to define a 'mesh' of linked points all over and around the component (see Figure 6–5). These are the points at which the necessary equations are going to be solved by the computer, and there may be a million or more of them on a complex problem! The mesh is assembled in such a way that critical or complicated areas are more densely covered with points than less critical areas, so concentrating the computing time on the bits that really matter. Mesh generation is the labour intensive bit, requiring hands-on control by the appropriately qualified expert. After that the computer is left to it, and later that day or the following morning, a new solution has been defined. It is then possible to output the fruit of the computer's number crunching labours in various forms, showing streamlines, surface pressure distributions, and other visual aids to studying the solution (see Figure 6–6), together with predictions of pressure values, and, of course, downforce and drag values.

CFD is being increasingly used by teams and manufacturers in the upper echelons of motorsport at the early, conceptual stages of the design process, and it isn't hard to imagine that a great deal of the car will be designed using CFD alone in years to come, as the technique is

Generic Benetton Formula 1 Car

Details of the Surface Grid in the Cockpit Region

Fluen
TGrid 2.3
Tue Nov 14

Figure 6–5 *The fluid dynamicist uses the CFD software to define a 'mesh' of linked points all over and around the component.* (Fluent Europe Ltd)

Figure 6–6 *CFD plot of a generic Benetton Formula 1 car showing streamline 'ribbons'.* (Fluent Europe Ltd)

developed, more powerful hardware speeds up the process, and experience breeds more confidence. For now, it is just one tool contributing to the design process, and to the refinement of existing designs, providing great images for the rest of us to admire! But whilst CFD generates data which enables aerodynamic efficiency to be predicted, the precise effect on performance is not calculated or measured. This facet used to have to be ascertained on track – until the advent of computer models which could predict on-track performance, that is.

Performance simulation is another form of mathematical modelling made practical by computers. Whereas the calculations for the performance of a car *at a given instant* could be done fairly easily with pen, paper, and pocket calculator, it is not the work of a moment. It follows, then, that to investigate varying configurations would take an extremely long time, and that analysing an entire lap, never mind a whole race, is not something a sane race engineer would contemplate. But once the mathematical methods for this type of analysis have been written – that is, the computer program has been written – a computer will happily churn out solutions for various configurations, such as different aerodynamic set ups, enabling a race team to predict the probable best aerodynamic set up for a circuit long before they get there. This has to be a vital advantage when practice and qualifying time is limited, and there just aren't enough hours available to work through a range of aero configurations, as well as the mechanical variables on a car, whilst at the track.

Performance simulation doesn't necessarily need to predict precise lap times for a given track, interesting though that may be. What really matters is that the *relative* effects of changes can be analysed, and that, with sufficient iterations, an idealised set up can be derived. For example, in general terms it is obvious that increasing the front and rear wing angles on a car will generate more downforce, and allow corners to be taken faster and braking to be left until a bit later. It is also obvious that straight-line speed will be reduced because of the increased induced drag. By feeding in different downforce and drag values, a performance simulation program will predict lap times in each case, and, theoretically, allow the ideal compromise to be selected, at least from the range of possibilities that were fed into the computer in the first place. What the simulation model cannot do is to take account of uncontrollable variables that might be encountered at a circuit, such as changing track temperature, or dust build-up, which will affect available grip. But rather in the same way that a wind-tunnel does not take account of gusty side winds which may be encountered in real life, this is actually of benefit to the analysis in that it allows changes to be tested out in equal conditions, something which rarely happens out on the track.

Performance prediction is done by modelling a variety of aspects that influence vehicle performance, and integrating them onto a 'map' of the track or circuit being studied. So fairly detailed knowledge of the venues of interest as well as the car is required. Things like the mass, dimensions, and roll stiffness of the car are needed, to calculate the forces and accelerations involved, and to work out the loadings on each tyre at any one instant (see Figure 6–7). An aerodynamic model is incorporated, probably based on wind-tunnel data, so that the influences on the tyre loadings and on straight-line performance can be worked out. And then there are models to calculate the accelerative performance of the car, using data on power curves and gearing, braking performance, and, perhaps most importantly, the tyres and their ability to transmit power, cornering forces, and braking effort to the road surface under constantly changing circumstances. Clearly the downforce to drag compromise plays a large role in this analysis, especially for high downforce formulae

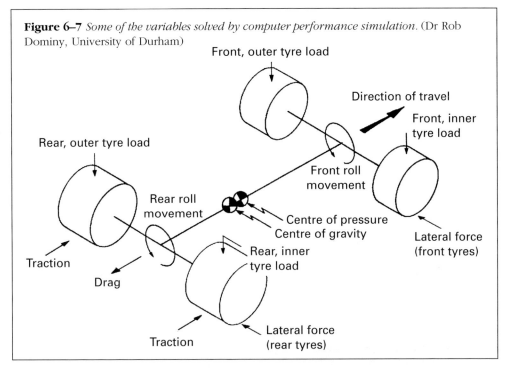

Figure 6–7 *Some of the variables solved by computer performance simulation.* (Dr Rob Dominy, University of Durham)

Front, outer tyre load

Direction of travel

Front, inner tyre load

Rear, outer tyre load

Front roll movement

Rear roll movement

Centre of pressure
Centre of gravity

Lateral force (front tyres)

Rear, inner tyre load

Traction

Drag

Traction

Lateral force (rear tyres)

like the top single seater categories of Formula 1 and CART/IRL.

In essence, the model might look first at a corner, calculating the theoretical maximum speed that could be carried around it, given that the corner radius is known, and the level of grip is fixed, perhaps, at some value measured on a previous visit to the venue. The analysis might assume steady state cornering with little or no tractive effort being fed into the driven wheels. Then, as the track straightens out, the model has as its corner exit speed the steady speed at which the car came off the previous corner, which is the speed that acceleration is assumed to begin from, and by calculating the acceleration that is possible from that speed, it is then possible to work out the speed at the end of the straight. All of this naturally takes into account the changing aerodynamic forces involved. The distance required to brake to corner entry speed can be worked out, and then the next corner follows like the first, and so on. The entire lap is built up in this way,

and the calculation of lap time is very simply achieved by dividing the lap distance by the average speed around the lap.

A race team equipped with this type of analysis tool can then feed in various aerodynamic configurations, and get the computer to work out the relative lap times achieved with each set up, thus allowing it to turn up to a circuit with pretty much the right settings to begin practice (see Figure 6–8). Hopefully all that will be needed from there is fine tuning to suit the prevailing conditions. Once again, the use of this particular tool is, currently, the privilege of the moneyed professionals, but it probably won't be too long before some enterprising software engineer with an understanding of motorsport competition produces an affordable program that will run on a home computer.

This chapter has looked at a wide range of analysis tools, from the simple and affordable to the complex and exotic. But it doesn't matter what your budget is,

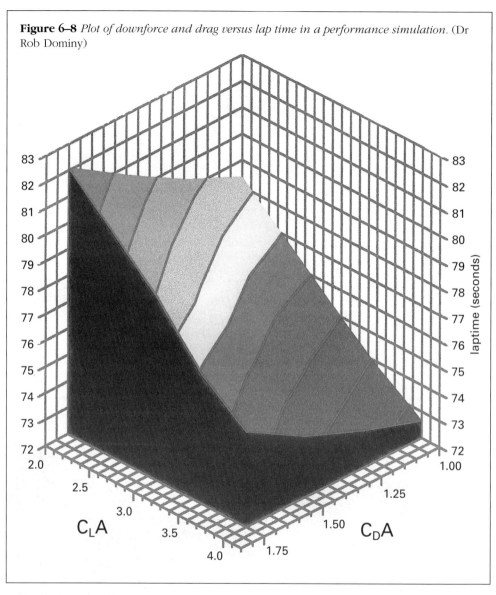

Figure 6–8 *Plot of downforce and drag versus lap time in a performance simulation.* (Dr Rob Dominy)

and which type of tools you are accordingly obliged to rely on. The prerequisite in all cases is to use the tools carefully, with common sense, and this will enable you to improve your understanding of your competition car's aerodynamics in ways that will help in turn to improve its performance. Further development will then, quite probably, require modifications or additions to be made to your car, and the next chapter will look at ways in which downforce-inducing and drag-reducing components can be made in the home workshop.

Chapter 7

You can make it

HAVING WORKED OUT what your competition car now needs in the way of downforce, and designed the items that you calculate will get you that downforce, it's now time to obtain the components. If you're lucky, you may be able to buy what you need from the manufacturer of your car, either new or second-hand, or from a company that makes the components, or possibly through the ads in your favourite motorsport weekly. But if you're not so lucky, or you just don't have the budget to go out and buy the bits you need, then you fit into probably the largest group of motorsport competitors – the ones who make bits for themselves, or who have a pal who makes them. Most self-sufficient competitors (or their pals) are able to work in wood, sheet metal, and, quite probably, glass fibre reinforced plastic (GFRP) too. If you have such skills, then pretty well any of the aerodynamic components mentioned so far in this book can be made in your home workshop, including wings, tunnels, and diffusers. This chapter provides

Aluminium – a popular choice for professionals and amateurs alike for wing construction.

brief 'how to' guidance on making some types of component in either sheet metal or fibre reinforced plastic (FRP), the latter definition being taken to include advanced composite materials, such as carbon fibre, which can be employed using home workshop tools and techniques.

But before we get into the practical stuff, a few friendly words of warning. It might sound rather obvious, but making components to create downforce and transmit that force into your competition car is a *safety critical* job. The components and their mountings have to be up to the job in terms of structural integrity, and need to be resistant, up to a point, to the abuses of a hard life in competition. These criteria would be easy to meet if it were not for the conflicting requirement of making the components as light as possible, in the interests of combining to enhance the car's performance, as we hope to, rather than impeding it. The loads that wings, tunnels, and so forth create are *substantial* at a car's maximum speed, and so the components have to be fit for purpose. Having said that, just about every other component on a competition car is safety critical too, so this should not put anyone off from having a go at making their own bits and pieces if they feel competent at working in the relevant materials. It isn't necessary to be a stress analysis expert to design and build something sturdy yet light, but it probably will be necessary to do some experimenting in order to gain adequate experience and knowledge to make, say, a set of wings – that is, if you haven't already got that experience. You may well be already sufficiently skilled to get straight on and start fabricating. Whatever category you fall into, hopefully this chapter will provide at least a few useful, practical tips.

Choice of materials

Choosing the most appropriate material for making a particular component will depend on a number of factors, such as your familiarity with a material (or your willingness to familiarise yourself with it) and the requisite fabrication methods; the structural and physical requirements of the component; the material costs in relation to your budget; and the number of repeat items you expect to have to make. The do-it-yourself enthusiast can draw on a variety of sources for appropriate construction methods, and although 'traditional' motorsports fabrication methods applicable to wood, metal, and glass-reinforced plastic are what most people rely on, it is also worth looking into model aircraft construction methods too, where high strength and light weight are top of the menu just as in our own field of interest. Full-scale aircraft design literature is also worth checking out too, as is the book about the Rutan-designed aircraft 'Voyager', the first to fly around the world non-stop (see Appendix 2).

Simple components, such as undertrays, or simple splitters, which are basically flat with little or no curvature, can be made from plywood, sheet metal, or from moulded FRP. Components with single curvature, that is, those which are curved or bent in one plane only, such as simple wings, can be made from sheet metal or FRP, whilst components with complex curvature, such as more sophisticated airdams/splitters, and wings with spanwise curvature, are probably best made from FRP, unless your sheet metal-work skills are very good and your workshop is well equipped. From this, it can be seen that FRP's have the widest applicability, yet for something simple like a flat panel that isn't going to need replacing very often it isn't always going to be worth the time and trouble needed to make a pattern, then a mould, and then the component. It may be that for items such as these, aluminium sheet or thin plywood make more sense. Such practical logic does not stop Formula 1 teams from making such essential items as clipboards from carbon fibre reinforced plastic, however, though one suspects that the material availability, and its

Carbon fibre reinforced plastic wings can *be made in the home workshop – this one was.*

pleasing aesthetics, have tended to over-come common sense!

But let's look at the making of wings as an example of a component that encompasses pretty well all the skills needed for making any downforce-induc-ing item. They can be made from sheet metal, most probably aluminium, over a sub-structure that can be made from wood, aluminium, or steel, or they can be made from FRP. This covers a range of different possible methods, but common to both 'technologies' is the need for a sub-structure that offers the wing ade-quate rigidity and strength, as well as a means of mounting it.

Sheet metal

In the case of the sheet metal wing, the skin is made generally of aluminium thin enough to be folded or rolled to the desired profile. This in itself would not provide a rigid or strong enough 'shell' to cope with the loads, so an internal struc-ture – comprising a number of 'ribs' shaped to the wing's sectional profile, stationed at locations across the span, together with one or more 'spars' running spanwise – is usually employed (see Figure 7–1). The ribs enable the skin to be attached in a way that maintains the proper cross-sectional profile, whilst the spars give the wing its spanwise rigidity, and are also used for attaching the skin (see Figure 7–2). A means of attaching the wing to the car has to be incorpor-ated too. Front wings are normally either mounted onto a tube which slides into bosses in the ribs, or, if of the underslung type, will have fore and aft plates bolted to the sub-structure (Figure 7–3). Rear wings are either mounted on plates either side of the centre line, similar to the underslung front wing principle, or via structural end plates which are bolted to the outer ribs, and to a support beam mounted on a strong part of the primary chassis, such as the end housing of the gearbox.

Ribs can be made from wood or from sheet metal. Hardwood can be cut to the required profile with a jig-saw, and screws and/or epoxy adhesive will form a good bond to the skin. But ribs are usu-ally made from aluminium of 20 or 22swg thickness (0.9 to 0.7mm), formed into a

Figure 7–1 *Rib and spar sub-structure.*

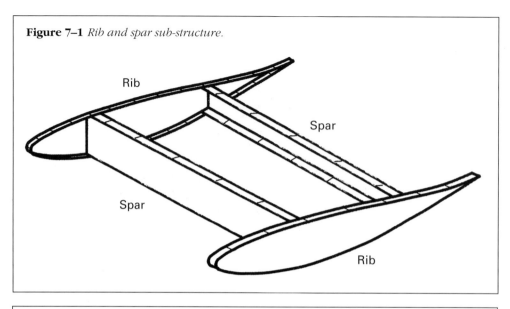

Figure 7–2 *Skin riveted to sub-structure.*

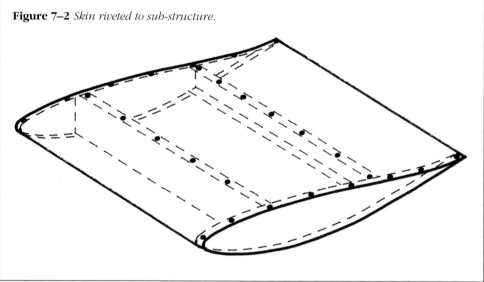

wing-shaped profile by beating over a solid former (see Figure 7–4). Thin sheet steel may be a wiser choice for a stronger, more fatigue-resistant structure. Spars are usually formed from thin sheet steel, perhaps in the range 18–22swg (1.2–0.7mm), and take a [-section shape that can be bonded and riveted to the upper and lower surfaces of the wing skin. Consequently their precise profile will depend on where, along the wing chord, they are positioned (see Figure 7–5). If the cross-tube mounting method is to be used, for example, for front wings slotting on to a tube mounted on a nose box, then the ribs will need to incorporate bosses into which the tube is a reasonably tight fit. These are likely to be made up from steel tube welded to a plate, which allows them to be riveted to the rib in the desired position – that is, approximately where the centre of pres-

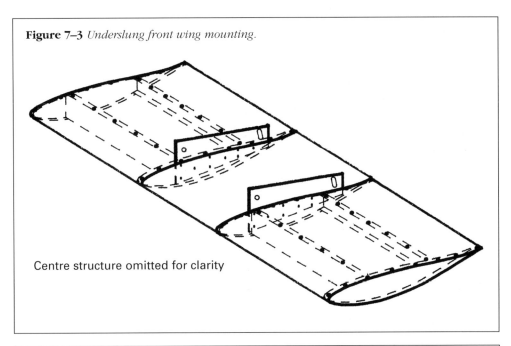

Figure 7–3 *Underslung front wing mounting.*

Centre structure omitted for clarity

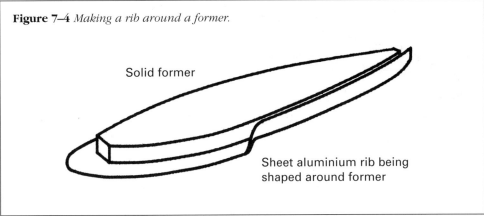

Figure 7–4 *Making a rib around a former.*

Solid former

Sheet aluminium rib being
shaped around former

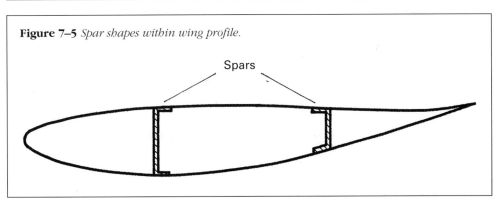

Figure 7–5 *Spar shapes within wing profile.*

Spars

sure is (see Figure 7–6). Any slack in the fit of the boss on the mounting tube can be taken up with plumbers (PTFE) tape or similar.

Aluminium (and other) wing skins need to be as light as they can be, so must therefore be as thin as possible. They must also be rigid enough not to distort under the forces and pressure changes to which they will be subjected, and need to be as dent-proof as possible. And naturally they need to be easily

worked, so that they can be made to adopt the required shape. Once again, thicknesses in the range 18–22swg (1.2–0.7mm) are most widely used, the latter being approximately 40 per cent lighter than the former, easier to fold and bend, and more prone to damage.

The wing skin is generally folded up out of a single piece, joined at the trailing edge by riveting (preferably with flush countersunk rivets) and/or bonding, and joined to the ribs and spars by similar

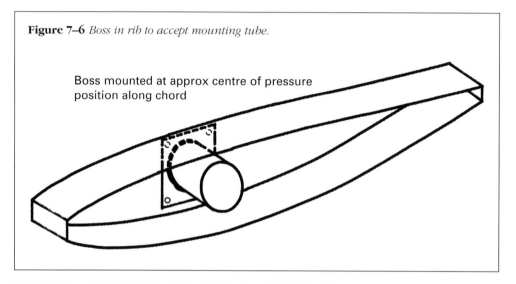

Figure 7–6 *Boss in rib to accept mounting tube.*

Boss mounted at approx centre of pressure position along chord

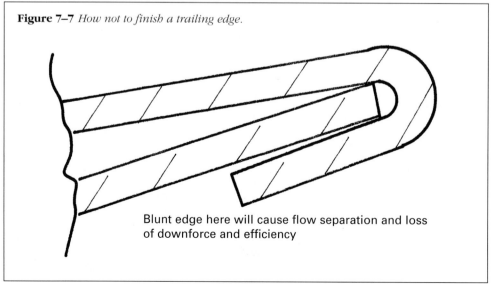

Figure 7–7 *How not to finish a trailing edge.*

Blunt edge here will cause flow separation and loss of downforce and efficiency attachment methods. Aluminium is not keen to be glued, and meticulous preparation of the surfaces to be bonded, in accordance with the adhesive manufacturer's instructions, is required if the joint is to be prevented from springing apart at the first signs of vibration and flexing on a moving car. Make sure that any joins are aerodynamically sound – it's surprising how many wings can still be seen, in paddocks where the entrants really should know better, with forward facing overlap joins on the lower surface of the trailing edge (see Figure 7–7). This is an aerodynamic no-no, and is *bound* to trip the airflow up and cause early separation, losing precious downforce and gaining undesirable drag. If there *must* be an overlap join, it is better to put it on the top surface, where it may act as a small Gurney flap and help slightly, providing that the trailing edge concerned is the rearmost one. It would not help to do this on the trailing edge of a mainplane ahead of a flap, where the required smooth, fast flow through the slot gap would be compromised. It helps, by assisting in making the wing's wake as small as it can be, to keep the trailing edge as thin and sharp as possible. It isn't always easy to achieve this *and* have a trailing edge which is structurally sound. If appropriate, a Gurney will help with the structural aspect.

Aluminium wings are reasonably cheap to make, and this is the principle reason for their enduring popularity amongst clubmen. But they do have the dual disadvantages of being heavier than necessary, and being visually – and probably aerodynamically – ruined by dents, to which they are, unfortunately, particularly prone. Stones thrown up from a car in front very easily damage the leading edge of an aluminium wing, as do inadvertent knocks in the paddock or the workshop. All that careful design effort and painstaking manufacture can therefore end up being completely compromised in the space of just a few meetings – or a few minutes, even. The problem is especially acute for front wings, though rear wings are not immune. And it is also fair to say that airdams and splitters, as well as rear spoilers and other downforce-creating components, are also prone to this kind of damage if made in sheet aluminium, though the effect on aerodynamic performance may not be as critical. The propensity to this kind of damage can be markedly reduced by switching to some kind of FRP construction, with the extra benefits of increased strength and rigidity, and some weight saving too, if required.

Fibre reinforced plastics

Most motorsport competitors are familiar with glass fibre reinforced plastic (GFRP), often just known as glass fibre. In its cheapest, simplest form, randomly laid

Front and rear CFRP wings on the Marengo hillclimber.

Shaping profile formers for the lower half of a wing pattern.

Hot wire-cutting polystyrene foam to shape around the formers.

fibres of glass ('chopped strand mat', or CSM) are held in a matrix of cured polyester resin, to provide a tough, durable, relatively light medium that can be 'laid up' in quite complex shaped moulds to make body panels, nose cones, undertrays, wings, and pretty well any of the components discussed in this book. Increased strength with decreased weight is achievable using woven glass fabrics, and further gains are possible if sandwich structures are created, using 'core' materials that markedly increase the rigidity of a component in relation to its weight.

Then we move into the realm of advanced composites, using reinforcement materials such as carbon fibre, which provides high levels of stiffness for a given weight, and kevlar, which offers high strength and amazingly tough abrasion and impact resistance. Light honeycomb core materials enable featherweight but rigid sandwich structures to be fabricated, and the structural properties of this group of materials are so superior to sheet metal and 'traditional' forms of FRP that, in top professional competition car manufacture, nothing else will do for the bodywork and aerodynamic items. But we shall see shortly how some of these advantages can be enjoyed by the home-based clubman, because there are techniques that allow advanced composites to be exploited using relatively simple technology.

First, let's go over the basics of making a component out of GFRP. The good news is that we can make just about any shape we desire. The bad news is that it takes lots of time, and it can get messy, smelly, and irritating! But the ability to start from a design drawn up yourself, rather than being constrained to a shape that someone else created, as well as being able to incorporate complex curvature, makes the whole exercise worthwhile. The process involves three basic steps: first, a pattern, or buck, has to be made, which is a full-size, exact replica of what the final product is going to be; second, a mould is made on the pattern;

and third, the component is made in the mould. Many people stop to wonder at this point as to why, having made an exact replica of the component, you don't just stop there and use that on the car. Well, in effect, that's what you do if you make an aluminium wing, for example. But one of the advantages of taking the time to make a mould in the first place is that subsequent components that exactly match the original can then be fabricated relatively quickly. This is especially useful for vulnerable components like nose-cones, airdams, splitters, and front wings that tend to need frequent replacement.

Taking the manufacture of a wing as an example once again, it is possible to use a variety of approaches to creating a pattern. First of all the three-dimensional shape has to be defined in some way, and then an outer surface that permits the laying up of mould materials onto it has to be created. The materials used for the pattern must also be compatible with those that are to be used for making the mould, and with the conditions under which the mould is to be cured. If the wing is a simple affair, with no spanwise curvature, then an aluminium skin can be used, perhaps bonded to an internal foam core or rib-and-spar structure. Remember that any surface imperfections are going to be transferred faithfully into the mould, so you might want to try to avoid using rivets on a pattern. Alternatively, and if a more complex shape is required, a foam core can be cut or sanded to shape around profile form-ers, and coated with a compatible resin to form a sealed, rigid surface. Polystyrene foam can be cut with a hot wire bow, then coated with epoxy resin (*not* poly-ester, which dissolves polystyrene), and finished with vehicle body filler prior to painting and finishing. Polyurethane foam can be coated with either epoxy or poly-ester resin. The finishing process is the time-consuming part, but it is well worth the investment in order to achieve the exact shape you were after. Having painted, flatted out, cut, and polished to a

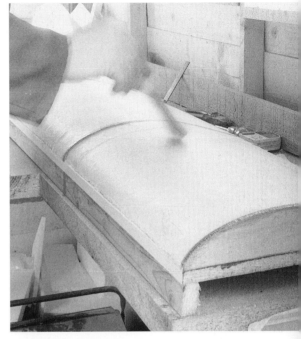

Coating the polystyrene core with woven glass fibre and epoxy resin.

Having applied body filler to the imperfections, the pattern is sanded to a 'perfect' finish.

gleaming surface finish, a mould release agent, which can be a wax or a liquid release agent that dries to an impervious skin, is then applied, and the mould making process begins.

Assuming for now that we are confined to ambient temperature moulding processes such as found in the DIY workshop, then the mould is most probably going to be made of GFRP based on a polyester resin system. This involves firstly applying a 'gel coat' to the pattern surface to give the mould a tough, shiny outer layer, and then allowing this to cure (a process initiated by the addition of a chemical catalyst to the gel). Layers of CSM are next laid up with catalysed polyester resin onto the gel coat, fully 'wetted out' with brushes and rollers to squeeze out all the air bubbles (well, most of them anyway), before being once again left to cure. An external reinforcing structure is usually fabricated onto the outside of the mould to ensure its rigidity once removed from the pattern. This can be done with GFRP over pieces of wood, or

Laminating the mould over the pattern.

metal tube. The mould needs to be allowed to fully cure before attempting to release it from the pattern, which means a minimum of 24 hours, and possibly a lot more in cold conditions. Completion of the curing process takes several days even in warm conditions.

Once the mould has cured, it can be prised off the pattern. This is a nerve-wracking process, usually rewarded by the sound of a satisfying 'crack' as the mould pops off the pattern, and the sight of a super surface finish to the mould needing the minimum of attention prior to component production. Occasionally things can go wrong, such as little patches of surface wrinkling on the mould, but problems like this are rare if you have followed the instructions provided by the makers of your supplies, and are easily fixed with body filler and a bit of time. Final preparation of the mould then consists of applying several coats of release wax.

Given that we are discussing the manufacture of wings, it is necessary to make moulds for the internal sub-structure components too. It isn't necessary to go for an aesthetically pleasing surface finish on ribs and spars, so there are some easy ways to make moulds for these items which avoid the need for pattern manufacture. A simple [-section spar mould can be made by screwing two pieces of plastic-coated and edged chipboard at the appropriate spacing onto a base of the same board (see Figure 7–8). If a spar does not have parallel sides, then an angle will need to be cut on one side of the mould, and prior to moulding this edge will require sealing with resin, filler, or even just clear adhesive tape (though not all such tapes are gel and resin compatible, so check this out before starting). The same type of board can be used for making rib moulds, if a wing profile shaped hole is cut out of one piece of board, and this is then screwed to a base board again (see Figure 7–9). Bosses for wing tubes can be made from a piece of the appropriate wing tube held in place

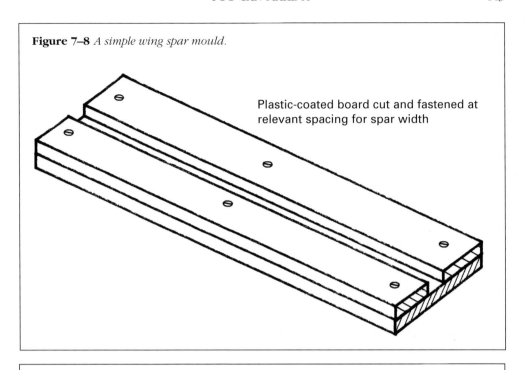

Figure 7–8 *A simple wing spar mould.*

Plastic-coated board cut and fastened at relevant spacing for spar width

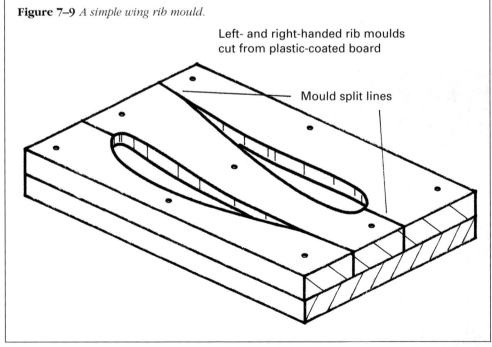

Figure 7–9 *A simple wing rib mould.*

Left- and right-handed rib moulds cut from plastic-coated board

Mould split lines

by double-sided tape in the rib mould. Note again that we have used a single step to make these moulds – it wasn't necessary to make a pattern first. Wax and release agent can then be applied prior to making the moulded compo-

Waxing the lower half of a front wing mould.

Applying clear gel coat to the waxed mould. Note the black gelled leading edge to hide the join!

nents, which are made using much the same process as described in GFRP mould manufacture above, though possibly using structurally better materials. More detail on manufacturing methods will be found in the books listed in Appendix 2, or can be obtained from the materials suppliers.

The wing skins, and the internals, can all be made satisfactorily in GFRP. It may be necessary to add some reinforcement to the wing skins in areas not supported by ribs or spars, and a range of 'core' materials can be considered here, including corrugated card ('poor man's honeycomb' as it has been called), balsa wood, and proprietary core materials like 'Coremat' or thin PVC foam. Honeycombs are not really very good with polyester resin because the resin bond is not strong enough. More of this later. However, there are means of making components in FRP that produce a stiffer, stronger, lighter and perhaps inevitably more expensive end result. The costs, however, need not be prohibitive, and these methods are therefore worthy of consideration, as the techniques can be applied to the wide range of downforce-inducing parts that we are interested in.

Advanced composites, in the motorsport context, are generally taken to include materials like carbon fibre, kevlar, and honeycomb core materials. 'Composite' actually only means 'made up of several parts', and the 'advanced' tag is added by those with a vested interest in maintaining a little bit of high-tech mystique. We'll ignore this as nonsense, and plough on regardless! How can the DIY clubman benefit from advanced composites? The answer, especially if GFRP technology and skills are already available to you, is *easily*. It is possible, despite a widely held belief to the contrary, to combine carbon and kevlar with the same types of polyester resin used for making glass fibre reinforced mouldings. Thus, although the reinforcing fabrics are a lot more expensive, cheap resin can still be used to get a pretty useful gain in component stiffness and strength, generally with a significant weight saving. If the carbon is laid up behind a clear gel coat then you can also enjoy the aesthetically pleasing, and very high-tech, appearance engendered by it to your wings or whatever; this, if nothing else, will get your fellow competitors mumbling behind your back!

If, structurally speaking, an even better result is desired then ambient temperature cure hand lay-up epoxy resins can be obtained which markedly increase strength and rigidity, and which also permit the adoption of honeycomb cores to make some impressively rigid yet lightweight components. Epoxy resin works with honeycomb, where polyester resin does not, because of its inherently greater bond strength. It will be evident that the contact area between a honeycomb and the surface to which it is to be bonded is very small, given that the contact is restricted to the very edges of the honeycomb material. Thus, to get a secure bond to such a small contact area requires a high bond strength, and appropriate epoxy resins offer this. Clearly some means of holding the honeycomb onto the surface to which it is to be bonded is necessary during cure. For simple flat or single curvature items, this can be achieved with mechanical pressure – in the case of a wing, for example, by putting the pattern, weighted down if necessary, back in the mould on top of the materials to be cured (with a suitable release film, such as polythene sheet, between the pattern and the epoxy-impregnated materials). For more complex shapes, a more complex solution – vacuum bagging – is required, which enables compound curvature mouldings to be 'sucked down' into a mould, thereby maintaining proper contact over the whole component area. The technique obviously requires a new range of consumable materials, such as release films, breather fabrics, and vacuum bag materials and sealants, together with a suitable vacuum pump and fittings. But

Applying the first layer of carbon with clear resin.

Applying black resin to Coremat sandwich material.

The sub-structure of ribs and spar is bonded in after the second ply of carbon is applied and cured.

The two halves are bonded together and clamped.

used with care it does ensure that complex, well consolidated, 'void-free' mouldings can be produced.

With the purchase of some more equipment it is also possible to use some really quite sophisticated materials to get a highly professional result from your composite mouldings. 'Pre-pregs' are reinforcing fabrics which have been pre-impregnated with resin, in exactly the right proportions to achieve an optimum end result, something which is virtually impossible to achieve in hand lay-up, where excess resin is almost always used. The pre-pregs are stored at freezer temperatures (around –15 to –18°C, 5 to 0°F), and are cured at elevated temperatures of around 60 to 120°C, or 140 to 250°F. Clearly, then, an oven is required to utilise pre-preg technology, and either a proprietary one can be bought – made to measure if desired – or a suitable one can be built using some ingenuity. The Multi-Sports Composites book *A Practical Guide to Composites* (see Appendix 2) is recommended if you want to get into pre-pregs. However, it is necessary to use materials in the manufacture of the mould, and to some extent the pattern, which are tolerant of these more extreme conditions. A GFRP/PE resin mould, for example, will only cope with temperatures up to about 90°C (195°F), and only then if care has been taken to vacuum out air bubbles during its cure; otherwise subsequent high temperature/low pressure cycles are likely to inflict damage to the mould. Appropriate 'tooling' pre-pregs may therefore need to be used for mould manufacture, which all adds to the cost. But the combination of vacuum, elevated temperature cure, epoxy resin systems and carbon fibre with honeycomb provides difficult-to-beat technology for the making of wings and other downforce-inducing bits and pieces.

It's worth pausing at this point to take a look at the relative properties of some of the materials discussed, to help in deciding which is the best material for a particular job. Some very simple tests

The finished item, with end plate fitted.

were rigged up in which equal size test strips of each material were cut, clamped to the workbench, and put under load with a suspended weight hanging from the end of the test strip. Deflections were measured, and relative specific stiffnesses (that is, weight adjusted), normalised to GFRP at 1.00, were calculated. The results are tabulated below, and shown graphically in Figure 7–10.

Relative stiffnesses of 2 ply laminates and 18swg aluminium

Material	Relative weight	Deflection, mm	Relative stiffness
CSM/polyester resin	1.00	35	1.00
Kevlar/polyester resin	0.94	22	1.69
Carbon/polyester resin	0.79	25	1.77
Carbon/epoxy	0.84	21	1.98
Carbon/Coremat/ polyester resin	1.87	1	18.72
Carbon/Nomex/ epoxy	1.27	0.5	55.12
Pre-preg carbon	0.78	35	1.28
Pre-preg carbon/ aluminium h'comb/ epoxy	1.27	0.35	79.05
Aluminium	2.62	2.5	5.34

What these simplistic tests did not take into account was the thickness of each sample tested, and this obviously has a lot to do with the stiffness of a given material. But nevertheless, the samples make for interesting comparison. For example, carbon in polyester resin is a lot stiffer than GFRP made from CSM in polyester. The biggest gains in stiffness come from using a core material, and Coremat^R is a cheap way of making a stiff laminate, whilst Nomex and aluminium honeycombs make the stiffest laminates tested here. Pre-preg carbon doesn't look very stiff, but having been vacuumed down, this sample was a lot thinner than the hand lay-up samples it is compared with, which undoubtedly gives a false impression. Interestingly, aluminium comes out fairly favourably in

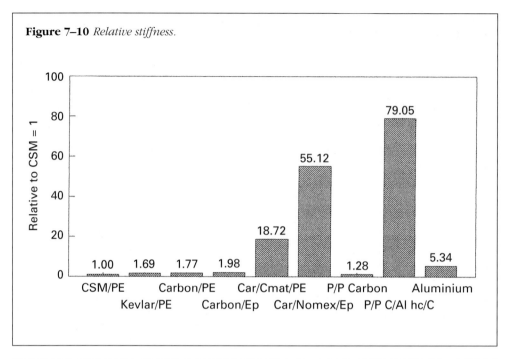

Figure 7–10 *Relative stiffness.*

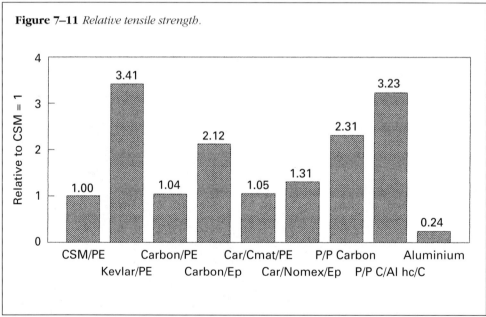

Figure 7–11 *Relative tensile strength.*

this comparison, but its greater thickness than the simple laminates gives a slightly misleading impression.

Load was added to each material either until breaking point was reached, or until the elastic limit had been surpassed, and the results were used to calculate the specific relative tensile strengths. These are shown in the table below, and in figure 7–11.

Relative tensile strengths of 2 ply laminates and 18swg aluminium

Material	Relative weight	Breaking load, kg	Relative strength
CSM/polyester resin	1.00	2.525	1.00
Kevlar/polyester resin	0.94	8.1	3.41
Carbon/polyester resin	0.79	2.075	1.04
Carbon/epoxy	0.84	4.5	2.12
Carbon/Coremat/ polyester resin	1.87	4.95	1.05
Carbon/Nomex/ epoxy	1.27	4.2	1.31
Pre-preg carbon	0.78	4.55	2.31
Pre-preg carbon/ alum h'comb/ epoxy	1.27	10.325	3.23
Aluminium	2.62	1.56	0.24

In the case of strength, the materials fall into a very different order, and kevlar comes out top. Clearly the switch from polyester resin to epoxy gives an increase in strength in the case of the carbon laminates. The pre-preg aluminium honeycomb sandwich again performs very well, and is the best performer overall in this group of samples. Aluminium sheet performs poorly on relative strength, taking up a permanent bend at relatively low load, although not actually breaking. Whilst this is also what allows it to be worked into folds and bends, it is also the property that leads to its propensity to dent.

To complete this comparison of materials, we should also look at relative costs. To make a reasonably fair comparison, the costs in the table below (and in Figure 7–12) are on a square metre basis, and are for made up laminates, including resin, catalyst where appropriate, and the fabric itself. The aluminium figure is based on a quote for 18swg (1.2mm) sheet from a randomly picked stockist. All the prices are based on those in the UK in 1997.

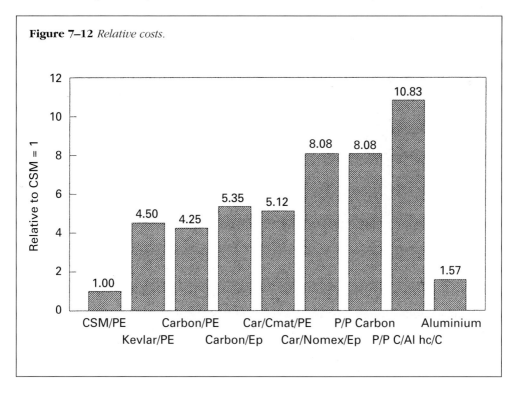

Figure 7–12 *Relative costs.*

Relative cost of 2 ply laminates plus 18swg aluminium

Material

CSM/polyester resin	1.00
Kevlar/polyester resin	4.50
Carbon/polyester resin	4.25
Carbon/epoxy	5.35
Carbon/Coremat/polyester resin	5.12
Carbon/Nomex/epoxy	8.08
Pre-preg carbon	8.08
Pre-preg carbon/alum h'comb/epoxy	10.83
Aluminium	1.57

The costs of the FRP laminates is a function of the materials cost, the resin consumption, and the resin cost. Clearly, the cheap form of GFRP is very cheap, whilst the use of advanced materials does add significantly to expense. But if a wing, for example, costs £50 ($80) in materials instead of £10 ($16), yet is half the weight and over five times as stiff as the cheap version, then that is surely an option worthy of consideration.

Before moving on to a brief look at how the professionals make composite components, it should be mentioned that FRP prototype components can be made by a one-step process if the item is shaped out of polyurethane foam, a material which is easily cut and sanded, and which is then covered with chopped strand glass fibre mat and polyester resin. Rough finishing may be all that is needed, using sanding blocks, files, and so on, plus the inevitable car body filler. Once the component has been tested – provided it survives the process – it can obviously then be used as the basis for a proper pattern. In this way, a range of different components can be made and tested relatively cheaply and quickly, and only when you are satisfied as to which component is the right one will the time be put into making the mould.

Professional techniques

The previous section on the DIY use of pre-pregs described techniques not all that far removed from the world of the professionals, the technology being, in fact, similar to that used by the leading motorsport manufacturers just a few years ago. But things move on, and top quality composite mouldings are cured nowadays in autoclaves, which, as well as permitting high temperatures and vacuum to be applied, also exert pressures of anything up to 100psi (7bar) onto mouldings during the process. Consequently the laminate consolidation, absence of entrapped air bubbles, and the optimum resin to fabric ratio all combine to produce components with a stiffness and strength outstanding for their light weight. This is just as well, considering these guys are also the best at creating large quantities of downforce. In a paper written in 1992, Brian O'Rourke, Senior Engineer of Composites at Williams Grand Prix Engineering (see Appendix 2), indicated that the front wing structure of the then-current Williams Formula 1 car applied a maximum load in excess of 1,120lb (5,000 Newtons), and the underbody and the rear wing *each* created over 1,345lb (6,000 Newtons) of download. Although rule changes have reduced these figures since that date, the forces involved are still very substantial, and experts like O'Rourke – whose background was in the aerospace industry before joining Williams in 1982 – are an essential part of the design team of a top racecar manufacturer.

But whatever levels of downforce you are hoping to achieve, do everything you can to ensure that your wings, or splitter, or whatever, are strong enough to do the job you expect of them. Their design and construction is entirely your responsibility, and neither the author nor the publisher will take any responsibility if anything goes wrong!

Chapter 8

Case studies

HAVING SPENT THE last seven chapters figuring out how aerodynamic devices produce downforce, how much of it there is, how you can try and quantify it, or its effects, and how to make components to create it, we'll spend this chapter casting an eye over some of the many different motorsport categories that permit the exploitation of downforce to one degree or another, and attempt to work out what is being done in each case. Doing so invariably raises more questions than answers, but that's no bad thing if it increases our general understanding of the principles involved. But it's well worth remembering that ideas – or the specific execution of ideas – which work on one car may or may not work on another. This is what makes the whole subject so fascinating, and means there is scope for all of us to try out new ideas – even ones cribbed from somebody else!

Competition cars can be said to fall neatly into two broad categories: open wheelers, which includes single seater racecars as well as drag racers, stock cars, dirt modifieds, and such like; and closed wheelers, which encompasses pure sports racecars as well as 'family' passenger-car based vehicles used in racing, speed events, and off-road competition like rallying. This classification is convenient both in terms of the obvious visual distinctions between the categories, and their totally different aerodynamic characteristics. We'll start with open wheelers first.

Open wheelers

Most open wheel competition cars are conceptually very simple – the idea usually is to create the most basic structure possible to carry the engine, transmission, and driver, and to transmit the power and control to the wheels. At least, that's how it started out. Over time, developments have taken place that mean that open wheel competition cars are amongst the most complex motorsports machines in the world. And this complexity is manifested in the application of aerodynamics to this most difficult generic group of vehicles. It is because of their very nature – open wheels – that the airflow around them is complicated, difficult to control, and hard to exploit. Yet, because the world's most technologically advanced competition categories are for open wheelers, this, ironically, is where the most money is spent looking for efficient downforce.

Literally as well as metaphorically, open wheels are a real drag! Over 40 per cent of an open wheeler's total drag can be caused by the wheels. The air flowing around an exposed wheel is turned into a turbulent mess behind it, which causes drag directly, and has a profound adverse influence on the flow over parts of the body in the wake of the wheels. This can further affect the vehicle's drag coefficient, its cooling ability, and the efficiency of downforce creation by the underbody and the rear wing(s). The front wheels also influence the flow over and under front wings, and this generally has a less than beneficial effect on downforce and its efficiency too.

But as well as creating large amounts of drag and messing up the airflow over the rest of the vehicle, rotating wheels also generate significant amounts of positive lift too. This is not a lot of use, but that's just the way it is – the Laws of Nature have determined that air accelerating over the top of a wheel and tyre causes a reduction in pressure on the top surface of the tyre, which creates an upwards force. To some extent this is mollified by the presence of the ground, and the ground's influence on a process known as the Magnus effect, which describes how cylindrical or spherical bodies which rotate during their travel through the air create a force component which is perpendicular to the direction of travel. The direction of the perpendicular force is governed by the direction of spin in relation to the direction of travel, and a cylinder in free air, rotating as would a wheel, would normally create a downward-directed force as the result of the Magnus effect, just like a tennis ball hit with top spin. However, a wheel is not usually in free air, and since the flow is blocked from travelling below the wheel, the air is forced to accelerate over it, and creates a lifting force. The Magnus effect, by virtue of the viscous friction between the air and the wheel, tends to try to retard the flow over the top of the wheel, and this reduces the lifting force somewhat, but unfortunately the lift is still positive.

So an open wheeled competition car is a difficult beast to make aerodynamically efficient. Let's take a brief look at a number of different open wheelers to see what their designers have done to get the downforce they need, and what measures they have taken to achieve that downforce as efficiently as possible. Almost inevitably we'll start off with an example from Formula 1.

Formula 1

All Formula 1 cars are beautifully pack-aged devices, with superbly crafted composite chassis and bodywork shrouding the engine, transmission, and driver compartments. Within the dimensional constraints imposed by the Formula's regulations, and the practical needs of installing the power plant and drive train, as well as the cooling demands imposed by those systems, the central portion of a Formula 1 car is as sleek as it can be. The chassis are as narrow as possible, given that a driver has to be accommodated comfortably in order to do an effective job, and given too that the structural needs are better met with as *wide* a chassis as possible! This conflict of interests between aerodynamics and structural integrity is one which severely taxes the ingenuity of the engineers charged with building a safe chassis that matches the shape derived from the CFD and wind-tunnel work. Though this central portion of the car may be sleek, the wheels do their best to disturb the visual and aerodynamic efficiency of the design, and the front and rear wings somehow always look like afterthoughts, even though they are carefully integrated into the overall package.

The photos show a Jordan Peugeot 196 in the pits at Estoril, Portugal, in 1996, a circuit that seems to favour a high downforce set up, with a number of fast corners where over 3G of cornering force is felt, and only one longish straight. At the front of the car, the Jordan used the virtually ubiquitous full width front wing, suspended from a raised nose-cone. The wing is, in effect, a two-element device, with single flaps, though the mainplane is a one-piece structure running the full allowed span of 55in (1,400mm). The centre portion of the front mainplane is slightly raised, which will reduce the wing's ride height sensitivity, and provide a cleaner flow to the central underbody region. The wing flaps are asymmetric in shape, with their maximum chord at the outer ends. The reduction in chord at the inner portion of the flaps will allow a better feed of air to the car's radiators,

The Jordan 196's front wing, an underslung asymmetric two-element device. (Tracey Inglis)

which were provided with air via twin ducts on this car.

The front wing end plate is very much a three-dimensional affair, with a horizontal lip at the bottom edge to reduce undesirable air spillage to the underside of the wing. The vertical lip at the rear edge of the end plate, together with the scalloped lower rear part, are to try to maintain an attached flow along the wing underside in this difficult area just ahead of where the wheel would be if it were bolted in place! Gurneys are attached to the rear edge of the flaps, and the team would alter the height of the Gurneys fitted, and possibly the angle of the flaps, to fine tune the aerodynamic balance of the car if that proved necessary. Behind the front wing, a vertical curved 'bargeboard' is visible. These items vary from car to car, and some teams use more than one, arranged in tandem. Their purpose is to reduce the adverse effects of the wheels on the airflow, and to smooth out the turbulent wake behind the front wheels. They redirect some air back behind the

wheel, thus reducing the wheel's wake and consequently drag. They also direct a smoother flow of air into the ducts feeding the radiators. Just visible in the head-on shots, but more clearly seen from behind, are pairs of curved vertical plates attached to the underside of the front wing mainplane, and extending towards the rear edge of the flaps. These are clearly shaped to steer the airflow on an outward curving path beneath the wing, which is in opposition to the natural tendency for the airflow to converge inwards between the wheels. One can speculate that this ensured a better attachment of flow to the wing's undersurface, and added to the effect of the bargeboards in re-attaching the flow behind the front wheels again.

Moving further back on the car, the regulatory requirement to have a flat underside between the rear edge of the front wheels and the front edge of the rear wheels begins on this car with the central, flat splitter just ahead of the inner radiator inlet ducts. The raised underside

of the nose structure meets the splitter at a point where the airflow would be at high pressure (a stagnation zone), and, as such, this splitter would feel a pressure on its upper surface, as distinct from the low pressure beneath it where the air would be converging and accelerating into the underbody area. Thus some downforce will be generated here. It is interesting how the splitter is then shaped to turn into the forward radiator duct here, with effectively an extension of the splitter leading back into the duct. The two ducts are tall and narrow.

The engine cover is a smoothly shaped shroud which, as well as providing an air feed to the engine's inlet airbox, has the job of providing as tidy a flow as possible

Left *Curved vanes beneath the front wing, seen from behind.* (Tracey Inglis)

Below *The beginning of the regulation 'flat floor' creates the under-cockpit 'splitter'.* (Tracey Inglis)

to the rear wing, given the disturbance caused by the region around the cockpit and the driver's head. The rear of the sidepods, integral with the engine cover on this car, is tapered in towards the centreline in order to allow the air to flow around the insides of the rear wheels. Two further devices modify and improve this effect. The curved fairing obviously steers the air more smoothly around the lower part of the rear wheels, whilst the 'winglets' – which were positioned ahead of the upper part of the rear wheels – would tend to divert the airflow over the wheels. These winglets, though still in use in 1997, have been much reduced in size, and are only permitted in certain areas ahead of the rear wheels, in order to reduce their contribution to down-

Right *The 'tyre shelf' and fairing.* (Tracey Inglis)

Below *The engine cover, rear sidepod cover, and 'winglets'.* (Tracey Inglis)

force. A flat horizontal extension to the underbody, the 'tyre shelf', protrudes into the space ahead of the lower part of the rear wheels (had they been bolted on), which 'taps' the high pressure zone that exists in front of the wheels, thus providing some extra, and relatively drag free, downforce.

The rear wing is a complex device consisting of, in effect, six elements. The upper section is a highly cambered three-element affair with a Gurney which tapers down at its outer extremities. The middle section is a two-element device with a complex shape to its leading section, incorporating some twist in its span-wise profile, and with a correspondingly complex shape in the secondary element. The rear warning light interrupts the span of this portion, as it does the lower single section element. The end plates provide the structural support for the wing, which attaches to the gearbox casing via the lower wing elements. There are forward extensions to the end plates which also support the inner edges of the winglets,

and as well as this structural role, these extended end plates also serve to isolate the disturbed flow around the rear wheel from the rear wing, so helping to keep the flow to the wing as clean as possible. The rear vertical edges of the end plates have an outward-turned vertical Gurney, which helps to keep the flow attached to the inside faces of the end plates, and this in turn helps to keep the flow attached to the undersurfaces of the wings. The topmost, rearmost part of the wing coincides with the same point of the end plates, which is, of course, as high and as far back as the rules allow. Notice too that the upper edge of the end plate extends forwards horizontally – this helps to prevent the high pressure air on top of the wing from spilling off, which would lead to some loss of downforce.

The complexity of the rear diffusers can also be clearly seen. The outer portions, which, as with all parts of the diffuser in Formula 1, are restricted to starting in line with the front edge of the rear wheels, are further restricted to ter-

Complex rear wing arrangement, and equally complex diffuser. (Tracey Inglis)

minating in line with the rear wheel axle line. They are thus extremely short at roughly 13in (330mm), and yet are still quite steep. Each side has a pair of intermediate vertical turning vanes to steer the flow in the desired direction. The central diffuser, which is permitted to extend as far back as the rear wing (19.7in or 500mm) behind the rear axle line, curves more gradually upwards towards the back. It is rounded in cross-section, with lips on the outer lower edges to prevent the unwanted sideways ingress of air. There are slots let into the 'roof' of the central diffuser to allow a bleed of air into this region to try to keep the flow attached, an absolutely crucial factor in the generation of underbody downforce on this type of car.

As this book is being finalised, it seems that the FIA is intent on introducing some sweeping changes to Formula 1 for the 1998 season in an attempt to slow down lap times, and possibly to increase overtaking opportunities. As well as introducing grooves into the tyres, in an effort to reduce their grip and slow down cornering speeds, the cars will also be approximately 8in (200mm) narrower overall. The reduction in width will have various knock-on effects, but aerodynamically it will mean that frontal area is reduced, which will enable top speeds to be higher, and it may also mean that less downforce, at least in the short term, can be generated, because it will be more difficult to get clean air to and from all the current downforce-inducing devices. It remains to be seen whether or not these aims will be achieved in the long run. It is certainly causing a lot of extra design and research effort at the time of writing, and, as with all major change, seems to be receiving a mixed response from teams and drivers as to whether it will produce the desired results. Time alone will tell.

Attention to detail is obviously the watchword in Formula 1, as it is in the world's other top single seater category, CART, or Indycar as it was known until 1996. As CART is a free chassis formula, and its competitor, the Indy Racing League, is, at the time of writing, a two chassis control category, we'll take a look at CART as being technically more interesting.

CART

The big difference between CART and Formula 1, aerodynamically speaking, is that CART still permits the use of underbody tunnels to generate a large proportion of the downforce. But because of the disparate nature of the events on the CART calendar, there are in reality four different configurations in which the car has to be optimised – superspeedway, short oval, road course, and street circuit – each with different aerodynamic demands. There are also quite specific rules for the different environments too, which ensure, for example, that only slim, single element rear wings which fit a box 12in by 1.5in (305mm by 38mm) in side view are run on the 200mph plus (320kmh) Superspeedways, or that two-element rear wings that fit a box 14in by 8in (356mm by 203mm), with an 8in radiused lower rear corner, must be used on road courses and short ovals. For 1997 also, a controversial rule to reduce underbody downforce in Superspeedway trim was introduced, which involved the retention of the standard underbody, but with the insertion of a triangular filler block which reduces the width of the tunnel exits. This was variously mooted as reducing downforce by anything up to 20 to 25 per cent overall.

The general configuration of a CART car has some similarities to Formula 1, but some differences too. Front wings must be mounted integrally with the nose-cone, and highly elevated noses are not permitted, so twin front wing sets are the norm, as shown in the photo of the 1996 Penske PC25 (in Superspeedway trim, on Goodwood's wet hillclimb course!). In common with Formula 1, though, the central portion of the front wings is raised slightly to give a better feed to the radiators and the underbody, and reduce the ride height sensitivity of the front wings. Front wing flaps (not used in Superspeedway trim) are asymmetric, as in Formula 1, with deeper chord at their outer extremities, which helps to mask the 'messy area' near the front tyres.

Bargeboards are not so prevalent in CART, probably because the sidepods start much further forward, and so assist the airflow to merge behind the front wheels without the need for supplementary assistance. The inlets to the tunnels on the different chassis marques employ various methods to funnel air into the tunnels themselves, whilst the inlets to the radiators are kept fairly small these days. Underneath the sidepods, the tunnel profile is dictated by regulations insofar as the maximum total cross-sectional area of the diffuser is defined (maximum diffuser dimensions being 36in wide × 6in high, or 914mm × 152mm), as is the overall length. The precise shape is for each constructor to determine from wind-tunnel testing. The tunnels are curved so as to direct the diffuser exit at the space between the rear wheels and the centrally mounted gearboxes, though tunnels are not permitted to extend beyond the rear axle line.

The upper surface of the sidepods contain radiator air exit ducts, together with variously positioned winglets – similar to those used in Formula 1 – ahead of the rear wheels. Flat 'tyre shelf' splitters ahead of the lower portion of the rear wheels tap the high pressure zone there. Winglets have come into common use now, to add a bit of their own downforce, and to tidy up the airflow around the rear tyres and to the rear wing. They are a 'bit more efficient' than the simpler 'ramps' that preceded them.

One particularly interesting facet of aerodynamic set-up that CART racecar engineers seem to pay more heed to than their counterparts in Formula 1 is running in traffic. Oval racing especially creates circumstances where cars have to be able to run nose-to-tail, overtake each other, run close to vertical concrete walls and do all of this without falling off the track. Whilst CART drivers, like Formula 1 drivers, are often heard to comment on the loss of front end downforce when running close behind another car, they seem to regard it as part of their job to optimise their car so that the effect is minimised, as far as possible, in order that they can overtake other cars. CART engineers obviously also play an important part in

The Penske PC25 car, in Superspeedway trim – not ideal for a damp hillclimb.

this process, so that the driver is able to do his job. This approach from engineers and drivers is not absent from Formula 1, but given Formula 1 cars' apparent inability to pass anything faster than a breakdown truck currently, either the problem is more severe, or else something else is wrong. Do Formula 1 drivers not possess the ability to overtake? Are they incapable of setting up a car to facilitate overtaking? Are the cars really too sensitive to running close together? Is it the circuits that are at fault? Whatever the cause of the problem, be it aerodynamic or otherwise, CART seems to offer more overtaking opportunities than Formula 1, so maybe their aerodynamic package is worth wider adoption . . . 1998 will give us the opportunity of comparing Formula 1's new 'narrow car with grooved tyres' concept with CART.

There are so many categories of open wheel competition cars that we will have to stick to looking at just a few other interesting cases here. Hopefully no-one will be offended by my omission of their particular category.

Formula 3

Constrained not only by the rules to running specified rear wing profiles, and a stepped flat underside similar to Formula 1, Formula 3 is also constrained by the limited power delivered by the restricted engines used in the formula. Although power outputs were raised from around 175bhp to somewhat over 200bhp in 1997 by increasing the engine airbox inlet diameter from 0.944 to 1.024in (24mm to 26mm), Formula 3 cars need to keep drag down, which means they cannot afford to run steep rear wings. The rules specify that a maximum of three rear wing elements, to stipulated profiles, are permitted, and this is manifested in a two-element upper tier, and single-element lower tier. The installation angle is adjustable, and it is up to each team and race engineer to establish the optimum setting for a given circuit. Front wings are

The Dallara F397.

two-element designs, with asymmetric flaps running only across the outer portions of the wing span.

One of the most successful current Formula 3 cars is the Italian Dallara marque, and it is no coincidence that the company carries out extensive wind-tunnel research in its own tunnel, capable of testing 25 per cent scale models. The Dallara features a raised nose, with front wing assembly mounted on the nosebox structure. The central portion of the wings is inclined downwards to give anhedral angle in order to feed the central underbody. The composite monocoque is narrow and sleek, and the sidepods are as low as they can be, given that the cooling radiators, which are laid down almost flat, need to have some inclination to the airflow to be effective. The upper bodywork tapers tightly around the engine and transmission bay behind the driver, whilst the engine cover is fairly low. The upper rear wing tier is attached via the end plates to the single-element cross-beam lower tier, which attaches to the gearbox end casing via

twin drop plates. The stepped floor between the wheels starts off with a small shadow plate splitter under the driver, and extends outwards beneath the sidepods, to ahead of the rear wheels to tap the high pressure there, just as Formula 1 and CART/IRL cars do. It is interesting to note that the bottom edge of the front part of the sidepods is radiused, whilst the rear part of the edge is sharp, and continues rearwards as the splitter plates ahead of the back wheels. The suggestion here is that air is being encouraged to accelerate under the front of the sidepods, and discouraged to flow laterally into the underbody region further back.

Formula 3 cars utilise fairly complex diffuser shapes, though nothing like as complex as in Formula 1. The diffuser is not permitted to start its upward incline until in line with the front of the rear wheels, and is limited in rearward extent in a similar way to Formula 1, the outer portions being restricted to the rear axle line, whilst the inner section may go back no further than 19.7in (500mm) behind the rear axle line. Vertical, curved vanes

A Formula 3 diffuser, with turning vanes.

are used to steer the airflow within the diffuser. Underbody downforce is critical to the performance of a Formula 3 car, and minor changes in ride height and rake angle radically alter the balance and overall grip level achievable by a car.

In 1995, the stepped underside was imposed on Formula 3, following the same rule change in Formula 1 and Formula 3000. Dallara reportedly discovered that, depending on the overall car configuration, between 17 per cent (on fast circuits) and 24 per cent (on slow circuits) of total downforce was lost by the adoption of the stepped floor from the previous single plane, very low ground clearance floor. However, there was a major benefit in much-reduced sensitivity to ride height and pitch changes, and the cars, though perhaps cornering a little slower, were said to be more consistent and predictable to drive. Clearly they were *very* sensitive before this rule change . . .

Formula Renault Sport

The interesting aspect of this category is that it is a true multi-chassis formula, with six different marques competing in the UK national series, and it is currently the only 'slicks and wings' single seater category on the Super Touring Car billing. The category also has national series around Europe, and the International Eurocup. As such, there is scope for the individual designers to go their own way on aerodynamics, and there is considerable variety of approach. The cars are powered by 2 litre fuel injected Renault Laguna engines, turning out around 170bhp, so once again, keeping drag down is crucial. In 1995, the year of the category's inception, the Italian manufacturer Tatuus produced an ultra-compact design, heavily influenced by the Dallara, which was to set the standard for the next two seasons. Although beaten to the 1995 title by Van Diemen, Tatuus swept to the 1996 titles in the international Eurocup and the national series in Britain, Germany, and Spain, with a chassis that underwent only minor revisions along the way.

A major contribution to the success of

The Tatuus RC97 Formula Renault Sport, a Dallara-influenced design.

the Tatuus was its very compactness. The car was some 9.5in (242mm) within the maximum permitted width, and the central chassis itself was made as narrow as possible, the dimensions effectively being defined by the mandatory fuel cell and roll hoop. The radiators were laid as flat as possible, and the low, sleek sidepods, very reminiscent of the Dallara's, helped towards a small frontal area.

The category specifies a control rear wing, which is a two-element design with the profiles dictated quite specifically. This effectively controls the total amount of downforce that can be generated by the wings because it would be pointless generating more front end downforce than was needed to achieve a balanced car. The front wing must be a single-element design, with specified maximum dimensions, and the leading and trailing edges must be continuous and parallel. This allows designers some freedom to choose what they believe will be an efficient profile, and indeed there is a range of designs across the different marques. Most cars carry the underslung single wing below a raised nose, and although this was specified by Tatuus too in 1997, most UK Tatuus runners continued with the twin front wings with anhedral centre portion set-up from the 1996 design.

The underbody is to the stepped plane design, but diffusers are not permitted, and this clearly restricts the amount of downforce that can be generated by this region. However, the relatively large flat area, when run with a slight rake angle, can create downforce if the ride height is low, and typically the centre section of the underbody will be run at ride heights of 0.39 to 0.59in (10 to 15mm) at the front, and 0.98 to 1.18in (25 to 30mm) at the rear. The stepped outer plane is, by regulation, 1.97in (50mm) higher than the centre section (the 'reference plane').

The trend set by Tatuus has now been followed by other marques, most notably Van Diemen, who in 1997 produced a superb, equally compact design, the RF 97 FRS, which at the time of writing was definitely catching the Tatuus in terms of competitiveness, and very likely to challenge for the UK championship.

Hillclimb and sprint

The so-called 'speed event' categories of hillclimbing and sprinting in the UK encompass a number of separate single seater classes, delineated according to engine capacity only. The rules pertaining to bodywork and aerodynamics are otherwise identical in each class, and, with few restrictive regulations, the category is perhaps one of the last to allow designers and innovators real freedom to try out new ideas and concepts.

The capacity splits for National Championship Hillclimbs, for example, are at 600, 1,100, 1,600 and 2,000cc, and dimensions and aerodynamic aids tend to progress logically with increasing engine capacity and available power. Ultra-compact and lightweight motor cycle-engined cars are most prevalent in the two smaller-engined classes, and downforce-inducing items consist generally of low camber, low angle of attack wings, often exploiting the maximum permitted spans of 59in (1,500mm) ahead of the front wheels, and 55in (1,400mm) behind the front wheels. There seems to be no general agreement as to whether single or two-element wings should be used, and indeed this would depend on the power a particular engine develops, the dimensions of the car, and the nature of the courses visited, as discussed earlier in this book. Some of these smaller-engined cars carry a rear diffuser panel, though – curiously perhaps, given that they are permitted – few utilise full ground effect sidepods. Although such structures would add some weight, careful materials selection and construction would keep this to a minimum, and could provide more downforce for little drag penalty. Having said that, the performance being achieved by makes such as Jedi and OMS, with limited ground effect exploitation, has severely embarrassed pilots of much more powerful cars in the bigger capacity

The Jedi is highly competitive in the small- and medium-capacity British hillclimb classes.

classes, the author included!

The 1,600 and 2,000 classes are populated by more powerful cars, and the trend is towards more radical wing profiles, with double-element wings prevailing, and triple-element rear wings on some cars in the 2,000cc division. The rear wing overhang rule, which allows a wing to extend as far back as 59in (1,500mm) behind the rear axle line, is exploited more in these classes too, as leverage on the rear wheels is sought without extra drag penalty. The rear wing can be expected to benefit from cleaner air if it is further back from the rear wheels too.

Ground effect sidepods are also more common in these middle classes, with no real inherent penalty in frontal area and drag, given that most cars need to carry a reasonable cooling matrix area to cope with the heat rejection demands of more powerful engines. As an example, the Pilbeam MP62 perhaps exemplifies the

The Pilbeam MP62 dominates the 2 litre British hillclimb division.

2,000cc hillclimb car best, with double-element wings front and rear, and twin ground effect tunnels that extend well past the rear suspension links. The cars are powered by engines typically producing near to 300bhp, which, on the majority of the courses visited, allows the wings to be set at moderately steep angles of attack.

The unlimited capacity class is dominated currently by cars fitted with ex-Formula 1 engines, some of enlarged capacity and producing prodigious amounts of horsepower. Drag thus becomes of little concern, the quest being for maximum downforce, steeply inclined, heavily cambered multi-element wings which utilise the full width and overhang being the order of the day. Rear wings tend to be at least a triple-element affair, and some cars use twin-element lower tiers as well. The need for silencers (which is not a restraint that encumbers Formula 1 cars) tends to fill a substantial part of the region below the rear wing, but although this must necessarily affect airflow adversely, it just has to be tolerated. Front wings, so far, have only been dual-element, though increased complexity is now appearing in the quest for a car

that can be balanced *and* run a substantial rear wing assembly.

Ground effect is generally, though not universally, exploited, the few extra kilos of sidepods and undertray being an insignificant penalty compared to the gain in grip and stability in the faster parts of some courses, such as the left-right wiggle over the finish at the Gurston Down course in Wiltshire, England, taken by the bravest at around 140mph (on a track little over 12ft, or 3.6m wide . . .). The ubiquitous Pilbeam MP58 and MP72 chassis utilise conventional tunnels on either side of the monocoque, whilst the Gould-Ralt, an ex-Formula 3 chassis, stays with the flat underside and rear diffuser of its progenitor.

Miscellaneous
It seems unfair to pay only lip-service to a few more categories, but to do justice to the plethora of categories around the motorsports scene would probably take several volumes, and there just isn't the space here. But it would be a foolish omission to leave out drag racing and stock-cars, and their oval racing cousins.

Drag racers, especially in the fastest classes such as Top Fuel, are incredibly

The Gould-Ralt, with its Formula 3-derived flat floor and diffuser, a Formula 1 style front wing, and a three-element rear wing.

rapid machines, built with one sole aim – to cover the standing quarter mile in the shortest time possible. With almost unbelievable power on tap, which hits the spectator as a shock wave as the driver reacts to the starting lights and launches the horizontal missile down the strip, downforce has a part to play in helping to maintain traction and stability. These devices reach 100mph (160kmh) in the blink of an eye, and around 300mph (480kmh) at the end of the quarter mile, so serious amounts of downforce can be attained for a large proportion of a run. Large three-element rear wings deployed high above and behind the rear wheels are utilised to squeeze the rear wheels onto the deck, whilst to try to prevent the astonishing power and torque from lifting the front of the vehicle, relatively small front wings are set way out, just ahead of the tiny front wheels, where their extended cantilever effect can counteract the torque-induced overturning moment.

The forces generated by the large rear wing are substantial at terminal speeds of 300mph (480kmh) – we only have to look at the size and wing profile to make a rough estimate that would indicate wing downforce in excess of 5,000lb (2,270kg) could be created. No wonder the tubular wing support structures are very substantial. Whole vehicle drag at the same speed will also be extremely large, using up a sizeable proportion of the 5,000 + bhp!

Stock-car racers are also well aware of the benefits of downforce, despite relatively limited maximum speeds on tight oval circuits. Indeed, these limited speeds mean they can virtually forget drag, and go for maximum downforce. This is generally achieved using highly inclined, large area, low aspect ratio single-element wings located directly above the driver compartment. It is highly probable that a great many of these wings are run at angles way above the critical stall angle, but nevertheless a performance benefit is clearly felt. A reasonably efficient wing built to typical stock-car dimensions ought to be capable of generating around 100lb (446 Newtons) at 50mph (80kmh), and four times that value at 100mph (160kmh), though whether such efficiency is attained on the car is perhaps debatable. Then again, if bolting the kitchen table to the roof at an inclined angle makes the car go quicker, it would be worth doing!

By contrast, the USA's 800bhp V8-powered Dirt Modifieds are specifically pro-

High terminal speeds mean large *quantities of downforce from Top Fuel dragsters.*

Stock-car wings come in one size only – extra large *and* steep! (John Colley)

Scalloped front end and wedge-shaped profile get some *downforce on this 'Dirt Modified'.* (Bob Perran)

hibited from using aerofoils, and may only use crude body-shaping to provide downforce. But again, they try their hardest to gain every scrap of downforce they can, by using scalloped front panels and wedge shaped side profiles, in a bid to be able to get the power down on the loose oval surfaces on which they race at up to 100mph (160kmh).

So that completes a somewhat brief round up of how downforce is obtained in open wheeler motorsport categories. In the next section we'll survey some closed wheel competition car categories.

Closed wheelers

Closed wheel cars are inherently less draggy machines as a rule, but in some cases are – or at least, were – capable of generating prodigious amounts of downforce, with much more efficient lift to drag ratios than can be achieved with a single seater. There are, however, very few closed wheel categories that allow an unfettered quest for downforce, and the cars that once produced the greatest lift to drag ratios – the late lamented sports prototypes like the Jaguar XJRs, the Porsche 956 to 962, and others discussed earlier in Chapter 5, which were capable of lift to drag ratios approximately twice as great as the best Formula 1 car – are a thing of the past. Nevertheless, it is interesting and instructive to look at the designs of today to see how downforce can be achieved even where regulations attempt to strangle it out of existence. Naturally, a category as broad as 'closed wheelers' includes sports and GT cars as well as passenger-based saloon/sedan vehicles.

Sports and GT

Although there is no longer a World Championship for Sports Prototypes as such, there are motorsport categories where what can be generically referred to as sports prototypes or sports/GT cars – if we take the definition to mean 'competition cars with enclosed wheels, nominally with two seats, and built specifically for

racing' – still compete. The USA's Professional Sports Car Racing category, formerly known as IMSA, is one such, and of course there is a class at the Le Mans 24 Hours specifically for sports prototypes. Other competition arenas in which sports/GT cars compete include categories in the UK such as Supersports 200, various regional GT championships such as the Castle Combe GT Championship, and hillclimbing and sprinting where the more general heading of 'sports libre' is used. The World Championship these days is for 'GT cars' nominally based on road-going vehicles, though if we are to believe press reports, it would appear that some manufacturers are creating their racing machines ahead of the road-going cars on which they are supposedly based! Whatever, with McLaren, Porsche, and Mercedes taking up the GT challenge, supported by Lotus, Panoz, Lister, and Chrysler, there is serious manufacturer involvement from around the world, and although downforce is restricted by the rules, aerodynamic trickery abounds. Consequently 'sports and GT' covers a wide range of categories and cars. Let's start by looking at a car built for the American IMSA series, as it then was, by that most famous of European manufacturers, Ferrari – the 1996 333SP.

IMSA/'Sportscar'

The 333SP, pictured here at the Goodwood Festival of Speed, is fairly typical of prototypes of today in general aerodynamic layout, the majority being open-topped, although some prototypes, notably the TWR Nissan at the 1997 Le Mans race, are closed. At the extreme front, the Ferrari has a small splitter with very low ground clearance, although note that the two portions of the splitter either side of the centre line have slightly increased ground clearance to prevent the complete blockage of airflow to the underside under extremes of pitch, thus maintaining a flow to the underbody at all times. The splitter is exploiting the high pressure region ahead of the blunt nose section and radiator inlet. The little dive plane extensions of the splitter on the sides of the nose actually mirror the profile of the underside of the splitter ahead of the front wheels, this sweeping upwards towards the wheels as mini-diffusers. The dive planes themselves, being inclined to the airflow, provide some downforce, and can also create beneficial vortex formations down the lower sides of the car which help to prevent unwanted lateral migration of air into the underbody region. The louvres atop the front wheel arches serve to allow high pressure air to leave the wheel well, and rejoin the main flow in the low pressure area above the curved wheel cover, which helps to reduce the magnitude of that particular low pressure spot to the benefit of lift reduction.

Further back, the bodywork swoops over the rear wheels, before curving back down again at the rear termination. This downward curving tail is common to all such prototype designs these days, and clearly serves to minimise the base area of the car, which in turn will lead to the smallest wake possible, with commensurate low form drag. This is a crucial aspect in long distance races, where fuel efficiency is vital to race tactics. Above the slender tail is a two-element, full-width span, high aspect ratio rear wing, of maximum chord and depth specified in the regulations, mounted on twin drop plates, which would tend to utilise only a low to medium angle of attack, again in the interests of low drag and good fuel efficiency. Under the car, the flat underbody dictated by the regulations extends from the front axle line to the rear axle line, and rear diffusers are expressly prohibited, though the floor ahead of the front axle line is free. The rake angle of the flat underbody is also free, which allows a modicum of underbody downforce to be generated. Other interesting details include the profile of the bodywork just behind the front wheels, helping lead air away from the cooling system and wheel wells. Note too the small split-

Ferrari 333SP from the 'Professional Sports Car Racing' category, formerly IMSA.

ters at the lower part of these areas, which will serve to isolate the underbody from the disturbed flow around the wheels as well as benefit from any pressure differential that exists above and below it. There have been a number of detail changes to the 333SPs that have competed since chassis 01 – illustrated here – was built, including a splitter which does not have the raised centre portion along its leading edge. However, the overall layout remains similar.

FIA GT

In the FIA's GT category, which forms the current World Championship, rule restrictions cap downforce, but, as in nearly all other competition categories, not the efforts of the designers to achieve the most downforce they can for the least drag. The three major makes contending this championship – the McLaren BMW F1 GTR, the Porsche 911 GT1, and the Mercedes CLK GTR – are all, superficially at least, remarkably similar in shape, though with detail differences. The

McLaren has been around the longest, and the 1997 car was the third evolution of the basic design. It has to be said, though, that the new long tail shape which McLaren brought in for the 1997 season was a response to the Porsche 911 GTR debuted at Brands Hatch, England, in September 1996. The Porsche raised the aerodynamics stakes with its extended rear end, and consequently much larger diffuser area and increased cantilevers, and the McLaren design, rather stumpy by comparison, just had to follow suit. Meanwhile, Mercedes put together their first GT package since the demise of the Sauber-engineered prototype cars of a few years ago, and it too bore the long tail shape pioneered in this category by Porsche.

The McLaren front end is now longer and shallower than the original design, to balance the additional rear downforce, but still sports a superficially simple splitter arrangement running right around the front. However, beneath lurks a complex front diffuser arrangement, with inter-

The Porsche 911 GTR upped the aerodynamic stakes in GT racing.

changeable panels for adjustment purposes. Dive planes extend upwards along the sides of the nose section, and these come in a range of sizes for fine tuning. Front wheel arch louvres help by letting high pressure air that builds up in the arch escape, and also by spoiling the high speed, lift inducing flow over the top of the arch. They also aid cooling since some cooling air is exhausted into the wheel arch. The shallow angle from the leading edge of the nose up to the roof, and the gentle downward curve from the roof down to the tail, ensures a low drag coefficient from the basic vehicle shape, overall C_D ranging from 0.50 to 0.60, depending on downforce set-up. The extended tail now sweeps upward in the form of a rear spoiler, which will help to create raised pressure over the rear deck, whilst this 'spoiler' juts out slightly beyond the sides to form inclined strakes, an addition shown to create additional downforce. Above the tail, at a separation approximating to the chord dimension, is the regulation single-element rear wing. A selection of wing profiles is available. Beneath the car, the regulation flat underside may be supplemented with a rear diffuser, and this freedom is exploited on the McLaren, as on the other cars in the category. The 1997 McLaren F1 GTR could generate anything up to 2,200lb (1,000kg) of downforce at 200mph (320kmh), and, with drag only increasing slightly, this gave an L/D increase of about 60 per cent compared to the 1996 car.

The Porsche layout is very similar to the McLaren's, the only obvious difference being the steeper windscreen angle carried over from the road-going 911 family progenitor of this latest model. This might be anticipated to create a little more form drag than the shallower fronted McLaren, but if there is a difference, it doesn't seem to show on the track.

The Mercedes, however, does have at least one significant visual difference, and that is the shape of the front airdam/splitter arrangement. In common with the Mercedes-built Class 1 International Touring Car which preceded the CLK GTR, the centre of the airdam is actually shaped into a venturi inlet, with a raised, radiused lower lip quite clearly shaped to accelerate the airflow under the leading edge of the airdam. The outer parts of the airdam are formed as a fairly conventional, if small, splitter. The Mercedes would appear to channel a much greater mass of air into its underbody using this device. In all other outward appearances,

In its third aerodynamic evolution the McLaren F1 GTR rose to the Porsche challenge in 1997.

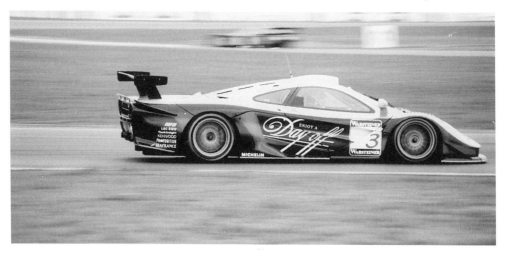

The Mercedes CLK GTR combines lessons learned in International Touring Cars and Group C sports prototypes.

though, the Mercedes seems to follow the general outline of the other two makes.

An interesting aside here is the strategy used by McLaren Cars Motorsport to derive a set-up for the unique Le Mans 24 Hour Endurance race. Basically they make an evaluation of the likely lap time that will be required to be competitive. This is then run through a PC-based lap time simulation program to produce a downforce requirement. This level of downforce is then set up on the wind-tunnel model, and reiterative testing is carried out to knock down the drag as much as possible at this level of down-force. This then yields the best attainable efficiency within the development time available, and produces the most efficient aerodynamic set-up the team can obtain, which the cars are subsequently fitted with. The strategy seems to have served them rather well since 1995 (when they won the event outright at their first attempt).

Supersports 200

Previously known as the Clubmans formula, Supersports 200 is no longer the exclusive preserve of front-engined, rear-drive, two seater sports racers. Mid-engined cars are now permitted too, and

though the front-engined cars are still eligible, it seems likely that the intrinsically better mid-engined layout is likely to take the category over completely in the not too distant future. As it is, in 1997 the mid-engined Mallock, Nemesis, Slique, and Phantom marques account for over half the grid.

Powered now by 200bhp (hence the '200' tag) Vauxhall engines, these sophisticated 'club' sports racers demonstrate some fascinating aerodynamic thinking, and one of the most interesting is the Nemesis RME 97. In overall peripheral shape, the Nemesis looks pretty much like a slightly scaled-down sports proto-type, but peer a little closer and you realise that this car is very sophisticated, packed with a plethora of aerodynamic details. Amazingly, however, it has not yet seen the inside of a wind-tunnel, in spite of its very advanced appearance, and it speaks volumes for the 'have a go' ingenuity of the team that designed and constructed it.

Starting at the front, the lower leading edge of the body is, in essence, a conventional front splitter, but with a raised central section. But what is not immediately obvious is what is behind the front splitter, beneath the front section cover.

The Nemesis RME97 is packed with clever aerodynamic details.

The lower part of the chassis in the centre between the front wheels has a further, low mounted splitter plate, and the shrouding above this splitter has been shaped to scoop the air which enters through the central front duct at an angle sideways, and out behind the front wheels. The thinking here was to make this section function like the under-cockpit splitter of a raised nose Formula 1 car. The team has tried running with a conventional low splitter at the front, which effectively blocks off the flow to this particular area, but this resulted in understeer at speed, indicating that the raised splitter feeding the secondary 'divider', as perhaps we'll refer to it, gave more front end downforce.

The body top curves gradually towards the cockpit surround, which is slightly higher than other cars in the category. Behind and above the driver's head is an airbox feed to the engine, and the airbox cover serves as a nicely curved fairing to tidy up the airflow behind the driver/cockpit region. The rear bodywork curves up and over the back wheels, then downwards again, as on sports prototypes, to minimise the base area of the car and keep form drag down. The rear wing is a widened Formula 3 two-tier affair, with a high aspect ratio, small chord, two-element upper tier, and single-element lower tier, beautifully crafted in carbon composite. The upper tier is attached to the lower tier by carbon composite end plates, and the lower tier is mounted via twin drop plates onto the gearbox end casing. The rear bodywork feeds air directly to the lower wing element, which itself is reasonably close to the underbody diffuser exits. The low pressure created beneath the lower wing tier will thus provide a lot of the driving force to keep the flow in the diffuser fast and attached, which in turn keeps the pressure in the underbody low.

The rules governing underbodies in this category require a flat bottom from the rear of the front wheels to the front of the rear wheels over the minimum chassis width of 32in (812.8mm), which means that the central part of the diffuser cannot start its upsweep until in a line with the rear wheel vertical front tangent. However, it would be permitted to start the outer portions of a diffuser ahead of this line as long as they were outside the 32in minimum chassis width.

Formula 750

The 750 Motor Club-run category tends to be a kind of traditional 'nursery' for budding innovators and designers, and is a rich source of interesting, often novel, and occasionally quirky ideas. But the fact that innovation and imagination is not only permitted, but positively nurtured – albeit within a framework of rules – is to the ultimate benefit of motorsport, a number of whose past and current top designers have cut their teeth in one of these excellent club categories, including Colin Chapman, Arthur Mallock, and Gordon Murray.

Formula 750 cars are low on engine power, yet it is interesting that there is no single line of thought as to what is the requisite aerodynamic route to follow, and the examples pictured here demonstrate some of the alternative solutions. The Jenniccar Mk 1, pictured in Chapter 3, combines a full-width nose-cone with short splitter and front-mounted radiator, with a single-element, low camber rear wing. The front wheels are shrouded with the so-called 'cycle' type mudguards. The Darvi Mk 5 (car 42a) takes 'the other' front end approach, with a narrow nose supporting a pair of single-element, shallow angle wings. The radiators are thus mounted in the side-pods, which by virtue of extending from just behind the front wheels to just in front of the rear wheels will also help to keep drag down by minimising the wake of the front wheels.

The Marrow takes an altogether different approach, and is clearly aimed at achieving the lowest drag coefficient possible. The all enveloping body covers the wheels almost completely, and indeed the rear wheels are shrouded by side covers too. The front sports the smallest of splitters on the lower leading edge of the body, which is balanced by small rear spoilers attached to the outer sponsons of the body. The radiator inlet is located in the nose. The cockpit is shrouded by a neat perspex half-bubble, and the compact dimensions of this car must make it one of the least draggy in the formula. It will create some downforce, by virtually sealing off the underside to all but the low pressure wake, and from the small splitter and spoilers, but in all likelihood the two 'winged' cars will generate more downforce, but with more intrinsic form and induced drag.

There are cars in the category now which take a hybrid approach, such as the highly competitive Darvi 877, which has a fully enveloping body and a con-

The Darvi Mk 5 uses the narrow nose with front wings approach.

The Marrow goes for the all-enveloped look.

ventional rear wing – proving, perhaps, that a compromise is always best.

Hillclimb and sprint

These categories cater for pretty well all types of competition car so they're going to keep cropping up in these case studies! There are basically two sports racing categories in hillclimbing and sprinting, namely Supersports and Sports Libre. The former reflects the change made in its circuit racing equivalent, and used to be known as Clubmans Cars, where Mallock U2s of various marks compete against occasional others such as Visions and Phantoms. Thus far the mid-engined revolution has not asserted itself on the hills or in sprints, and the front-engined cars remain not only eligible but prevalent. Sports Libre caters for two seater racecars that do not fit into Supersports, and is split into varying capacity classes. Thus, as might be expected, aerodynamic appendages tend to vary according to available horsepower.

There are differences between the downforce-inducing attachments of hillclimbing Supersports cars compared with their circuit racing front-engined brethren. Take the cars illustrated in the photos, for example – a hillclimbing Mallock Mk 21/24 (car 238) and a circuit racing

Mallock Mk 28 (car 39). The hillclimber has a totally different nose section, with an altogether steeper incidence angle, and this reflects the lower speed regime in which the car operates, where this type of nose will create more downforce than the sleeker, later model used on the circuits. However, there is a further contrast of note – the hillclimber has no front radiator inlet, whereas the circuit car utilises a front radiator inlet in the nose-cone. In this case, the hillclimber's radiator is actually located across the back of the car, open to the wake, and with a NACA duct in the body top feeding it. The short duration of hillclimb runs (typically 30 to 50 seconds) enables adequate cooling from this system without risk of overheating, whereas the circuit car would possibly overheat with a somewhat restricted feed of cooling air to the radiator. So, whilst the hillclimber's nose might be thought to create more drag than the circuit car's, this may not be the case, and the hillclimber may well have a better lift to drag ratio. They utilise rear wings of the same single-element, high aspect ratio type – both running at relatively shallow angles of incidence – and other details are very similar.

The smaller capacity Sports Libre class has become the domain of larger motor

A hillclimbing Mallock Mk 21/24 compared with . . . a circuit racing Mallock Mk 28.

cycle-engined cars such as the OMS. The aerodynamic layout follows sports proto-type thinking, the all-enveloping body-work tapering down at the tail to reduce drag, with a full width rear wing, and an underbody diffuser, which here has two outer extensions as well as a pair of inter-mediate vertical vanes in the main dif-fuser. Further forward, louvres above the front wheels can be seen, and the car is balanced aerodynamically with a small front splitter.

Further up the Sports Libre range in engine capacity and power output is the Pilbeam MP43 – the one pictured is pro-pelled by a four cylinder 2.8 litre Hart 428R. The body is a particularly low line shape on this car, but follows general sports prototype profiles again. Interestingly, though, despite the engine's respectable output, and the car's generally low drag shape, it seems to carry very modest downforce-creating components. The body above the adjustable front splitter is far from being a blunt shape, which means there will only be a small stagnation zone here. This will be good for keeping drag

The OMS small capacity Sports Libre hillclimber bristles with interesting features.

down, but the splitter will not have much in the way of high pressure over its top surface. Equally, the rear wing, though full width and of high aspect ratio, is a low camber, shallow angle of incidence device. Thus the conclusion is that this car will not be creating large amounts of downforce. Pilbeams have always been

This Pilbeam MP43 seems to do best in low downforce trim.

renowned for having high mechanical grip, and this particular car is highly competitive in its class. But would it be quicker still with more downforce? Apparently not. The car is softly sprung, and having been tried with much stiffer suspension, it sets its best times with soft set-up. This effectively precludes running high downforce, and even as it is the wing has to be trimmed back, its Gurney removed, and the splitter shunted back to its shortest setting for faster tracks to prevent the car bottoming. So this is an object lesson in 'more is not necessarily better'. The car is fast in a straight line, however, often getting quicker speed trap figures than considerably more powerful single seaters. However, one still cannot help but wonder whether, if its chassis could be made to work with stiff springs, it might not go quicker with greater downforce . . .

Passenger-car based competition vehicles

Notwithstanding the vast array of vehicles in the previous two categories, this group of vehicles probably covers more motorsport competition environments than any other, encompassing circuits, ovals, hills, sprints, short ovals, dirt ovals, drag strips, and special stages. It also covers cars that would have once been capable of carrying anywhere between two and five people, and includes sports cars and coupés as well as family cars – in other words, just about anything that was produced originally with conventional transport in mind, and which has been used as the basis for a competition car. Once again we'll just dip into a few example classes to see what goes on.

NASCAR

It has been said in the past that the NASCAR Winston Cup is the most successful racing series in the world, though ironically in the first half of 1997 one man has won the majority of the races, something of an uncommon occurrence in this tightly regulated category. It is, indis-

putably, the category with the biggest following in the United States, and this has to be in large part because it guarantees good, unpredictable racing – usually. And yet Winston Cup cars are fundamentally technically very simple, which the regulatory body 'fiddles with' on a frequent and on-going basis in an effort to keep things equal between the Ford Thunderbirds, the Chevrolet Monte Carlos, and the Pontiac Grand Prix. Perhaps the phrase 'fiddles with' could be misconstrued – the technical people in charge of the series impose small changes to things like spoiler heights and airdam ground clearances to try to make the cars as evenly matched in performance as they can, and to prevent any unwanted escalation of lap speeds. Of course, this comes in for serious criticism from teams who are adversely affected by a change, and glowing praise from those that gain benefit! Winston Cup cars run at very high speeds on some of the tracks they visit, and yet the only devices they are allowed to use to counteract lift are front airdams and rear spoilers. Splitters are not permitted, nor are smooth or profiled underbodies. Furthermore, the cars have to be able to run in traffic, in *very* close company, with vertical concrete walls on the outside, at speeds up to 200mph.

The simple shape front airdams have specified ground clearances for each make of car, 'normalised' to the Chevrolet, which means the others are adjusted to try to match performance to the baseline, which in this case is the Chevy. For example, in mid-1997 the Ford Thunderbird had to have a 4in (101.6mm) airdam ground clearance for all except the Superspeedways at Talledega and Daytona, where all cars had to use 3.5in (88.9mm) clearance. Chevrolet were allowed 3.75in (95.3mm) clearance, and Pontiac 3.5in. These are minimums, so if a team felt inclined it could raise the airdam clearance. Smooth underside panels are not permitted behind the airdam, just a 1in (25.4mm) return, which isn't of *any* value in generating downforce, it seems.

As for rear spoilers, there is a minimum angle specified of 45° for the Superspeedways, and teams can run them steeper than this if they wish, whilst at all other tracks the rear spoiler angle is free. Drag peaks at a spoiler angle of around 67 to 68°, so the teams can take a view on the level of aerodynamic efficiency required, and run the things just as steep as they dare, usually in the 60 to 70° range. The height of the spoiler is controlled and is measured using templates, with tight minimum and maximum limits. Each car make has a different specified spoiler height, which in mid-1997 were 5.75in (146mm) for the Ford, 6in (152.4mm) for the Chevy and 6.5in (165.1mm) for the Pontiac, and these are also changed as required by NASCAR to equalise performance. The exception to this is that all cars have to run a 6.5in spoiler at the Superspeedways.

Other aspects of the aerodynamics are also tightly controlled, including roof height, rear deck height, and the floor-pan, which is the same on all cars and is based on a 1960s Ford Thunderbird pan! The regulations are kept tight in order

not just to try to keep performance level throughout the field, but also to keep tabs on safety. So downforce figures, whilst not huge, are sufficient for reasonable stability. At 200mph (320kmh) figures quoted by Penske Racing South, who run the Miller car of Rusty Wallace, are 950lb (432kg) in 'high downforce' configuration, giving a drag coefficient of around 0.400, whilst in Superspeedway trim around 520lb (236kg) would be representative, at a c_D of 0.320, as measured in a full-scale fixed ground wind-tunnel. It is interesting to note that routine wind-tunnel testing of these cars is done over a yaw range of 3° nose left to 1° nose right, which is the range considered to be seen on high banked tracks. The effect of yaw on performance is critical, and teams strive for a consistent balance across this yaw range to give the car stability, and the driver the confidence he needs to run at high speed.

These figures should be considered relative to the car's considerable weight of 3,500lb (1,591kg). It is also worth noting that the engines put out around 740bhp in 'normal' configuration, whilst at the Superspeedways, controversial car-

NASCAR controls the Winston Cup rules very closely.

burettor restrictors keep horsepower down around the 430bhp mark. This helps to explain why a lower drag coefficient is especially important for Talledega and Daytona. As part of the low drag package for the 'restrictor races', the 'fender width' – or width across the front wings – ahead of the front wheels is reduced, whilst for tracks requiring high downforce it is increased. For the one lap qualifying runs, it is customary to tape over the radiator and brake cooling ducts to reduce drag, and also to gain some front end downforce. The safety measures taken by NASCAR to try to prevent cars flipping over when they get out of shape at high speed were discussed in Chapter 3.

So NASCAR controls its rules, especially those relating to the production of downforce and drag, in a different way to just about every other racing category in the world, and it certainly provides close, exciting action. Is there a lesson here for other regulatory bodies?

Touring cars
Up until the end of 1996, what started as the German Class 1 Touring Car Championship, and subsequently became the FIA-controlled International Touring Car (ITC) championship, produced some of the most sophisticated touring cars ever seen. Ultimately it may have been that the cars' very sophistication, and associated high costs, contributed to the demise of the category at the end of 1996. But although no longer current, these spectacular cars are still fresh in the memory, and deserve to be looked at, especially as they carried some interesting aerodynamic features.

In the last year of the ITC, three manufacturers were involved: Alfa Romeo, Mercedes, and Opel. Each produced very distinctive cars, with their own particular downforce-inducing and drag-reducing ideas. Taking the Mercedes first, at the front end this car featured a venturi inlet, clearly aimed at accelerating airflow under the front lip of the car (see Chapter 5). The rules allowed short profiled 'underwings' as far back as the front of the front tyres. They also allowed flat undersides (panelling of the underside was permitted) to be run with a suitable rake angle, and rear diffusers. Thus, although there were claims from one of

The Alfa front end allowed control of cooling air.

the manufacturers in the category that only a very small percentage of total downforce could be created by the underbody of a Class 1 Touring Car, there was obviously considerable scope to make the whole underbody actively contribute to downforce production. Clearly, Mercedes, along with the others, were attempting just this. Outlets visible at the sides of the 'airdam', ahead of the front wheels, are the cooling air exhausts from the forward-mounted cooling matrices. Popular on touring cars because they allow more efficient extraction of cooling air than just letting the air find its own way out, it is said that these side vents do, however, create a large and rapid change in flow direction, and an effective increase in frontal area.

The Alfa had a rather more conventional front end, in touring car terms, with a low mounted splitter. But notice that the underside of the splitter is generously radiused, so that air that was going to pass beneath it would do so accelerating smoothly so as to aid pressure reduction underneath the front lip of the car. Above the splitter, notice the vertical vanes to control the flow of air to the cooling matrices, and notice too the cool-

ing outlets ahead of the front wheels, also complete with vertical and horizontal 'shutters'. These vanes could be moved to keep control of engine cooling, but clearly would also affect aerodynamic efficiency.

The Opel had a front end which was half-way between the Mercedes and the Alfa, with a radiused splitter which had a slightly raised centre portion. Earlier Opels with flat splitters had apparently been very pitch sensitive, to the extent that as the splitter dipped onto the ground under forward pitch and blocked off the flow beneath, significant front end downforce was lost. The raised centre section overcame this problem. Rotatable vertical shutters can also be seen in the Opel's radiator inlet orifice. The outer ends of the splitter turn upwards onto the wheel arch extensions to divert airflow upwards and outwards.

All the cars exploited the rules that allowed 3.94in (100mm) wide sill extensions to be fitted to the lower edges of the body between the wheels. With the main part of the floorpan being required to remain at the same height as the original passenger car, these sill extensions obviously formed a kind of skirt that

And the Opel was different again.

helped prevent the unwanted sideways flow of air into the underbody region. At the rear, wings were allowed to be two-element devices that, in side view, would fit a 7.87 × 7.87in (200 × 200mm) rectangle, whilst diffusers were restricted in length by the flat underside regulation, and to a maximum height level with the wheel centres. Each manufacturer had clearly gone to considerable lengths to improve the flow in their diffusers with the aid of vertical vanes.

Reported values of downforce for ITC cars were not especially high, being in the region of 195 to 390lb (89 to 177kg), which for a category with a minimum weight of 2,288lb (1,040kg) represents between 8.5 and 17 per cent of the cars' weight.

Super Touring cars

The rule-makers and the manufacturers of what used to be known as Class 2 Touring Cars, but which are now known pretty much the world over as Super Touring cars, are (in mid-1997) having a hard time balancing the arguments for and against the use of downforce in the category. Though restricted to airdams, splitters, and small single-element rear wings to produce downforce – supplemented with a few tricks here and there but with little extra being achievable from the underside – there is nevertheless a lobby watching from the sidelines which firmly believes that downforce has ruined the racing in the formula. There is another body of people, which includes some of those much more intimately involved, which thinks that downforce has not made that much difference to the racing because, relatively speaking, so little downforce is generated, but that it *has* evened out the cars' performance. The reality is probably that the quality of racing – that is, the relative lack of overtaking – may well owe more to grippy tyres and drivers who appear unwilling to allow others past without a barging match. But whatever the truth here, the fact is that Super Tourers are currently

allowed to generate some downforce, although reports on the attempts at drawing up new rules for 1998 would indicate that it may be cut back somewhat in the future. It would seem doubtful that there will be an instant improvement in the amount of overtaking.

Currently, the front airdam/splitter assembly may not protrude beyond the plan periphery of the vehicle, so it cannot stick out beyond the forward-most part of the front bumper. Further, it may not reach any closer to the ground than 1.77in (45mm) when measured statically. Underneath, it is permitted to panel the underside of the airdam/splitter as far back as the front wheel centre line, though behind that the underside of the original car's floor may not be altered. However, there is scope to make fuel tanks and exhausts that smooth out the underside to some extent. At the rear, and above deck, the single-element wing must fit, in side view, a rectangle 5.9 × 5.9in (150 × 150mm), and not extend rearwards beyond the plan periphery, nor beyond the sides when viewed from the front. Restrictions are therefore fairly tight. However, there is scope for much attention to detail, and most teams now conduct a fair amount of model wind-tunnel testing each winter, prior to homologating their aerodynamic packages for the next season. Adjustment to the aerodynamic devices are not permitted at all, so once a package is homologated, a team has to stick with it for the season – getting the off-season R&D work right is consequently imperative.

Rather like the medium-sized family cars that Super Tourers are based upon, the general shape and form of the front airdam and splitter arrangements have tended to look similar during 1997. There has been a general trend towards the raised centre section along the splitter, though in detail each design is quite different. Perhaps the most elegant is the Peugeot, but in each case it would appear that the aim is to accelerate the air beneath the front part of the splitter,

The Honda Accord Super Touring car.

whilst tapping the high pressure stagnation zone in front of the blunt front of the cars with the upper face of the splitter. There is also a degree of sameness about the side vents in the airdams, which exhaust a proportion of the cooling air down the vehicles' sides, in a way that is likely to generate beneficial vorticity. What is not evident from the pictures here is that some cars have mini-diffusers ahead of the front wheels, where the splitter extends rearwards and sweeps upwards slightly towards the wheel axle line.

Rear wings vary in shape and profile too. Most are not like simple aerofoils in shape at all, and appear to have features that, at first glance, do not look very efficient, such as the vertical step part-way back on the underside of the Renault Laguna's rear wing. Similarly, the rather extreme Gurney on the Vauxhall Vectra rear wing seems, when compared to the wing chord, to fly in the face of accepted wing practice with respect to Gurney height as a *small* percentage of wing chord. But these wings are not operating in a particularly good environment, given

that they are shrouded by the passenger cabin and are severely restricted in size. Clearly, one of the benefits of being able to conduct a wind-tunnel test programme is that radical ideas can be tried out, and if they produce an efficient gain – that is, some downforce for not much extra drag – then they can be adopted. Without the benefit of that ability to try things out, the chances are that much less radical-looking solutions would appear.

Earlier in this book, estimates of Super Touring car downforce quoted from 1996 indicated that between 120 and 130lb (55 to 59kg) was typically being generated at 100mph (160kmh). Progress was apparently made prior to the 1997 season, with suggestions that perhaps 20 per cent more downforce had been found for the same drag, which would mean a figure of 145 to 155lb (66 to 70kg) was being generated. This is around 7 per cent of a front wheel drive Super Tourer's 975kg minimum weight, so downforce is still relatively modest. These downforce figures would rise by 2.25 times at 150mph (240kmh). Crucial to performance, however, is downforce efficiency, so keeping drag down for a given level of downforce is vital, perhaps even more so than absolute downforce itself.

Rally cars

In recent years, World and National Championship rally cars have been governed by Group A regulations that required the aerodynamics to remain the same as on production vehicles. So if a car had a rear spoiler, or whatever, then it could be retained for rallying, but it could not be altered or improved. The only changes permitted were the fitting of engine and transmission guards underneath the relevant components, which at least had the secondary benefit of smoothing out of the underside. The most important aspect of the aerodynamics of a rally car, though, were – and in reality still are – to ensure that adequate cooling air gets to the various systems that require it. But recent changes to the rules have seen the introduction of 'Kit Cars' to Formula 2's 2 litre, two-wheel drive division, and latterly the 'World Rally Car' variation on the turbocharged,

four-wheel drive theme. Both of these new categories have effectively allowed a bit more freedom to play with aerodynamics to produce some actual downforce – or at least, to reduce some of the natural lift that occurs at speed on most production cars. Aerodynamic devices are restricted to remain within tight dimensional restraints, and their location is strictly controlled as well. But new components may now be homologated each year, so it is likely that we will see year on year developments in this area.

In the Kit Car category, the most discernible difference compared to the basic Formula 2 predecessors is that a rear aerofoil is permitted, which is able to generate some downforce despite the small size limits imposed. British Rally Championship front runner VW evaluated their first kit car rear wing in their windtunnel in Wolfsburg, Germany, prior to homologation, and the drivers reported that the cars were more stable at high speed. Similarly in the World Rally Car (WRCar) category, the freedom to homologate a specific design of aerody-

The VW Golf Formula 2 rally 'Kit Car' rear wing.

namic package encouraged manufacturers to spend time in wind-tunnels. Ford reported that even though the rules prohibited rear wings of the size of the rear spoiler on the road-going Escort Cosworth, the design evolved produced more downforce for less drag than the previous 'whale tail' device. Subaru also reported that their WRCar actually generated downforce, as opposed to positive lift on the earlier Group A model, and this produced a car which retained the same balance at high speed as at low speed. The earlier car had been prone to high speed oversteer, so was obviously generating lift at the rear.

Front spoilers are, in effect, practically restricted by the relatively soft, long travel suspension used on rally cars, especially for gravel stages, and by the rough terrain that they compete on. Clearly a really low ground clearance front airdam would be quickly destroyed. Nevertheless, effort has obviously gone into shaping the front ends of the WRCars, not just to ensure adequate cooling, but to maintain an aerodynamic balance at speed.

Hillclimb and sprint

Once again the speed event categories crop up! It is, of course, a total coincidence that the author has spent the last 19 or 20 years in and around this particular sporting arena . . . The speed events cater for passenger cars with a range of engine capacities in the so-called Modified Production classes. The previously discussed Sports Libre division also caters for certain 'passenger-car based' vehicles which are deemed to be modified too much to be classed as Modified Production cars, but because of their production roots, we are going to look at them here.

The ubiquitous Lotus/Caterham/Westfield 7 derivatives are amongst the most prevalent and competitive cars in these classes, although there are some

This fearsome Westfield 7 is adorned with aerodynamic addenda!

exceptional alternatives successfully competing too. But one of the most radical-looking of the Westfield brigade is the fearsome 5.3 litre V8-engined variant shown here. Looking more like a Mallock Supersports than its Lotus 7 progenitor, this Westfield has obviously had some serious effort put into obtaining downforce. At the front, the nose is very reminiscent of the front of the Mallock discussed in the closed wheeled sports/GT section, with the radiator orifice left unencumbered, but the full-width spoiler-cum-splitter diverting air up and over the wheels and onto the cycle type mudguards, probably to the benefit of drag and downforce. Notice the circular inlets to feed air to the front brakes. The mid section of the car remains much as the original, though the tonneau cover has been left over the passenger space, a move that would tend to reduce drag a little. At the rear, a spoiler runs across the

full width of the car, and has what is effectively a vertical Gurney on its trailing edge. The underside has certainly not been ignored, with an upswept diffuser with side panels and three intermediate vertical vanes to control the airflow in this region.

At the more modest end of the budgetary scale is the 1.4 Rover Metro shown here. However, this is a particularly fascinating car because it is owned by Graham Kendall, the engineer who runs the MIRA full-scale wind-tunnel, who shares the car with daughter Claire. Not surprisingly, the car has been in the wind-tunnel. Various downforce-inducing features are fitted, including the front airdam/splitter, those longitudinal fences along the bonnet, lowered side skirts, and a small rear spoiler on top of the tail gate. The cooling inlet area has also been reduced. The modifications took the car from having positive lift front and rear to

MIRA wind-tunnel Project Engineer Graham (and daughter Claire) Kendall's Modified Production Metro. (Claire Kendall)

one with some genuine downforce at the front and virtually zero lift at the rear. The Metro was tested at stages, first with just the front airdam/splitter, and then with all the other features fitted. The pre-modification data were not measured.

At the first stage, with just the front airdam/splitter, the car gave the following coefficients:

$C_D = 0.364$
$C_{Lf} = -0.037$ $C_{Lr} = 0.138$

After the fences, skirts, rear spoiler, and cooling area reduction had been added, the figures were:

$C_D = 0.384$
$C_{Lf} = -0.099$ $C_{Lr} = 0.020$

The effect of the fences was tested independently too, moving the C_{Lf} from −0.072 to −0.099, and the C_{Lr} from 0.035 to 0.020.

These figures illustrate a number of interesting points. First, within the constraints of the rules – which effectively prohibit much in the way of a rear spoiler on this type of modified production car – it is harder to get as big a reduction in lift at the rear as it is at the front. Nevertheless, quite significant changes have been made to the lift coefficients front and rear with only a slight increase in drag, and the car is more stable at higher speeds now. The front end is obviously producing actual downforce. Another particularly interesting point is the benefit that accrued from the bonnet fences, with improvements in both front and rear lift coefficients, whilst a very small improvement in drag was recorded too. To try to explain where these benefits came from, one has to assume that, at the front, preventing air from spilling off the bonnet sides has increased the flow over the high pressure separation area at the rear of the bonnet, and that this may have enlarged the width of the separated flow region, so increasing the pressure on the bonnet rear. And at the back, it

may be that the rear spoiler gets a better feed of air too, as more air is being forced over the roof line, and that this has had a similar effect to the bonnet region, with a larger high pressure separation bubble ahead of the spoiler on the rear of the roof. As for the very slight drag reduction that also occurred with the fences, perhaps the reduced spillage off the sides lessened the formation of drag creating vortices down the sides of the car. The results obtained with the fences are another example of how it is virtually impossible to generalise about aerodynamics – if these fences were to be fitted to a more curvaceous medium size family car, such as the ones that form the basis of Super Tourers, the possibility exists that positive lift would increase as more air was accelerated over the roof!

Lastly in this category, we have to stop and admire this Audi Quattro, a replica of the cars built to tackle the Pikes Peak Hillclimb in Colorado, USA. Because of the extent to which this car does *not* look like a production Audi, it has to run in the Sports Libre category, but it clearly *is* based just as much on a passenger car as any Super Tourer or Winston Cup car. It just has a lot of aerodynamic bits stuck on it – everywhere! It also has 600+ flame belching turbocharged brake horse-power, and four-wheel drive, and it is a truly spectacular car! At the front, the Quattro sports a large front airdam/splitter protruding well in front of the main body, and leading up from the outer ends of this, onto the tops of the extended wheel arches, are fences – once again. Running boards between the front and rear wheel arches will tend to tidy up the flow somewhat between the rather bluff arch extensions. And then at the rear there is a twin-tier aerofoil arrangement, each tier comprising a triple-element wing. With the kind of horsepower available, and the speeds likely to be seen in the British hillclimbs in which the car now competes, drag is just not an issue. But downforce is.

Just as this book was nearing comple-

Tom Hammonds' Pikes Peak Hillclimb replica Audi Quattro on the rather less daunting Gurston Down Hillclimb, Wiltshire, England.

The Audi's rear wing certainly does what it's supposed to! (MIRA)

tion, owner Tom Hammonds put the Quattro in MIRA's full-scale wind-tunnel, and some of the results of a fascinating set of tests were released for publication. In the configuration in which the car was first put in the tunnel, the rear wings and overhang were creating over 400lb (180kg) of downforce at the rear wheels, whilst in spite of the considerable front spoiler size, a small amount of positive lift was being felt at the front wheels. Clearly the airdam would have been creating some lift reduction, but the effect of the rear wing, together with its cantilever action, was causing a rearward bias to the centre of pressure. So a series of experiments was performed, which culminated in adding a 2.36in (60mm) deep extension to the bottom edge of the airdam along its front and around its sides, combined with a small decrease in the inclination of the rear flaps. This basically shifted about 200lb (91kg) of downforce from the back to the front axle, giving an approximately equal split of downforce front and rear. The car has a forward-biased weight distribution, so although not perfect, this downforce distribution should have provided a better balance at

speed. Plenty of 'paddock advisers' had been sceptical of the benefits of this car's aerodynamic appendages, it seems, but Tom Hammonds reported that the result of this shift of downforce was to make the car feel significantly better balanced. And far from adding to the car's drag coefficient (0.56), the new airdam extension actually reduced it somewhat, 3bhp less being absorbed at 100mph – enough, the Audi's owner affirmed, to cut the lawn with!

Hot Rods

The closed wheel cousin of the stock-car which pounds the short ovals of the UK is known as the National Hot Rod. These are generally based on one or other of the small hatchbacks like the Peugeot 205, Renault Clio, or Ford Fiesta, and with speeds within the tight confines of a stadium oval reaching 75 to 80mph (120 to 130kmh) on the straights, there is scope for some downforce to be attained. There is, however, one fundamental aerodynamic difference between a Hot Rod and pretty much any other competition car based on a passenger vehicle, which is that Hot Rods race without any

Removing the rear wing from a Hot Rod causes big problems. (Cars & Car Conversions)

window glass. This makes them more akin to open top sports/GT cars in a sense, and frontal areas will obviously be effectively reduced in comparison with the road-going originals. The flow over the vehicle is going to be totally different to the car with windows, and in all likelihood there will be reduced lift from the basic body. But downforce-creating additions are also permitted, and consist of the airdam/splitter set-up at the front, with minimum ground clearance defined by a rule that says no part of the body may touch the ground when all the tyres are deflated, and single-element wings with Gurneys and end plates, or swept up spoilers mounted at the top of where the tail gate would have been at the rear, no part of which may extend more than 6in (152.4mm) above the roof.

Cornering speeds are obviously considerably less than the maximum speeds feasible on straights, and whilst there might have been a feeling that downforce was not particularly significant, the driver of a car similar to the one pictured here reported that in a back-to-back test, removing the rear wing caused serious rear brake locking problems. To state the obvious, braking starts at the highest speed attained, and ends at corner entry speed. The experience of rear brakes locking up illustrates the fact that, at least at the speeds at which braking commenced, there was sufficient downforce being created by the rear wing to markedly increase the tractive capability of the tyres (drivers of cars with large amounts of downforce, such as Formula 1 cars, have to learn to ease off the brake pedal to cope with the reducing amount of grip as downforce reduces with decreased speed). So, once again, even in the relatively low speed environment of short oval racing – as in, say, hillclimbing – it would be wrong to underestimate the performance benefits that accrue from exploiting downforce.

Chapter 9

Final thoughts

A balancing act

We've spent quite a while looking at how downforce is created, how components for exploiting it can be made, and what devices are used in various competition categories in order to exploit it. So, by now you may well have designed some new, improved (you hope) downforce-inducing parts, and have perhaps even made them and fitted them to your competition car. But before rushing into that first race, or run, or stage, or whatever it might be in your chosen branch of the sport, think about spending some time testing, if it's at all possible, in order to compile a database of reference settings. You will be able to use these wherever you compete, whether you've been there before or not, and whatever weather and track conditions you encounter. It will *not* be possible to get the set-up for a given venue right first time every time, but if you take the trouble to establish a table of settings, from low downforce to high downforce, that you know gives you a balanced set-up, you'll be one step nearer to doing better than your competitors who haven't bothered. The assumption here is that your aerodynamic aids are adjustable, and that the chassis can deal with the downforce you have decided to put on it.

Perhaps one of the most sensible things you can try and do is to separate the mechanical balance of your car from the aerodynamic balance. It's a regular cause of surprise how many people try to overcome a mechanical chassis imbalance by making an aerodynamic change, or vice versa. This doesn't necessarily refer to the upper echelons here, where the race engineering practices are a law unto themselves. But, for example, there wouldn't seem to be any logical reason, in any category, for trying to cure a low speed chassis imbalance by making aerodynamic changes. You might mask the effects of the imbalance at higher speeds, and this might give the illusion of a good set up on a fast course. But wouldn't it be better to have a chassis that was mechanically balanced first, then aerodynamically optimised as well? OK, life is never so simple or convenient that such a state of affairs is always going to be possible. And there are, undoubtedly, branches of motorsport and particular venues and occasions when it is advantageous to have a car that, say, oversteers at low speed, but is neutral at high speed. But for the sake of compiling a set of aerodynamic data that can be called upon to cover different venues and conditions, and which enable a ball park first guess at what will be needed, it is better to get the aerodynamically unaided chassis balanced first.

So how about starting that first or next test session with the downforce-inducing appendages removed? This might be difficult in the case of an underbody with radiators and so forth mounted on, so this simplistic approach isn't going to work for a lot of cars that rely heavily on underbody downforce. But it will be effective for a lot of others, so go on, take off the front and rear wings, and go and see if the chassis is balanced. If it isn't, then fiddle with the springs, dampers, tyre pressures, and anti-roll bars until it is balanced. Hopefully, adjustments needed from venue to venue will be relatively minor after this exercise. Then you've got a baseline to start assembling aero data, because any changes you make now to the car's balance at medium and high speed will be due to downforce adjustments.

With front and rear downforce aids now fitted, there are different ways in which you can approach the first test run. It depends on how confident you are about the probable balance that the wings, or spoilers, are going to give you, but a 'safe' start point is one which will create a dynamically stable handling condition, which is to say, medium and high speed understeer. So set the front to 'minimum downforce', and the rear to whatever position you believe will outperform the front. If this means putting the rear to 'maximum downforce', then do that. Then go out and try the car. If you encounter understeer in the faster corners – and hopefully you will – you can then back off the rear downforce until you get the car balanced. Once you've done this, you have established your minimum downforce, aerodynamically balanced setting. If the understeer is still present with the rear wing or spoiler at its minimum setting, then you will need to increase the front downforce setting until the understeer is eradicated.

Now you can increase the rear wing or spoiler, run the car to sense the understeer again, and then adjust the front until the car is once again balanced. This provides you with another point of balance which is giving more downforce than the first set up. If you keep reiterating this process until you reach the maximum rear downforce setting you can practically achieve, you will then have your reference table of balanced settings from minimum to maximum downforce. Naturally, you will have been recording lap or run times during this process, to see which set up gave the best result on the track you were testing on. This will give you a good idea of the level of downforce that will be needed at other tracks you go to. If you have been able to do some data logging as well, even better, because you will be able to study the changes in cornering and straight-line speeds, and compare segment and lap/run times.

This is a thoroughly simplistic, not to say time-consuming, approach to aerodynamic tuning, and also puts wear and tear on the car. But the information compiled in this way will avoid the need for guesswork later on, when, say, you come back to the same track that you tested on, but it's raining and you want to put on all the downforce you can. All you have to do is look up the relevant front wing or spoiler setting that balances the maximum rear setting, set it, and you've saved precious practice time, which can now be used for learning the track in the wet instead of searching for a balance.

Research and development
There are two reasons why you might want to try out new ideas on your competition car – one is natural curiosity, and the other is that you perceive the need to improve. Both are entirely valid justifications for experimenting, and it is only by actually doing so that you find out what works and what does not work on your particular car. You *can* rely on others with the same model of car trying things out first, and you can then follow their successes and ignore their failures. But this won't ever get you *in front* – copying never does. The only way to get ahead is to try to find that elusive 'unfair advantage', which means thinking about what might work, making it, and trying it. But don't ever burn your bridges, or be too proud to revert to your old set-up if things don't work out. There are far more blind alleys than yellow brick roads in motorsport!

'It's good to talk!' Ferrari aerodynamicist Willem Toet and top designer Mike Pilbeam in deep discussion.

Remember too that, as the British Telecom advert says, 'it's good to talk'. Discussing ideas is one of the best known ways for expanding your knowledge.

In conclusion

Hopefully this book has pooled sufficient information and ideas – based as it is on the wide experience of the engineers, academics, and fellow competitors who have helped in its compilation – to be of some value to anyone with an interest in motorsport, but especially to those who are, like the author, interested in how

you can 'work the wind' to help you go faster. Above all, though, I hope it is now evident that it is very difficult to generalise on a great many aspects of competition car aerodynamics. What works on one car may not work on another, apparently very similar car. Trial and error are an essential part of the development process, at any level of the sport. So if, having read this book, you discover something that makes you go quicker, then that's great. If, however, you go slower, don't blame me. Just say 'That's motorsport', and try something else!

Good luck.

Appendix 1

Some wing data

A SMALL SELECTION of wing profiles and their lift characteristics are listed here. The source for the data is Abbott and von Doenhof's classic text *The Theory of Wing Sections* (see Appendix 2), from which the graphs have been plotted and the drawings of the wing sections reconstructed. These examples are offered merely to show some of the effects of different configurations. The texts listed in Appendix 2 provide many more profiles for study.

The NACA 4415 profile is one of the simplest single-element sections, and is relatively easy to make in aluminium or FRP. It is one of a family of simple profiles of different thicknesses and cambers. As can be seen from the graph of lift coefficient versus angle of attack, the profile provides moderate lift at 0°, climbing to a peak C_L of 1.42 at 12°, the stall angle. But note that this data is actually for two-dimensional – that is, infinite span – aerofoils. At realistic aspect ratios, stall angle is likely to be greater. However, the precise stall angle on a competition car will depend on the flow conditions in which it is located, and is

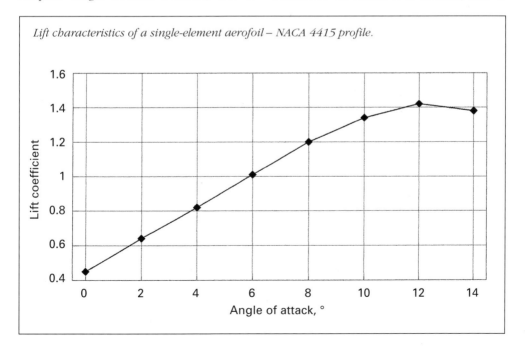

Lift characteristics of a single-element aerofoil – NACA 4415 profile.

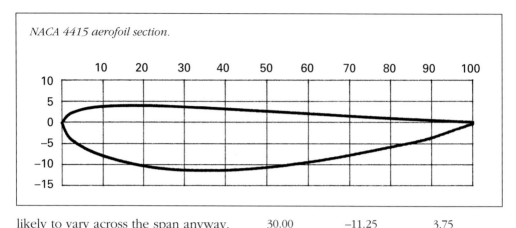

NACA 4415 aerofoil section.

likely to vary across the span anyway.

The ordinates to enable manual plotting of this profile at any size are as follows:

% from LE	Lower surface	Upper surface
0	0.00	0.00
1.25	–3.07	1.79
2.50	–4.17	2.48
5.00	–5.74	3.27
7.50	–6.91	3.71
10.00	–7.84	3.98
15.00	–9.27	4.18
20.00	–10.25	4.15
25.00	–10.92	3.98
30.00	–11.25	3.75
40.00	–11.25	3.25
50.00	–10.53	2.72
60.00	–9.30	2.14
70.00	–7.63	1.55
80.00	–5.55	1.03
90.00	–3.08	0.57
95.00	–1.67	0.36
100.00	0.00	0.00

The NACA 63_2–415 section is an altogether more sophisticated profile. It provides lower profile drag than the NACA 4415 in the C_L 0.2 to 0.8 range – that is,

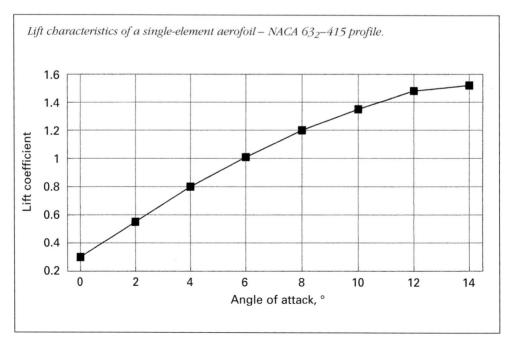

Lift characteristics of a single-element aerofoil – NACA 63_2–415 profile.

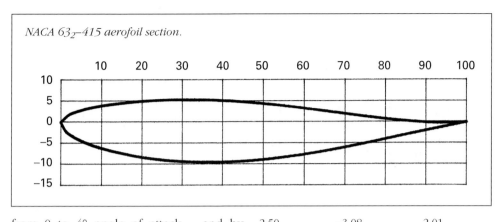

NACA 63_2–415 aerofoil section.

from 0 to 4° angle of attack – and by virtue of a more efficient shape has a higher stall angle (14° in the two-dimensional case), enabling a higher maximum C_L of 1.52 to be generated, as can be seen from the graph. The shape intuitively looks more efficient than the 4415, and this is born out by the data. It would be harder to make in aluminium than the 4415, but no different if FRP was the chosen construction medium. The ordinates for this profile are as follows:

% from LE	Lower surface	Upper surface
0	0.00	0.00
1.25	−2.07	1.24
2.50	−3.08	2.01
5.00	−4.34	2.85
7.50	−5.35	3.50
10.00	−6.11	3.94
15.00	−7.37	4.59
20.00	−8.29	5.03
25.00	−8.94	5.32
30.00	−9.26	5.41
40.00	−9.40	5.14
50.00	−8.76	4.40
60.00	−7.51	3.29
70.00	−5.85	2.00
80.00	−3.91	0.80
90.00	−1.93	−0.08
95.00	−0.96	−0.22
100.00	0.00	0.00

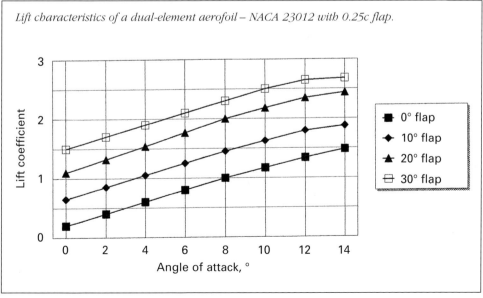

Lift characteristics of a dual-element aerofoil – NACA 23012 with 0.25c flap.

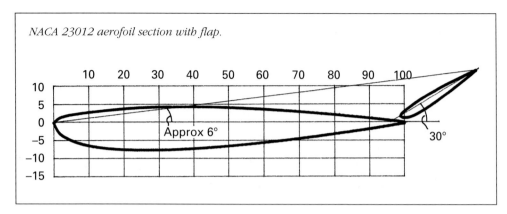

NACA 23012 aerofoil section with flap.

The dual-element aerofoil illustrated here is based on a combination of the slightly bizarre NACA 23012 wing section, with a flap to the same profile but of chord 0.25 times the size of the mainplane chord; this is not precisely as shown in Abbott and von Doenhof, but serves to illustrate. The data from which the graph was derived are as shown in Abbott and von Doenhof.

It can be seen that a wide range of lift coefficients is possible with this dual-element configuration, from a minimum of about 0.2 to a maximum shown of around 2.6. The absolute maximum is not much higher than this, given that the largest tolerable flap deflection is around 40°, and gains in lift get smaller with increasing flap angle at the upper extremes of the usable range. Notice also that the stall angle starts to reduce at the higher overall angles with a steep flap angle too, a fact which is not surprising given the rapid change of direction that the airflow is being asked to take in these circumstances. Clearly the efficiency with which a dual-element design actually functions will be controlled by the profiles used, and notably by the relative positioning of the flap and the mainplane. See Chapter 4 for more details.

The triple-element configuration illus-

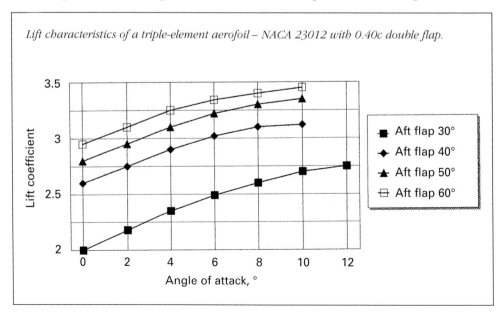

Lift characteristics of a triple-element aerofoil – NACA 23012 with 0.40c double flap.

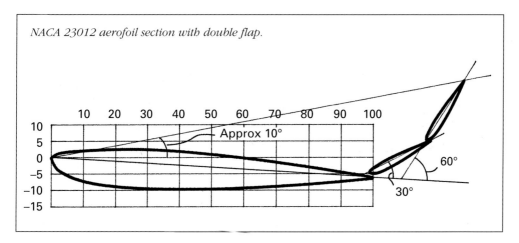

NACA 23012 aerofoil section with double flap.

trated here is shown as a NACA 23012 section mainplane with a 0.40c double flap consisting of a pair of scaled down 23012 sections. This is not as shown in Abbott and von Doenhof – the configuration illustrated there has more complex but undefined flap shapes. So again, the simple flap shapes shown here are generic, and for illustration only. The data in the graph are as shown in Abbott and von Doenhof.

The graph shows that this triple-element wing with the settings described takes over, more or less, from where the dual-element wing leaves off. The lowest aft flap setting of 30° – the same deflection as the fore flap – still performs better than the highest dual-flap setting shown in the previous graph. There is then a large increase in lift coefficient at the next increment of aft flap deflection, followed by decreasing gains in C_L at larger aft flap angles. The stall angle decreases with increasing aft flap deflection, being at around 10° for all the higher flap inclinations. Once again, the precise efficiency will depend on the installation, and also on the geometry of the flaps in relation to the mainplane and each other.

Appendix 2

References and recommended reading

* Indicates books which catalogue wing profiles.

*Abbott, I.H. and von Doenhof, A.J., *The Theory of Wing Sections*, Dover, 1959.

Allen, J.E., *Aerodynamics: The Science of Air in Motion*, Allen Bros & Father, 1986.

*Althaus, D. and Wortmann, F.X., *Stuttgarter Profilkatalog*, Vieweg, 1981.

Anderson, J.D., *Fundamentals of Aerodynamics*, McGraw Hill, 1991.

*Benzing, E., *Ali/Wings*, Automobilia, 1991.

Campbell, C., *Design of Racing Sports Cars*, Chapman and Hall, 1976.

Cimarosti, A., *The Complete History of Grand Prix Motor Racing*, Guild, 1990.

Dymock, E., *The Guinness Guide to Grand Prix Motor Racing*, Guinness Superlatives, 1980.

Henry, A., *Brabham – The Grand Prix Cars*, Hazleton, 1985.

—, *Grand Prix Car Design and Technology in the 1980s*, Hazleton, 1988.

Herbert, P. and Harvey, D., *750 Racer*, Patrick Stephens, 1996.

Houghton, E.L. and Carpenter, P.W., *Aerodynamics for Engineering Students*, Edward Arnold, 4th edition, 1993.

Howard, G., *Automobile Aerodynamics*, Osprey, 1986.

Hucho, W.H., *Aerodynamics of Road Vehicles*, Butterworth, 1987.

Katz, J., *Race Car Aerodynamics – Designing for Speed*, Bentley, 1995.

Kermode, A.C. (updated by Gunston, B.), *Flight Without Formulae*, Longman, 5th edition, 1989.

—, (revised and updated by Barnard, R.H. and Philpott, D.R.) *Mechanics of Flight*, Longman, 10th edition, 1996.

McCormick, B.W., *Aerodynamics, Aeronautics and Flight Mechanics*, Wiley, 1995.

Nye, D., *McLaren – The Grand Prix, CanAm and Indy Cars*, Hazleton, 1988.

Rudd, T., *Tony Rudd: It was Fun! My fifty years of high performance*, Patrick Stephens, 1993.

Scibor-Rylski, A.J., *Road Vehicle Aerodynamics*, J. Wiley & Sons, 2nd edition, 1984.

*Simons, M., *Model Aircraft Aerodynamics*, Argus, 3rd edition, 1989.

Smith, C., *Engineer to Win*, Osprey, 1985.

—, *Tune to Win*, Osprey, 1987.

Staniforth, A., *High Speed, Low Cost*, Patrick Stephens, 2nd edition, 1973.

—, *Race & Rally Car Source Book*, Haynes, 2nd edition, 1989.

Taylor Wilde, M., *A Practical Guide to Composites*, Multi-Sport Composites, 1995.

Terry, L. and Baker, A., *Racing Car Design and Development*, Motor Racing Publications, 1973.

Wiley, J., *Working with Fiberglass – Techniques and Projects*, Tab, 1986.

Wills, J.A., *Glass Fiber Auto Body Construction Simplified*, Dan R. Post, 1964.

Yeager, J., et al, *Voyager*, Knopf, 1986.

Articles and papers

Ansell, J., 'Aerofoils', *Short Circuit*, September 1996.

Dominy, J.A. and Dominy, R.G., 'Aerodynamic Influences on the Performance of the Grand Prix Racing Car', *Proceedings of the Institute of Mechanical Engineers*, volume 198, 1984.

—, 'The Power of Simulation', *Racecar Engineering*, volume 6 number 2, 1996.

Dominy, R.G., 'The Influence of Slipstreaming on the Performance of a Grand Prix Car', *Proceedings of the Institute of Mechanical Engineers*, volume 204, 1990.

—, 'Aerodynamics of Grand Prix Cars', *Proceedings of the Institute of Mechanical Engineers*, volume 206, 1992.

Duncan, L.T., 'Wind-Tunnel and Track Testing an ARCA Race Car', *Vehicle Aerodynamics, Recent Progress, SAE SP 855*, 1991.

Frère, P., 'The Force is With Them', *Car Design and Technology*, August/September 1991.

Henry, A., 'Mr Downforce', *Car Design and Technology*, April 1992.

Jeffrey, D., Xin Zhang and Hurst, D., 'A Wind-Tunnel Investigation of Aerofoils Fitted with Gurney Flaps', *MIRA International Conference on Vehicle Aerodynamics* 1996.

Katz, J., 'Aerodynamic Model for Wing Generated Downforce on Open Wheel Racing Car Configurations', *SAE Technical Paper Series 860218*, 1986.

McBeath, S., 'Tunnel Visions', *Cars & Car Conversions*, November 1994.

—, 'Wind Cheaters', *Cars & Car Conversions*, June 1995.

—, 'Have a Go Aero', *Cars & Car Conversions*, March 1996.

—, 'DIY Composites', *Racecar Engineering*, volume 7 number 3, 1997.

—, 'An Empirical Method for Wing Set-up', *Racecar Engineering*, volume 7 number 4, 1997.

Nelson, G., 'Flight Control', *Racecar Engineering*, volume 4 number 5, 1995.

O'Rourke, B.P., 'The Design and Manufacture of Grand Prix Racing Car Components Employing Composite Materials, *Proc. Verbundwerk*, 1992.

Scarlett, M., 'Broadley Speaking', *Car Design and Technology*, February 1992.

Wright, P.G., 'The Influence of Aerodynamics on the Design of Formula 1 Racing Cars', *International Journal of Vehicle Design*, SP3, 1983.

Magazines which frequently discuss competition car aerodynamics, and are generally worth reading, include *Racecar Engineering, Autosport, Cars & Car Conversions* and *Race Tech*.

Glossary of terms and abbreviations

WORDS IN *ITALICS* within the definitions have their own individual entries elsewhere in the glossary.

Aerodynamics The study of the interaction between air and solid bodies moving through it. In the context of this book, the 'solid bodies' are competition cars and their ancillary components.

Aerodynamic force The force created by a vehicle's movement through the air. It is the combination of aerodynamic *drag* and aerodynamic *lift*.

Aerofoil Synonymous with 'airfoil', an aerofoil is, strictly speaking, the transverse cross-section of a *wing*. But in motorsport it is usually regarded as just another word for a wing.

Airdam A device to block off some of the airflow to a vehicle's underside region.

Angle of attack The angle between an aerofoil's *chord line* and the incident airflow.

Anhedral The angle between an aerofoil and the horizontal when the *wing* is inclined downwards from its mounting.

Aspect ratio The arithmetic ratio of the *span* dimension divided by the *chord* dimension.

Attached flow A regime in which the airflow follows the contours and surfaces of the body it is flowing around.

Bargeboard A generally vertical, curved plate positioned behind and between the front wheels of an open wheeled competition car, its purpose being to steer and control the airflow.

Bernoulli's Theorem In essence, where an airflow accelerates – around a body, for example – the local pressure reduces.

Boundary layer A layer of static to slow moving air adjacent to the surfaces of a moving body. Friction between the body and the surrounding air holds back the flow nearest the surfaces, whilst the air further from the body in the *mainstream* flows past at unabated speed.

Camber An *aerofoil* with one surface curved more than the other is said to have camber.

CART Championship Auto Racing Teams Inc, the regulatory body for the Indycar World Series.

Centre of pressure The point at which the aerodynamic forces on a body appear to act, and at which there is no aerodynamic moment. It is analogous to the centre of gravity in mechanical terminology.

Chord The distance between an *aerofoil*'s leading edge and its trailing edge.

Chord line A line joining the leading edge to the trailing edge.

Computational fluid dynamics (CFD) The use of computers to calculate complex fluid dynamic equations to solve theoretical flow problems around bodies.

C$_D$ Abbreviation for *drag coefficient.*

C$_L$ Abbreviation for *lift coefficient.*

C$_P$ Abbreviation for *pressure coefficient.*

Data acquisition Also known as data logging, this is the electronic sensing and recording of engine and chassis parameters to provide information on car and driver responses and behaviour.

Density The mass per unit volume of a substance. In the case of air, this book uses the convention that the density of air is 0.00238lb per cubic foot (lb/ft^3). Strictly speaking this should be 0.00238 'slugs' per cubic foot, where 1 'slug' equals 32.17lb mass.

Diffuser The divergent section of a duct which slows down an airflow. On a competition car it is an upswept panel or panels at the rear of the *underbody*, or at the rear of *tunnels.*

Dive plate An inclined plate attached to the front of a vehicle to modify and adjust the airflow.

Downforce The opposite of aerodynamic *lift*, sometimes referred to as negative lift.

Downwash The part of the airflow turned downwards by an *aerofoil.* In the case of a downforce-inducing aerofoil, the downwash occurs just in front of the aerofoil.

Drag That component of the *aerodynamic force* which is parallel to, but opposes the movement of, a body through air. *Form drag, induced drag* and *skin friction drag* are all components of drag which can affect vehicles.

Drag coefficient or C$_D$. A 'dimensionless' value (one without units) that allows the comparison of *drag* incurred by different sized and different shaped bodies.

Δ The Greek letter 'delta', used to represent an incremental change in a parameter: for example, **ΔC$_D$** would be a change to a *drag* coefficient.

End plate Also sometimes known as a spill plate, a more or less flat and vertical sheet of rigid material attached to the ends of an *aerofoil.*

FIA The Federation International d'Automobile, the ruling body of world-wide motorsport based in Paris, France.

Flap Part of a multi-element *aerofoil*, set just above (on a racecar) and behind the main element, for the purpose of supplementing aerodynamic downforce.

Flow visualisation General term for methods by which the airflow around a body is made visible.

Fluid Usually a gaseous or liquid substance which is capable of flowing. Air is a fluid under normal conditions.

Form drag That portion of a body's *drag* caused by the horizontal component of the overall *pressure distribution.* Form drag – sometimes called pressure drag – therefore results from higher pressure occurring on the front of a body than on the rear. A 'tear drop' shaped body thus has low form drag, whilst form drag is significant on most vehicle shapes.

Frontal area Generally taken to be the area of the front view 'silhouette' of a vehicle, though sometimes simplified as width multiplied by height.

Ground effect The aerodynamic modification of the airflow beneath a vehicle caused by its close proximity to the ground. All cars operate in ground effect, though not all exploit the effect beneficially.

Gurney flap A small strip attached to the trailing edge of an *aerofoil*, perpendicular to the upper aerofoil surface, for the purpose of supplementing aerodynamic downforce.

Induced drag That portion of *drag* caused by the generation of lift (or downforce).

Indycar A generic name for *CART* and *IRL* racecars.

IRL Indy Racing League, a competitor category to *CART*, whose cars are broadly similar in overall form to CART's.

Laminar flow Flow in which layers of air adjacent to a body slide smoothly over each other.

Lift That component of the *aerodynamic force* which is perpendicular to the direction of a body's travel, directed vertically upwards or downwards.

Lift coefficient or C_L. A dimensionless value that allows the comparison of lift incurred by different sized and different shaped bodies. A positive lift coefficient represents *lift*, whilst a negative lift coefficient represents *downforce*.

Lift to drag ratio The arithmetic ratio of *lift* divided by *drag*, often used as a measure of a vehicle's aerodynamic efficiency.

Mainstream That part of the airflow around a body which is far enough away to remain undisturbed by the body's passage. Thus the 'mainstream velocity' will always be equal, though opposite in direction, to the body's velocity.

Moving ground wind-tunnel A *wind-tunnel* equipped with a belt which simulates the ground passing beneath a car. This enables the simulated air speed to be matched to the simulated ground speed, allowing the realistic modelling of airflows adjacent to the ground, and underneath vehicles.

NACA National Advisory Committee for Aeronautics, the predecessor of NASA, the USA's aerospace agency. Among other things, the NACA catalogued a vast number of aerofoil profiles.

NASCAR National Association for Stock Car Auto Racing Inc, the regulatory body for the Winston Cup, the USA's premier racing series.

Pitch That motion of a vehicle in which the front moves up and down relative to the static position.

Pitch sensitivity The magnitude of aerodynamic downforce can markedly alter with changes to front ground clearance as the result of *pitch* movements. This can affect the vehicle's performance and 'feel'.

Plan area The area defined by an overhead view 'silhouette', or in the case of rectangular aerofoils, the *span* dimension multiplied by the *chord* dimension.

Pressure Air pressure is all around us, and results from collisions between air molecules and bodies that the air surrounds. When a body is stationary, and there is no air flowing past it, the sum of the pressures on a body balance out. However, when a body moves through the air, the pressures can change, and – in the case of an aerofoil, for example – *lift* and *drag* forces occur as the result of changes to *pressure distribution*.

Pressure coefficient or C_p. A dimensionless value which acts as a means of indicating the local pressure at some point of interest around a body, and which is independent of air velocity.

Pressure distribution The representation of local pressures at points all over a body moving through the air. The sum of all the pressures felt by a body is the *aerodynamic force*.

Pressure gradient As air is accelerated over, say, the forward part of a vehicle, the pressure reduces (*Bernoulli's Theorem*). A region of falling pressure constitutes a 'favourable pressure gradient'. Where the airflow starts to slow again, the local pressure rises, constituting an 'adverse pressure gradient'.

Profile drag Aerofoil catalogues list the profile, or 'section' drag coefficients, relating to theoretical infinite span, two-dimensional aerofoils. These make for useful comparison between aerofoil shapes, but the drag caused by an *aerofoil* in practical use depends principally on how much *lift* is being created, which governs the formation of *induced drag*.

Rake The inclination of the underside of a vehicle. A positive rake would generally be thought of as the front being lower than the rear.

Reynolds Number A dimensionless value which is proportional to the air speed of a body multiplied by 'some characteristic length', such as a vehicle's overall length, or, for an *aerofoil* being studied in isolation, the aerofoil *chord* dimension. The Reynolds Number is used to indicate scale effects.

Ride height Synonymous with ground clearance in this book, the ride height can be taken as the size of the gap between a vehicle underside and the ground.

Roughness Describes the variation of, for example, the underside of a vehicle from an 'average surface'. Thus, a production vehicle with cavities and protrusions has a rough underside, whilst a panelled-in racecar has a smooth underside.

Separated flow A regime in which the flow no longer follows the contours and surfaces of the body it is flowing around.

Skin friction drag That portion of *drag* caused by friction between the air and the surface of a body. In the case of vehicles, it is generally a very small contributor to overall drag.

Skirt A device for bridging the gap between a vehicle's sides and the ground for the purpose of controlling the airflow under the car, and sealing it from the flow outside.

Slat Part of a multi-element *aerofoil*, set just ahead of and below (on a racecar) the leading edge of the main element, for the purpose of supplementing aerodynamic downforce.

Slot The gap between *aerofoil* elements, eg between the main element and a *flap*.

Span The side to side dimension of an *aerofoil*; its width.

Splitter A generally flat, horizontal, forward-protruding extension to an *airdam*.

Spoiler Any device whose purpose is to 'spoil' a fast, low pressure flow over a vehicle in order to reduce or reverse positive *lift*.

Stagnation point A point, usually near the front of a moving body, where the air velocity is zero, and the pressure is high (the pressure coefficient is 1.0).

Strake A flat plate, usually inclined to the horizontal, attached to the sides of a vehicle to modify and adjust the airflow.

Streamline The mean flow path of an air particle past a moving body. Streamlines are often depicted graphically as a set of curves around an object defining the flow directions.

Throat The narrowest part of a *venturi*.

Turbulent flow Flow in which layers of air adjacent to a body do not slide smoothly over each other, but mix and swirl instead. The overall average speed of the flow may be the same as in a laminar case, but the streamlines within a turbulent flow are much more complex.

Turning vanes Flat or curved plates, usually mounted vertically, whose purpose is to steer and control an airflow.

Tunnel A generic name for three-dimensional underbody *venturi* sections, especially when mounted in pairs, one either side of a central chassis/engine/transmission unit.

Tyre shelf A flat, horizontal, low-mounted plate extending in front of the rear tyres of an open wheel racecar, usually an extension to the *underbody*.

Underbody General term for the underside of a competition car.

Underwing General term for a profiled underbody, whether comprising *tunnels*, or flat floor and *diffuser*.

Upwash The part of the airflow deflected upwards by an *aerofoil*. In the case of a downforce-inducing aerofoil, the upwash occurs behind the aerofoil.

Venturi Strictly speaking a narrow tube joining two wider sections of tube, whose purpose is to accelerate flow and cause a reduction in pressure. In a competition car context, venturi is synonymous with *tunnel*.

Viscosity Resistance to flow, or to motion through a fluid, and analogous to mechanical friction.

Vortex A rotatory motion in a parcel of air.

Wake The disturbed air behind a body moving through the air. The air within the wake tends to move along with the body.

Wicker Another term for a *Gurney flap*.

Wind-tunnel A room or chamber through which a fast airflow is pulled over a car or a scale model of a car, for the purpose of aerodynamic data gathering.

Wing In motorsport, a synonym for *aerofoil*. It is a device for creating *downforce* and displaying sponsors names!

Yaw The motion of a vehicle about a vertical axis in such a way that it points in a slightly different direction to its direction of travel. Thus, an oversteering vehicle, with its tail out, is running at a yaw angle.

Index